I0644661

Anthony Bourdain, Filmmaker

Contemporary Approaches to Film and Media Series

A complete listing of the books in this series can
be found online at wsupress.wayne.edu.

General Editor

Barry Keith Grant
Brock University

ANTHONY BOURDAIN, FILMMAKER

TODD KENNEDY

WAYNE STATE UNIVERSITY PRESS
DETROIT

© 2026 by Todd Kennedy. All rights reserved. No part of this book may be reproduced without formal permission.

ISBN 9780814352922 (paperback)
ISBN 9780814352915 (hardcover)
ISBN 9780814352939 (ebook)

Library of Congress Control Number: 2026937671

Cover art and design by Brad Norr Design.

Published with the assistance of a fund established by Thelma Gray James of Wayne State University.

Wayne State University Press rests on Waawiyaataanong, also referred to as Detroit, the ancestral and contemporary homeland of the Three Fires Confederacy. These sovereign lands were granted by the Ojibwe, Odawa, Potawatomi, and Wyandot Nations, in 1807, through the Treaty of Detroit. Wayne State University Press affirms Indigenous sovereignty and honors all tribes with a connection to Detroit. With our Native neighbors, the press works to advance educational equity and promote a better future for the earth and all people.

Wayne State University Press
Leonard N. Simons Building
4809 Woodward Avenue
Detroit, Michigan 48201-1309

Visit us online at wsupress.wayne.edu.

For Bri

I wanted adventures. I wanted to go up the Nung River to the Heart of Darkness in Cambodia. I wanted to ride out into a desert on camelback, sand and dunes in every direction, eat whole roasted lamb with my fingers. I wanted to kick snow off my boots in a *Mafiya* nightclub in Russia. I wanted to play with automatic weapons in Phnom Penh, recapture the past in a small oyster village in France, step into a seedy neon-lit *pulquería* in rural Mexico. I wanted to run roadblocks in the middle of the night, blowing past angry militia with a handful of hurled Marlboro packs, experience fear, excitement, wonder. I wanted kicks—the kind of melodramatic thrills and chills I'd yearned for since childhood, the kind of adventure I'd found as a little boy in the pages of my Tintin comic books. I wanted to see the world—and I wanted the world to be just like the movies.

—Anthony Bourdain, *A Cook's Tour: Global Adventures in Extreme Cuisines*, 2001

To be a filmmaker, you have to lead. You have to be psychotic in your desire to do something. People always like the easy route. You have to push very hard to get something unusual, something different.

—Danny Boyle, in an interview with *The Daily Telegraph*, 2009

CONTENTS

PREFACE

Anthony Bourdain's death altered the course of my life in ways I never could have anticipated. While his shows were among the few television programs I routinely watched, and my family shared a deep interest in travel, food, and film, I would not have described myself as a "fan" of Bourdain, per se. And I certainly would not have thought that I might end up writing a book arguing he is best understood as a filmmaker, and an important one at that. Nor would I have imagined being emotionally impacted by anything happening to him in real life. I enjoyed his shows, but I did not take them particularly seriously. After his death, that all changed in rapid progression.

At the time of Bourdain's death, my wife, son, and I were living in Donostia–San Sebastián, a place we have visited and resided in intermittently since our marriage. June 8, 2018, was the first sunny day we had seen in almost a week. We made plans to celebrate by taking our six-year-old to his favorite playground before going to the *pintxo* bar at Ganbara Jatetxea to try, for the first time, a dish Bourdain considered one of the best in the world: *hongos*, prized mushrooms in the north of Spain, perfectly grilled and simply served with a raw egg yolk and griddled slices of foie gras. We were excited. As we left the playground, walking through Donostia–San Sebastián's newer, sleeker city center en route to the old town and Ganbara, I instinctively checked my phone and saw a headline that stopped me in my tracks: Anthony Bourdain had committed suicide near Strasbourg, France.

Standing in a foreign country in which Bourdain was not as well known, at a time of day when most of the United States was asleep, surrounded by happy people enjoying the weather, reading such news made for a jarring experience. By the time we reached Ganbara, we were in tears. Even as the US woke up, and reactions to Bourdain's death dominated social media, we felt isolated and alone. A sense of impenetrable loss overwhelmed us for days. Bourdain came to be the only thing we were able to think or talk about, and we could not even articulate why.

That inability to understand our feelings was the driving force for feeling isolated in our grief. Plenty of people were mourning Bourdain—the responses dominated North American media, both mainstream and social—but I felt disconnected from that. Not only was I on a different continent, but I have also always had the peculiar trait of not being particularly interested in celebrities. I do not tend to read articles about their private lives, follow them on social media, or seek to interact with them. It is, perhaps, a byproduct of my profession. As an academic, I have been trained to admire people's work without developing a fantasy that I know them. While I respect that I am the peculiar one, I had never understood friends and family who seemed emotional about the "loss" of famous strangers. So, my feelings about this dead celebrity floored me. It simply baffled me to find myself, days later, sitting at a bar on the side of a mountain with a beautiful view of the Basque coast, still bawling about the loss of a man I had never met, and I had no tangible answer as to what made him different from all the other celebrity deaths that left me unmoved.

As I struggled to understand my emotions, I started to think about what it was about Bourdain that meant so much to me, what it was that, apparently, I had intrinsically felt yet only had become aware of in his absence. Very quickly, I started to zero in on the way he was one of the few examples of a person who took a wholly interdisciplinary approach to how they imagine the world. Academics love to talk about interdisciplinary approaches, as do some artists. Typically, however, this simply results in attempts to forge, or sometimes even force, a conversation between two, or maybe three, disciplines, usually through the lens of the one the person is most comfortable with. Bourdain never limited himself. He merged, almost seamlessly, a myriad of lenses—filmic, culinary, artistic, literary, musical, political, historical—into a unified, articulate argument each and every week. The influences were not in competition, nor differentiated. For Bourdain, they were the same and worked in congruence. I deeply believe the ability to see and express things so holistically is a rare, but absolutely essential, skill. More than anything, I realized the reason Bourdain was able to both see and articulate his arguments this way was through his deep love—and thorough understanding—of how filmic texts make meaning. Film, for Bourdain, was a window to everything. Suddenly, evaluating his work in retrospect, it felt consequential. And so, like every stereotypical professor ruminating on a topic, I decided to offer a class. Naively, I had no idea what would come next.

At that stage, the course was tentatively titled "Anthony Bourdain and His Influencers," and the concept was relatively simple: each week would pair an episode with the films or novels Bourdain referred to in it, and we would study the relationship between the two. I was worried the course might not attract enough students, so in mid-September I took to Twitter to advertise it. Within an hour the tweet had generated a record number of responses for an account which, at the time, I primarily used as a recruitment tool for my university's film studies concentration. The tweet spread widely enough that it came to the attention of a freelance travel journalist who had contacts at CNN, and she asked for an interview. If I was shocked to find my course the center of a lengthy, thoughtful piece that ran for multiple days atop CNN's news page,[1] I was completely blown over by what came next: interviews for articles in *USA Today*, *People*, *Food & Wine*, *Travel & Leisure*, the Associated Press, every newspaper in my region, about a dozen online news sources catering to travel or food, and even a lengthy interview with a podcast dedicated to high school pedagogy.[2] As a film scholar heretofore best known for scholarly articles about feminist theory and Sofia Coppola, I was, to be honest, a little uncomfortable in such a spotlight. I had the eyes of international mass media, my university president, and just about everyone I knew on a class that had thus far barely moved past the proposal level.

I felt a sense of urgency. I was on a mission. I spent my spare time reading, watching, and researching all things Bourdain as I set to work improving the syllabus—making the class more intellectually rigorous, broader in scope. I overthought every detail and loaded the course with more work than I typically would ever consider assigning. And then, thank goodness, I was met with energized, highly motivated students who brought their own diverse perspectives, from a wide range of majors: literature, culinary arts, film, mass communications, and studio art.

The more I studied Bourdain, the more I thought about his work; the more I listened to and learned from what my students thought, the more I came to realize the importance of his work. Moreover, the more I discussed and explored his legacy, the more the way that most news sources described his work seemed superficial by comparison. Travel-TV and food-TV host, chef, television personality: all were technically accurate, but all seemed insufficient means of understanding what Bourdain had achieved. I had taken superb filmmaking for granted watching Bourdain over the years, and I had never realized, until I scrutinized his shows, just how strong that filmmaking was—just how relevant, consequential, and ahead of its time it felt.

I began writing this book on August 29, 2021, as Hurricane Ida made landfall near Port Fourchon, Louisiana, eventually shifting our New Orleans home on its foundation and causing extensive damage, which dominates our time and finances to this day; it was also the sixteenth anniversary of Hurricane Katrina. When we lost power, I typed feverishly while the walls shook, knowing I had limited time before my battery died. I wrote most of the first chapter during those fleeting hours and finished it in a state of hyper-focus while on "hurrication" in the South Carolina Lowcountry, where we stayed with friends until our home regained electricity and was deemed inhabitable by an engineer. In that time, it was not lost on me just what an irrevocable void exists in our society, and what is at stake when there are not enough people who can make cohesive arguments stretching across disciplines, offering underrepresented cultures across the globe representation in the face of global homogenization, colonization, political turmoil, or in the case of South Louisiana, climate change. Suddenly, Bourdain's absence, or more precisely the absence of his voice, his films, seemed profound.

In the years since Bourdain's death, various books and films have helped shape his legacy, ranging from biographies by Laurie Woolever[3] and Charles Leerhsen,[4] to a memoir by one of his longtime directors, Tom Vitale,[5] a bio-documentary by Morgan Neville, *Roadrunner* (2021), and a narrative biopic by Matt Johnson, *Tony* (2026). The works are all earnest, engaging, and provocative. Yet, I cannot help but feel there is more to be said. These works focus their energy on explaining Bourdain's life and the behind-the-scenes reality of how the shows were made, and they share a common opinion that his work was important, but they do not spend a lot of time exploring, examining, or explaining why; rather, they assume it is an opinion they share with the audience so they can mention it as they return to their explorations of the myth of Bourdain. I am more interested in his work, where I feel his lasting achievement and legacy lies.

My first film mentor, Robert Sklar, made a career defining and exploring what he called the Hollywood "dream machine,"[6] focusing, specifically on the way film, as a medium, harnesses powers and abilities to shape the spectator's thinking in ways no other medium can. Bourdain was a master of understanding and using those tools, even as he often used them to expose and deconstruct traditional, mainstream filmmaking. My goal in this book is to show how and why that attempt matters.

ABBREVIATION CODES

ACT: *A Cook's Tour* (Food Network, 2 seasons, 2001–2)

NR: *No Reservations* (Travel Channel, 9 seasons, 2005–12)

TL: *The Layover* (Travel Channel, 2 seasons, 2011–13)

PU: *Parts Unknown* (CNN, 12 seasons, 2013–18)

S–Season **E**–Episode: e.g., S1E1 = season one, episode one*

* Numeration excludes preseason hype episodes such as "Prime Cuts."

I
FILMMAKER

INTRODUCTION

> Really, in the best-case scenario, we're trying to make a different independent film every week that looks different than the one before it, that doesn't fall into a pattern, that has its own stand-alone look, sound, editing style, camera style, lighting scheme.
>
> —Anthony Bourdain, *CityBeat*[1]

The opening moments of the first episode of Anthony Bourdain's first hour-long television show begin in black and white, with a handheld camera jostling its way down the streets of Paris following the show's host. Bourdain's dialogue invokes the French cinematic history that the camerawork references, particularly the nouvelle vague (New Wave). Specifically, Bourdain reminds us that the Paris he imagines, *his* Paris, was forged by the filmic images of the city that dominated his youth. This opening sequence, he tells us, "is the way I wanted this show to look."[2] Almost immediately, however, the screen turns to color and a more mainstream television camera style as Bourdain reminds us "unfortunately, this is television." The remainder of the episode (NR S1E1) mostly follows a traditional approach, and what we are left with is a joke emphasizing the space between the way Bourdain wishes to convey Paris and the production realities and corporate restrictions that determine a food-based television travel show. What is ironic about this joke, however, is that the opening sequence embodies precisely what Bourdain eventually achieved, namely a style of documentary filmmaking that actively defies and rewrites the rules not only of television genre, but of the medium in general. Furthermore, this type of documentary filmmaking routinely deconstructs notions of authenticity as it explores the way the filmmaker, and his film, is shaped by everything he has seen and read prior, much like Bourdain's New Wave imagination of Paris. Thus, when imagined as "a different independent film every week," as Bourdain wished, we are left with high-quality filmmaking that asks, and sometimes even answers, some of the most pressing questions in contemporary cinema.

For all the varied attempts to understand, praise, or minimize Bourdain's work, the focus on understanding his shows through the lens of various television genres seems fundamentally limiting, not only because of his proclaimed desire to imagine his episodes as independent films, but because it ignores the cinematic nature of his work. As Bourdain wrote in a guest column published in *Hollywood Reporter* the week before his death, "if it's not clear from my shows over the past 16 or 17 years, I like movies. I love movies."[3] Across four television programs—*A Cook's Tour* (Food Network, 2001–2), *No Reservations* (Travel Channel, 2005–12), *The Layover* (Travel Channel, 2011–13), and *Parts Unknown* (CNN, 2013–18)—Bourdain consistently asked his crew at Zero Point Zero Production to push boundaries well beyond what was considered normal, or even possible, for the television of his era. More than anything, however, to focus on television genres such as food, travel, and even politics misses the fact that the unifying force between the show's disparate interests almost always came from a perspective defined by cinema. As Bourdain said in an interview with *IndieWire*, also published the week before his death, "It's always been, to one extent or another, a stealth food show. We pretend it's about food. It rarely is. We always talk about films first, before we head to a location, for visual cues, for sound, for editing. We love nothing more than duping, emulating, or riffing on a film that few of our audiences have actually seen."[4]

In truth, however, it was rarely mimicry. Instead, Bourdain harnessed cinematic powers to visually reference the films that shaped his worldview so he could, in turn, shape how we saw the world through his own films. To return to the *CityBeat* interview quoted in the epigraph, the question that sparked Bourdain's invocations of independent cinema insisted *No Reservations* contained elements of "escapism" and "truthfulness." Bourdain's response playfully alters the first term and artfully dodges the second: "Escapism? Yeah, that's a goal. I'd like to be able to disappear into an episode. I'd like people to disappear into the places that we go. I'd like them to feel the way I felt or the crew felt when we were there."[5] Instead of an escapism of travel, Bourdain's diction changes the implication to one of an escapism into the filmic text, and into an open dialogue about the presence of the filmmaker within that filmic text. And this, as I will return to later, has profound implications for how we imagine the presence of a documentary filmmaker within their own work. As Bourdain proceeds to admit in that same interview, "Often, before we even pick what country we're going to, we start with a movie that we love and start thinking about where we might apply that look."[6] Elsewhere, Bourdain claimed he spent the most time between shoots talking about movies with his crew—citing directors such as Michelangelo Antonioni, François Truffaut, Akira Kurosawa, Federico Fellini, Jean-Luc Godard, and John Cassavetes. As such, when hiring crew, he stated, "I can't even start a conversation unless you're already familiar with those guys . . . There's a baseline: do you really like films? It's a requirement. With some directors, if you don't know them, that's weird."[7] For Bourdain, his work was always more about film, and how film shapes how we see the world, than it was ever about travel.

These are some of the reasons why the central aim of this book is to suggest Anthony Bourdain is best understood as a filmmaker, and that his life's work is more relevant and more complex when imagined as cinema. More than that, I hope that by putting some of his best work under the microscope, dissecting it and placing it in conversation with the breadth of film history, theory, and culture, I will also demonstrate that his work is not only cinematic, but important cinema. I think Bourdain's films largely reposition long-standing conversations about authenticity within documentary filmmaking, reimagine the subgenre of ethnographic filmmaking as a worthwhile social and cultural construct, largely deconstruct the Western, male gaze, and make those heady concerns relevant, pertinent, and accessible to a wide swath of mainstream audiences. Meanwhile, Bourdain does so not in spite of posing his programs as "stealth" food shows, but, rather, because of it. As his longtime director of photography, Zach Zamboni, claimed, "food has been the secret weapon we've had to get you to the table. People are like, 'you know, it's a food show.' Um. Kind of. Not really. But it's amazing what him being with CNN and being a food show . . . the access that's given us. It just diffuses things enough."[8] In short, the heightened access to remote and volatile locations offered by CNN (as well as larger production budgets), coupled with interviewees being disarmed by the food genre, all harnessed by a filmmaker with a keen understanding of how filmic texts make meaning, provided Bourdain and his team a unique opportunity to produce great art.

My point is not to create a false hierarchy between film and television; the quality of a work of art is never defined by its medium. Rather, the goal is to situate Bourdain at the forefront of a larger movement that transformed television's aspirations, a transformation that is too often imagined solely in narrative terms. Many scholars identify a "new golden age"[9] of television beginning with HBO's *The Sopranos* (1997–2007) and peaking in the 2010s. In this period, television shows began to employ higher production values and embraced plot themes and New Wave narrative techniques traditionally reserved for the silver screen. Series such as *Deadwood* (HBO 2004–6), *True Detective* (HBO 2014–present), *Lost* (ABC 2004–10), *Mad Men* (AMC 2007–15), and *The Wire* (HBO 2002–8) moved toward high-quality, digital filmmaking (sometimes even widescreen) and relied on increasingly complex plots, nonlinear editing, extended one-take shots, moral ambiguity, non-heroic protagonists, and the embrace of metaphor, both in plot and cinematography. In so doing, television became increasingly cinematic. Or, as Francis Ford Coppola phrases it, those who grew up in the 1970s wanting to make films like the ones he made "weren't permitted to" by the studios, so they "did it for television."[10] But nonfiction television often remains in the periphery of these discussions, in part because the period coincides with the birth of reality TV, a decidedly uncinematic genre. Bourdain's nonfiction television, however, shares the aims of the aforementioned narrative shows, and, in hindsight, Bourdain was not only a part of this movement, he was at its center.

This book's first section navigates the primary terms of debate. I begin by addressing what seems, at first glance, an audacious claim: that a television personality who did not direct his own programs and who had no filmmaking experience prior to his first show could be considered a filmmaker. Beginning with a survey of the historical debate around authorship in cinema, particularly as Bourdain would have understood it, the chapter on auteurship argues Bourdain exploited this history—as well as his spectator's desire for a tangible author—to perform an imagined role that brings questions about documentary film form to the forefront. Thus, I situate Bourdain's career, in part, as a response to the filmmakers who most influenced him: the international directors referred to earlier in this introduction, as well as American New Wave directors like Francis Ford Coppola and Terrence Malick, and, potentially most important for understanding Bourdain's relationship to both narrative and documentary filmmaking, Werner Herzog.

The next chapter addresses the central element of what makes film a unique art form: cinematography. This chapter traces Bourdain's obsession with cinematography and the way it shaped his approach. While I spend time looking at episodes where he talks to cinematographers, this chapter is most interested in the way Bourdain demanded a unique visual style for every location, and the way that visual style was almost always inspired by a film or filmmaker Bourdain wanted to use to interrogate the preconceived notions both he, and the spectator, have about a location. At its heart, every episode's narration, editing, and approach were almost completely dictated by the cinematographic style Bourdain chose for the location—a style that, again, changed almost every single episode. As noted by Zamboni, one of Bourdain's directors of photography, "we carry a lot of gear . . . we've gone into a shoot with eleven different types of cameras before."[11] Instead of a "typical" documentary shoot, Zamboni continues, where "you're trying to capture reality as it happens . . . picking up the camera to apply your sense of blocking and framing to improve on reality," the allegiance to a unique visual style forces a "whole new level of discipline" as "you're almost going against your own basic cinematic instincts."[12] Not only was cinematography the defining element of Bourdain's approach, but he wanted the spectator to be constantly aware of the control that cinematography has upon them, often breaking the fourth wall and drawing attention to the cinematography as it is created.

The third chapter situates Bourdain's films within the disparate categories his work participated in, paying particular attention to ethnographic filmmaking. Despite Bourdain's critiques of ethnographic filmmaking, the genre is the context that compels the most complex and interesting discussion of what his films have to say. This chapter traces the history of ethnographic films, particularly the work of Timothy Asche and Jean Rouch, but it also looks at non-ethnographic documentaries, such as Werner Herzog's *Grizzly Man* (2009), to provide rare context for what Bourdain eventually achieves—namely, an attempt to forge a new approach to ethnographic filmmaking through New Wave, avant-garde, and anti-authenticity approaches more commonly found (traditionally, anyway) in narrative cinema. Due to Bourdain's emphasis on cinematography, it should be no surprise some of his most direct commentary about his approach to documentary filmmaking, and the ethical questions therein, are found in the same episodes I discuss in chapter 2, but this chapter's primary push applies that conversation across the breadth of his work. For instance, I discuss how the man-on-the-street interviews he developed for the much-maligned *The Layover* came to influence, shape, and inform the approach he perfected in *Parts Unknown*. In short, while the previous chapters seek to convince the reader that Bourdain is in fact a filmmaker, this chapter provides context for the larger argument that he is an *important* filmmaker.

Having grounded the terms of debate for viewing Bourdain as a filmmaker, the second section explores Bourdain's influence upon the genres in which his work is typically pigeonholed. Even as I argue he is best understood as an ethnographic documentary filmmaker, I assert his work has much to say about (and is already shaping the future of) travelogues, personal cinema, political documentaries, and food films. The section's first chapter demonstrates Bourdain's mistrust of, and at times open disdain for, travelogues, a multidisciplinary genre that manifests itself in travel writing, photography, fine art, and travel TV. I explore Bourdain's ambivalent relationship with travel, its impact upon the environment and local culture, and the way he found the notion of paradise a dangerous social construct. Chapter 5, the chapter on personal cinema, compares three episodes centered on Bourdain's biography, tracing how his approach evolved. Rather than relaying simple autobiography, Bourdain used his experience to shed light on the world around him, again like an ethnographer. The chapter on political documentaries traces Bourdain's increasing confidence in foregrounding politics, particularly after unexpectedly finding himself trapped in a war zone in Lebanon, which eventually evolved into an outright embrace of political filmmaking. More than anything, Bourdain began to express what he had always thought—that food is, by nature, political—and began to articulate a political ideology working from the bottom up, focusing on everyday people doing everyday things. The chapter on food films details Bourdain's denial of food-film (and food-TV) genre conceits, in terms of content, style, and film form, paying particular attention to episodes dedicated to single restaurants, El Bulli and Noma.

The third and final section, Dégustation, examines six episodes, not only to make a case for their stand-alone quality, but also to explore a range of approaches, topics, and styles so the reader can apply these discussions to understanding any of Bourdain's other films. Where the first two sections use breadth of scope to understand Bourdain as a filmmaker, the Dégustation asserts there is far more to be learned taking an in-depth look at his best work under a focused approach. For this reason, I believe this section is the most revealing precisely because it evaluates and understands episodes within the very context I (and Bourdain) claim them to be: independent films. It is essential to remember that while I make the case that these episodes are representative of his best work, such discussions are arbitrary by nature, and this is not meant as a ranking or ordinal system. I am not declaring these to be the six "best" episodes, per se. I picked them not just for their complexity and quality, but also to provide a representational sampling of his work in terms of location, approach, style, and focus.

I choose the term *dégustation*, which traditionally refers to a multicourse, pre-set tasting menu at a chef-driven restaurant, not only to glibly draw upon culinary references, but because two specific connotations of the word serve as lenses for understanding Bourdain's performance of his chef-auteur role. First, *dégustation* connotes pleasure, which allows me to open a discussion of how the filmic gaze is traditionally (and sometimes problematically) tied to visual pleasure, reinforced by mainstream film form.[13] I argue Bourdain eventually achieved a cinematic approach that created an alternative form of pleasure as it exposed and deconstructed the Western gaze. In fact, such a disavowal of that Western gaze becomes the primary focus of the last four chapters of the Dégustation, as well as the book's conclusion. Second, *dégustation* connotes at least an imagined sense of control, asserted by the chef, similar to a filmmaker. In *No Reservations*' "Spain" (NR S4E17), Bourdain is offered two tasting meal options at Restaurant Mugaritz, one titled "150-minutes rebel," the other "150-minutes submit." Bourdain asserts, "No question it's submit. Cooking is about control. About dominating your environment, about controlling the forces of nature. Eating, for me, is about submission." If one were to replace cooking with filmmaking, and eating with watching a movie, I would argue there would be no better articulation of how Bourdain saw film, and the relationship between filmmaker and spectator he constantly exposed, challenged, and upended.

I begin the Dégustation using "Hong Kong" (PU S11E5) to model how the exploration of a single episode concretizes the broader discussions begun in previous sections of this book. In "Hong Kong," Bourdain borrows his visual style from Wong Kar Wai, contrasts it to that of the photographer Simon Go, includes multiple moments that draw the spectator's attention to the construction of cinema, and debates the ethics of all these filmmaking decisions on-screen with cinematographer Christopher Doyle. In short, each of Bourdain's primary thumbprints exhibit themselves, in unison, in a single episode. My discussion of "Montana" (PU S7E4) is representative of episodes where Bourdain chooses a literary figure as his central influence, in this case the poet and novelist Jim Harrison. Yet, even with a literary focal point, Bourdain's camera and editing choices move the discussion to filmic references, in this case classic 1950s Hollywood Westerns, as he repositions the genre's romantic imagination of the West into something defined as social rather than ruggedly individualistic. Essentially, "Hong Kong" and "Montana" are clear examples of how it is not just that Bourdain's work is made more complex by placing it within larger, filmic conversations, but also how his work can reshape those preexisting conversations.

The remaining chapters explore episodes that reference cinematic visual styles to, in turn, invoke, expose, and eventually thwart the Western filmic gaze. In so doing, Bourdain turns cinematic history on its head as he embraces and emphasizes difference while simultaneously refusing to allow his camera to render that difference exotic. In my opinion, given the weight of cinematic history and tradition, this may be his single most impressive achievement. In my discussion of "Rome" (PU S8E9), I show how Bourdain approaches one of the most cinematic cities in the world and uses its film history, borrowing from Pier Paolo Pasolini, to develop, and differentiate, his own lens. Bourdain's camera de-exoticizes Rome, taking an overly filmed, overly visited, and overly romanticized tourist destination and making it seem foreign once again. With "West Virginia" (PU S11E1), he approaches a domestic location that is, itself, largely defined by outsiders' gaze and stereotypes, and treats it as a "foreign" location to be studied and respected. Bourdain utilizes a visual style—uniquely borrowed from such diverse influences as Hollywood sports movies and the avant-garde filmmaker Bruce Conner—to expose and deconstruct stereotypes imposed by a history of visual culture. His episode in Donostia-San Sebastián (PU S9E2) approaches an ancient Basque culture, which predates modern conceptualizations of Europe, and mirrors Basque cinema's transition from a performance for a Spanish gaze to a global one, both in the ways Bourdain uses visual references to Basque cinema and in how he pointedly contrasts his approach to his previous depictions of Donostia-San Sebastián in *A Cook's Tour* and *No Reservations*. Finally, with "Bhutan" (PU S11E8), Bourdain takes his attempts to remove the Western gaze to their furthest extreme, a location so remote, so rarely visited or filmed, that it seemingly exists with no Western conceptualizations, one of the last "exotic" locations on earth. Bourdain builds on the styles used in Darren Aronofsky's films to destroy any need to exoticize or to depict Bhutan as existing—or performing—for a Western gaze.

This book suffers from several biases, but biases I intend to expose, just as Bourdain's films were so interested in exposing his own. The most prominent one is that I believe Bourdain's work got better, and more complex, with time, experience, and experimentation. In fact, I believe he was creating his greatest work at the time of his death, which only heightens questions about what might have been. For this reason, while I talk at length and use examples from throughout his career, my discussion is heavily weighted toward the second half of his career. Specifically, more than half my primary texts—and all six of the episodes that constitute the Dégustation—come from *Parts Unknown*, and, even within that, my selections are weighted toward the later seasons of that program. I think it is true that most filmmakers are judged by their best work, even if it should always be understood within the context of their entire filmography. I therefore see no reason to approach Bourdain differently. His best work not only shows him at his best, his most articulate, his most polished, it also sheds light on ways of better understanding the rest of his work as well. As Eric Kohn wrote for *IndieWire* after Bourdain's death,

"Bourdain was a modern-day auteur, discovering his creativity in piecemeal. It felt like he was just getting started, and on the verge of a new chapter as a unique filmmaking talent . . . Bourdain's parting gift to the world is a jolting realization of how much we needed him, and the excuse to continue to scrutinize the achievements he has left us."[14]

In the introduction to the book version of *A Cook's Tour* (2001), from which I pull this book's opening epigraph, Bourdain naively lists romantic adventures he wanted to experience and builds to a crescendo: "I wanted the world to be just like the movies."[15] In so doing, Bourdain inadvertently articulates the way cinema shapes our worldview in ways both conscious and subconscious. The more Bourdain traveled and interacted with the world, the more he seemed to become not only aware of, but also keenly interested in, the space between representation and subject. In time, as his filmmaking talents grew, so did his ability to explore, expose, and interrogate the ways artistic representations, particularly cinematic ones, shape spectators, much as they had shaped his youthful imagination and travel ambitions. Thus, by the end of his career, Bourdain was consistently making art that was *about* that filmic construction far more than it was about each episode's specific location. That interest, that obsession, with how film makes meaning, and the real-world implications of a society similarly shaped by film, came to be the driving force behind his work, affording Bourdain a means of asking the questions he wanted to explore as he pushed the boundaries of television and created unique art with something different to say.

The last episode to include his narration, and the last episode he had a full hand in shaping, aired three months after his death. The episode, "Kenya" (PU S12E1), documents Bourdain's trip with comedian W. Kamau Bell, and it marked Bell's first visit to the nation from which his ancestors were taken against their will. The duo's itinerary ranges from the urban streets of Nairobi to the sweeping vistas of the Lewa Wildlife Conservatory to a visit to a remote Maasai village. The final scene shows Bell experiencing what appears to be a heartfelt, emotional interaction with dancing Maasai warriors. Despite the highly cinematic nature of the shot, on the surface it smacks of a naive, Western imagination of authenticity. Yet, as the camera returns to views of the plains and the credits begin to roll, the audio track moves to Bourdain's narration: "Who gets to tell the stories? This is a question asked often. The answer in this case, for better or for worse, is, I do. At least this time out. I do my best. I look. I listen. But in the end, I know it's my story—not Kamau's, not Kenya's, or Kenyans.' Those stories are yet to be heard." Thus, in the final voice-over of his career, Bourdain asserts the central truth of all documentary filmmaking, that the story can never be impartial, balanced, or fair—that it is always the story the filmmaker chooses to tell. Many documentary films have worked to expose and interrogate this truth, but few have done so as thoroughly, as articulately, and as fruitfully as the films Bourdain was making toward the end of his career. That story, that perspective, is the story I aim to tell.

1
AUTEURSHIP

> I'm very fortunate to have, for the better part of my entire television career, unlike anyone else I know of in television, I've been free to do whatever I want, to make the shows I want anywhere I want with whom I want in any style I want. First, I don't know any other way, and by now, I won't have it any other way. . . . By the same token, when you are given that much freedom and you have essentially no interference and nothing but support behind you, what you don't want to do is get lazy and bored and sloppy. To me, I'd much rather not make TV at all, or even make unsuccessful TV, than make competent television. It's very easy to make a conventional travel or food show at this point. It's like shooting porn. It's the same shot sequence. The same limited terminology. You know how all the little pieces work. Where you have to start and where you have to end. I detest competent, workmanlike storytelling. And the times that we do that I'm very unhappy with that. I'd rather fail.
>
> —Anthony Bourdain, *Fast Company*[1]

At first glance, calling Anthony Bourdain a filmmaker, let alone suggesting auteurship, seems outlandish. Bourdain entered adulthood as a college English major who rarely attended class and dropped out altogether after his sophomore year. He began working in kitchens, graduated from the Culinary Institute of America, and spent more than two decades as a chef. When, at forty-four, he finally wound up in front of a camera, it was, essentially, by accident. Looking for material to drive a second memoir after *Kitchen Confidential* (2000) topped the bestseller's list,

Bourdain set out to tour the world "in search of the perfect meal,"[2] and, partially to secure funding, allowed a two-person crew to film his journey for a Food Network reality show. Bourdain began *A Cook's Tour* uncomfortable, inexperienced, and almost antagonistic in front of the camera. Even as his skills, as well as his involvement in the creative process, dramatically increased over the ensuing eighteen years, he never directed any of his own work. In the end, however, the control he did assert over his show, born of that very antagonism, allowed him to exploit expectations of authorship in a way that makes the spectator aware of their desire to have him define a "foreign" place via its cuisine, aware of his limitations to do so, and then uses those contradictions to create a brand of filmmaking defined by its reliance on an unreliable auteur. Therefore, while I hesitate to outright *call* Bourdain an auteur, his relationship to auteurship is fundamental to understanding his work.

The consequence of Bourdain's approach is what I define as a chef-auteur who draws on skills learned both in the kitchen and on the film set to interrogate auteurship. Zach Zamboni, one of Bourdain's long-term directors of photography, inadvertently makes a similar argument:

> You can see [his time as a chef] influence the way his show works . . . You have an idea about a dish, where there is collaboration certainly involved in making that dish, but there is a goal there, there is something you are trying to achieve, it is not a random taste or texture you want, it is a specific thing, and if you don't figure out how to organize people or inspire people either by the carrot or the stick to get that thing then it's not going to get accomplished . . . It's gotta be done this way.[3]

What's more, Bourdain's efforts to assert control, and his occasional failures at doing so, are highlighted within his episodes to make the spectator aware of the limitations of his influence and skewed perspective, as he, instead, makes television *about* film's limitations. Bourdain thus argues filmic representations always render a place unknown, to spectator and filmmaker alike.

Bourdain's disavowal of "competent" television that shows the same places in the same ways eschews the kind of romanticism seen in travel writing, particularly by American writers in Europe during the interwar period and the filmic travelogues that came thereafter. While I will return to the subject of travelogues in chapter 4, I mention it now because I think one such travelogue, Richard Wright's *Pagan Spain* (1957), is particularly relevant because of the way Wright approaches his subject. For instance, unlike Ernest Hemingway, Wright actively thwarts a desire to be charmed by flamenco and bullfights, and yet, unlike Thomas Woolf, he cannot bring himself to wholly condemn the Spanish people for their allegiance to Francoism and the Catholic church. For Wright, to see Spain was to adopt (and embrace) many different, and often conflicting perspectives: tourist, US and African American outsider, ethnographer, journalist. Rather than simply seeing these roles as oppositional, he created a text *about* those oppositions. As Wright experiences a Spain he says "looked and seemed Western" but "did not act or feel Western,"[4] he describes walking a "mental tightrope" that left him "free, in a fashion, to depict what I saw."[5] To this day, critics struggle to categorize this book precisely because of the way it is at least as much about Wright's subjectivity, and the implications therein for travelogues as a genre, as it is about Spain. Bourdain's strategy of invoking a genre only to challenge it by embracing multiple perspectives seems to walk a similar tightrope, and Bourdain's medium, coupled with his growing awareness of how to effectively use cinematic tools, allowed him to emphasize the juxtaposing perspectives in ways unavailable to Wright.

In this chapter, I offer a brief history of auteur theory, paying special attention to the ways in which Bourdain would have understood it. I then proceed to the "Congo" (PU S1E8) and "Hanoi" (PU S8E1) episodes as a means of demonstrating how Bourdain routinely used his understanding of—and the spectator's desire for—authorship to develop (and call attention to) his own, distinct, approach. Specifically, I choose these episodes because the locations are so central to Bourdain and to the authors that influenced him, and even more so, because of the way Bourdain proceeds to make filmic texts that transcend direct homage to authorial influence.

Bourdain never saw himself nor let himself be seen, as *just* a chef, journalist, tourist, traveler, ethnographer, or auteur; rather he fashioned himself as all of these at the same time, as he sought to draw the spectator's attention to the competing, subjective views, to see what *he* saw rather than what they wanted him to see. As such, Bourdain's films are best understood as reflexive documentaries often more about the act of documentary filmmaking than the subject itself, and it is for that reason his relationship to auteurism offers such a revealing lens for understanding his life's work.

The idea that Bourdain "exploited" auteurship to his benefit comes directly from the spectator's imagination of a director/author/chef who can tell us everything we want to know. Bourdain consciously plays all these roles as he repeatedly reminds us that every role brings with it limited knowledge; thus, he will never give us what we want. Filmically, the interrogation of this inability to provide a concrete whole manifests itself through invocation, and denial, of auteurship. As Cecilia Sayad writes in her book *Performing Authorship*, we have in many ways moved from an era of seeing "auteurs as 'constructed, called into being, by institutional forces,' thereby constituting a function 'generated by that system' to auteurs asserting their identities through the textual representation of their artistic processes."[6] Sayad analyzes narrative filmmakers like Jean-Luc Godard and Woody Allen, but also, pointedly, documentary filmmakers like Werner Herzog, Agnès Varda, and Errol Morris, focusing primarily on how they insert their bodies and voices into their films to create an open examination of auteurship. In so doing, she argues, "authorship becomes something to be earned . . . authorship not as a condition to be either reached or missed, but as a journey . . . thus the idea of performing authorship, of emphasizing the dramatic rendition of the struggle to communicate and a process that values the ephemeral, exterior, and erratic aspects of artistic expression."[7] Bourdain's journey toward auteurship is therefore a far more interesting study than trying to answer questions of rather or not he could or should be *labeled* an auteur, and, as I will explore using "Congo" and "Hanoi" as examples, his performance of auteurship builds on a tradition of auteur theory to reconsider the very nature of documentary filmmaking.

I think it is no coincidence that auteur theory first was codified in the pages of *Cahiers du Cinéma*, the French film journal that employed many of Bourdain's favorite filmmakers, such as Godard, François Truffaut, and André Bazin, the filmmakers who went on to be the driving force of the nouvelle vague. The movement challenged cinematic tradition as it used realism as an aesthetic (rather than an endpoint) to draw the spectator's attention to the fact realism is an unattainable goal for any art form, even if film's ability to bend time, image, and sound often provide the spectator an illusion of that reality. New Wave film techniques essentially turn the lights on in the theater and make the audience aware that they are, in fact, watching a film. New Wave directors tended to shoot on location with nonprofessional actors, used pastiche to invoke and mock traditional genre conceits within the narrative of their own films, took an amoral approach to their non-heroic protagonists, trended toward ambiguous endings, and used awkward and jarring editing techniques like jump cuts that both sped up time and shook any sense of verisimilitude. At the heart of this experimentation was the assumption that the director was the author of their work, that the spectator should be aware of that director's presence and perspective in the work, and that one should be able to recognize common themes and tendencies across their filmography.

The position of director has received special attention since the birth of cinema, and a connection between the quality of the director and the quality of a film entered French criticism as early as the 1940s, but Truffaut's 1954 essay "A Certain Tendency in French Cinema" served as a shot across the bow of traditional ways of looking at cinema. Defining his theory of auteurship in contrast to the dominant "cinema of quality" in France at the time, Truffaut directly attacked, by name, some of France's most respected filmmakers. Truffaut chided the "technical,"[8] "competent"[9] nature of their work, claiming they chose to ignore cinema's multisensory potential in deference to "faithfulness"[10] to the literary text or screenplay. Specifically, Truffaut claimed, "under the cover of literature—and of course quality—they give the public its habitual dose of smut, non-conformity and facile audacity."[11] Shades of this can be found in Bourdain's own assertion, in the second half of this chapter's epigraph, that he "detest[s] competent, workmanlike storytelling," equating it with porn. Thus, *Cahiers du Cinéma* promoted the idea it was the director's job to be an auteur, to push boundaries, to let his or her vision drive the film and challenge accepted notions of filmmaking.

While New Wave critics freely admitted that, more than any other artistic endeavor, films are collaborative efforts, their romantic view of authorship insisted the all-powerful director remained the unifying force. A common analogy to explain this idea is that of an orchestra, wherein, "the instrument that a conductor plays is, in fact, the orchestra. The orchestra members depend on the conductor to keep time and let them know when and with what emphasis to play. The conductor organizes the performance, and it is therefore up to her or him how the composition will be realized."[12]

Critiques of the inconsistency between sole authorship and collaboration have been present from the beginning. Within three years of Truffaut's article, *Cahiers* critic André Bazin offered a mild rebuke, cautioning auteurship's "exclusive practice leads to another danger: the negation of the film to the benefit of praise of its *auteur*."[13]

Pauline Kael, film critic for *The New Yorker* magazine from 1967 to 1991, went further, consistently chiding auteur theory for privileging the director as sole author of a collective work. Feminist theorists, and later race and sexuality theorists, aptly argue auteur theory privileges white, male voices. Yet, while all these critiques have successfully labeled auteur theory problematic, it remains one of the most central (and arguably useful) concepts in film studies, and even many of its harshest critics have been slow to reject it outright. For example, despite their relevant critiques, feminist film critics have found themselves "caution[ing] against [the] hasty dismissal of the authority of the author precisely because such status provides for both a critique of the power relations attending the position of the author and locates a site of pleasure and political identification."[14]

Compelled by a desire to retain auteurship as a useful lens while responding to fair and accurate attacks, many critics thus broaden the definition of what constitutes an auteur beyond just the position of director, considering screenwriters, actors, and more brazenly, occasionally even producers.[15] As Bruce Kawin argues, "if that redefined *auteur* method leaves us examining the politics of Capra, the conflict of guilt and desire in Hitchcock, or the social vision of Ford, there will be no problem—as long as we do not forget that none of these individuals can be given absolute credit for and title to the films they guided to completion."[16] In other words, the *idea* of authorship sparks important and relevant discussion, but can only be taken seriously when grounded in an awareness of the lack of autonomy typically held by any one force in the making of a film. Despite the fact we rarely talk about television hosts in such a manner, there are cogent reasons to contemplate Bourdain in such a light.

The first thing to consider about Bourdain's relationship to authorship is the fact writing was always central to his identity. Long before he turned to television, while he was still only known as a chef, he was already a writer. His first novel, *Bone in the Throat* (1995), was published five years before *Kitchen Confidential*, and he had been writing manuscripts long before that. By the time of his death, he had published five works of fiction, four memoirs, two cookbooks, and a nonfiction, feminist reevaluation of "Typhoid" Mary Mallon. He began writing much of his own narration on *A Cook's Tour*, and wrote even more of it as his career progressed. By *Parts Unknown*, he wrote his own narration exclusively. He also worked as a screenwriter for the show *Treme* (HBO 2010–13). For all their de-emphasis of screenwriters, nouvelle vague directors were obsessed with writing their own scripts, or, when doing so was not possible, adjusting the scripts they purchased to claim co-writing credits. This tradition carried over to the leaders of the American New Wave, directors like Francis Ford Coppola, Robert Altman, Terrence Malick, and Martin Scorsese, all of whom had direct influence on Bourdain. To the degree to which script clearly lays at the heart of the filmmaking process, Bourdain was the clear voice of his scripts, and the quality of those narrations is the result of his experience and abilities as a writer, his first form of artistic expression outside a kitchen.

The second thing to consider is the degree to which Bourdain eventually attained a level of freedom and autonomy rare not only in television, but often elusive to even the most auteur-minded filmmaker. Bourdain produced, wrote, and starred in his programs. He had massive input in hiring, cinematography, and editing processes. Bourdain also chose most of his own soundtrack for each episode, the vast majority of which was original score (rare for television); by the time of *Parts Unknown*, Bourdain personally commissioned his own, nontraditional theme song working with longtime friends and collaborators Queens of the Stone Age.[17] In short, he had more control and freedom over the end-product than most directors. Bourdain's insistence on, and ability to achieve, such autonomy began early in his career. Asked about "positive instinct decisions" in the last recorded interview before his death, Bourdain talked about *A Cook's Tour*: "I did not give Food Network the show they wanted. And I said no a lot to what seemed like a lot of money . . . What's good for you in the short run is very often not good for you in the long run."[18] Such a stubborn resistance to yield artistic freedom drove his moves, first, to Travel Channel, and later to CNN. At each stage, Bourdain leveraged his growing celebrity, fame, and the gravitas each afforded him, to demand contract terms that increasingly guaranteed larger budgets, more access to remote locations, and the autonomy he refers to in this chapter's epigraph, the "free[dom] to do whatever I want, to make the shows I want anywhere I want with whom I want in any style I want."

The third thing to consider is the degree to which Bourdain was able to successfully exert control over a collaborative process. Zamboni's description of Bourdain's chef-auteur attributes came about after discussion in an interview about the need to work collaboratively. In Zamboni's words, "In the kitchen and on the set, the power of entropy is really real, it is always working, things will turn to chaos" making it difficult for a chef (or filmmaker) to "impose [his or her] ideas."[19] Thus, Bourdain embraced a collaborative aesthetic in which he actively used everyone's ideas to help shape his voice, his vision, his performance of auteurship, leading them with the same carrot-and-stick approach needed by chefs, filmmakers, and orchestra conductors. As Bourdain himself asserted, "Everybody on my crew understands that if they have an idea—like I'd like to tell this story backwards or I'd like to shoot this entire show on a cell phone, or black and white, or Panavision, or 16mm film—let's make it happen! I will support that. And I work thankfully in an environment where the people around me will support that."[20] Over the course of eighteen years, he did just that, typically highlighting and crediting team members when they came up with ideas.

The unifying effect of these elements is the degree to which they all go back to how Bourdain approaches his subject matter from a cinematic perspective. As I discuss in the introduction, cinema lies at the heart of his approach to everything, and his shows are often an overt reflection or exploration of the way cinema shapes the spectator's, and more often Bourdain's, view of the world. This gaze is present at every level of Bourdain's approach, even assembling collaborators. In the last interview before his death, asked what he "looks for in assembling a team that works for you," Bourdain answered, "You've got to love movies, got to know your cinematographers, because if I start talking about Vittorio

Storaro and you don't know who the fuck I'm talking about, we're going to have a problem, and you've got to work hard . . . everybody understands that we all expect each other to do our best work every episode . . . the people who take that challenge seriously do well and stick around. And the ones who turn in competent work do not because I abhor competent work."[21] So, again much like Truffaut, Bourdain wanted to push beyond technical competency, to do something new, something innovative, something collaborative, something that employed every possibility of film as an art form.

Bourdain's relationship to auteurism evolved as his filmic talents and artistic control expanded, and he often performed his auteurship on-screen in ways that actively explored the potentials and limitations inherent in auteurship. Almost every episode was, in one way or another, a self-conscious exploration of how a single film, or group of films, shaped Bourdain's imagination of the subject and location. Often, however, it was his obsession specifically with auteurship itself that dominated those expectations. For example, every trip Bourdain took up a river seemed to require Bourdain to refer to (and compare himself to) Werner Herzog's *Aguirre, the Wrath of God* (1972), or *Fitzcarraldo* (1982).

Both representative examples I offer in this chapter, "Congo" and "Hanoi," are structured around direct references to filmic and literary texts, but we see them from various vantage points: from their influence on Bourdain's "image" of these places, the way in which those images and their influences have problematic and colonialist implications, and how what we do with those implications is left on-screen for us to contend with, devoid of easy answers or facile rhetorical questions. This was true of Bourdain's work, to some degree, from the beginning. But, by these *Parts Unknown* episodes, he used influential references in a manner that was far more subtle, more nuanced, more effective. Collectively, the episodes offer insight about how Bourdain sought to reimagine cinema in a forty-minute television show in which he performed the role of auteur.

In retrospect, Bourdain's desire to use CNN's budget and connections to get to the Democratic Republic of the Congo in *Parts Unknown*'s very first season should have been a foregone conclusion. Joseph Conrad's *Heart of Darkness* (1899) was one of the most influential novels of Bourdain's youth, and the American New Wave film it inspired, Francis Ford Coppola's *Apocalypse Now* (1979), which shifted the setting of Conrad's story to Cambodia during the war in Việt Nam, was among Bourdain's favorite films. In fact, Bourdain's colleagues claim it was a bit of an obsession,[22] a film he could not stop talking about, and that obsession was born out in his work as well. Almost all eight (yes, eight) episodes set in Việt Nam make direct reference to *Apocalypse Now* or *Heart of Darkness*. Bourdain even shot an episode in southern Italy (PU S10E8) largely as an excuse to interview Coppola. Two early episodes, one set in Cambodia (ACT S1E6) and one in Việt Nam (ACT S1E4), include quasi-narrative scenes in which Bourdain literally, and awkwardly, recreates scenes from *Apocalypse Now*. The latter ends with Bourdain, sick and moaning, in a mosquito-netted hotel bed, under a loud ceiling fan, moaning "the horror, the horror." Recalling those early episodes, Bourdain claimed in a 2013 interview, "I thought never in a million years will I have the opportunity to see Việt Nam or Cambodia or do this Joseph Conrad, *Apocalypse Now* thing. This was my opportunity. On my way to finding the perfect meal I was looking for some off-the-road adventures. I had a plan for Việt Nam that I was going to reenact the story arc of *Apocalypse Now*, a foolish, over-romantic notion perhaps."[23] That is not to say he abandoned playing on such influences for the point of humor, however. For instance, a late *Parts Unknown* episode, unfinished before his death, "Asturias" (S12E2), includes a narrative sequence in which cartoon versions of Bourdain and two chef friends re-create a scene from *Apocalypse Now* and tie it to the cheese caves Bourdain had just visited. But this scene is still notably different from *A Cook's Tour*. The production values are higher. It is less awkward, more filmic. More than anything, it is a brief comic interlude that neither deviates from nor domineers over the tone of the episode at large; rather, it fits seamlessly into the larger narrative structure.

One would anticipate that the choice of Congo as a location would inspire a focus on the literary text, *Heart of Darkness*, since it was the setting of the novel. On the surface, that is precisely the case. Whereas the entire episode is framed around quotations from (and references to) the novel, Bourdain never directly mentions *Apocalypse Now* by name and refrains, completely, from anything that would overtly shift the spectator's focus away from the Congo and directly onto Coppola's film. Yet, its presence, or, more precisely, its impact on Bourdain, dominates. The first narration we hear after the opening credits is Bourdain's voice claiming, "Everyone gets everything he wants. I wanted to see the Congo, and, for my sins, they let me." The narration is a direct quotation, without citation, from *Apocalypse Now*'s opening lines, altering the word "mission" to "Congo." The original score clearly refers to that of *Apocalypse Now*, as does the cinematography, which invokes Coppola's throughout the episode. Bourdain's narration then shifts to the dominant quotation from Conrad, which Bourdain cites as Conrad's "alter ego, Marlow." Bourdain begins, "When I was a little chap, I had a passion for maps. At that time there were many blank spaces on earth."[24] Suddenly, however, mid-narration and without pause or change of tone, Bourdain reverts to his own voice, retaining only a single word ("hankering") from Conrad. Bourdain continues, "but there was one yet. The biggest, the most blank, that I had a hankering after. This, then, is the Congo. The size of all Western Europe combined, it should be Africa's wealthiest nation. But people forget, or never even knew, that the twentieth century's first holocaust happened here." Bourdain links this holocaust to Belgium's King Leopold, of whom, Bourdain reminds us, Conrad's fictional Kurtz was an arm. As Bourdain continues to tell Congo's history throughout this sequence, the images and soundtrack speed up to a crescendo taken straight from the filmic text, *Apocalypse Now*.

The episode thus serves as a treatise on auteurship—Bourdain's, Conrad's, Coppola's, and, most importantly, how Bourdain's relationship to Conrad and Coppola determines how he understands, or admittedly fails to understand, Congo, as well as how the Western world has failed to understand Congo for at least a century. The blurred lines between Bourdain's narration and that of Conrad and Coppola's, paired with repeated images of Congolese standing silently on the riverbank staring back at the camera, first in silhouette, and then fleshed out, emphasize the way one's authorship, one's perspective, is never entirely one's own. The competition between these perspectives prevents us from ever fully experiencing other ones. Bourdain's perspective, which shapes that of the spectator's, was shaped by Coppola's, whose perspective, in turn, was shaped by Conrad's. Conrad, as an early Westerner imagining an "exotic" unseen (by Westerners) land also surely had his perspective shaped by a history of exoticism. Such a competition between perspectives, created by history and genre, prevents any person, any author, from having complete control over his narrative or where it will go. Bourdain means this artistically, in terms of how the narratives we have read and watched shape the ones we create, but also physically, as the realities of shooting a film in the Congo are actively emphasized on-screen in Bourdain's film.

Much as the logistical nightmares Coppola faced filming *Apocalypse Now* became part of the film's legend (as well as its marketing), Bourdain's struggle to control his own story in the face of obstacles is central to this episode. Bourdain, moreover, emphasizes them within his narrative, making his agency and control (and lack thereof) a central theme. For example, before the opening credits, Bourdain opens with a short sequence shown out of chronological order, in which the entire production team helplessly waits as locals try to repair a ferry before nightfall. Later, Bourdain discusses bumpy roads, the lack of food sources for the crew, the dearth of refrigeration, the danger posed by rebel groups, and the danger of flying on an airplane in Congolese airspace in bad weather. We see Bourdain bounce down these roads. We see him scared to board the plane. We see him struggle to cook his crew dinner before nightfall. All this not only draws the spectator's attention to the fact they are watching a film, and the impact the filmmaker's presence has on the "reality" being documented, but it also allows Bourdain's own body, on-screen, to consciously shape our view of his auteurship, and its limitations. As Sayad claims, this insertion of a filmmaker's own body, their own physical presence, serves as their "particular way for the emphasis on the gesture towards expression, while their bodies contribute to our sense that the amalgam of sounds and images we see on the screen can be traced back to a locatable human source."[25]

Bourdain makes no bones about the fact this episode is about *his* journey, born of his own hubris. Opening an episode that emphasizes poverty and genocide by proclaiming "everyone gets everything he wants" actively draws attention to Bourdain's privilege, not just as Westerner, but as filmmaker. His sins, one is left to surmise, are those of a filmmaker, and the "they" who afford him this privilege, are those for whom he has committed those sins, namely his bosses at CNN. Production difficulties cause Bourdain to be hours late for a meeting with Pierre Musala Abeka, chief of the Wagenia tribe, and Bourdain fails to understand, until later, the significance of the gift Abeka gives him, a gold bracelet that had been in his family since before colonial times. Bourdain draws attention to his own failings, however, sitting on his boat and self-mockingly asking in a New York society type tone, "So, where'd you get the bracelet? Oh, an African king gave it to me on the Congo River. Where'd you get yours?" Elsewhere, near the end of the episode, a Congolese library director tells Bourdain, in French, colonial times were "the best time they were living." Apparently not wanting to influence such volatile words in either direction, Bourdain refrains from subtitles (which have been present throughout the episode), choosing to let the man's translator speak for him. Bourdain says nothing in the moment. Instead, he asks in voice-over, "What do you *say* to someone who suggests that Belgian colonialism might have been the good times?" He lets the man's claims, no matter how abhorrent Bourdain finds them, stand for themselves, as he draws attention to that choice by asking what right a white, Western filmmaker would have to say anything at all.

In short, the degree to which the entire episode is driven by Bourdain's performance of auteurship, born out of influence from the authors whose work affected him, lies on the surface and at the core of the episode. No matter how empathetic or nonexploitive Bourdain aims to be, he admits in the final narration, "Rotting bridges, makeshift ferries. It's an adventure. Fortunately, ours was a good adventure. The Congo was a place that's always fascinated me. This is a trip I've been wanting to take since I've been writing stories or making television. But what I found was something unexpected. I met a lot of people who, for a long time, have been waiting, hoping for things to get better. A lot more hope than there's any right to expect." Then, as the camera shifts to Bourdain looking out his New York City apartment window, the sound of car horns crashing in, he concludes, "when all is said is done, I wanted to go to the Congo. And I did." Bourdain uses editing, sound, cinematography, and mise-en-scène to comment upon his own narration, to emphasize how we should comprehend that narration, to make sure we are aware of the privilege inherent in his cinematic "adventure." In fact, answering Truffaut's call to value cinema over script, most of Bourdain's arguments in this episode—about Congo, about Conrad, about Coppola—subtly remain in the periphery, outside the primary narrative. Unlike earlier in his career, he *uses* Coppola to shape how we see our own failure to see Congo.

Much as I argue Bourdain's approach suggests no film can provide a wholly accurate depiction of any subject matter, his goal is not to accurately depict locations like Congo. Or, more precisely, he believes the most accurate method of depicting a place like Congo is to critique the ways we, as spectators and as a society, have failed to see Congo and the ways that failure has been shaped and exacerbated by filmmakers who represent Congo within the context of an illusion of an accurate, complete depiction. As I explore throughout this book, Bourdain typically uses filmic devices to draw attention to the incomplete nature of his filmic depictions, but what episodes like "Congo" and "Hanoi" demonstrate is the way his deconstruction of passive cinema is present even at the level of one's imagination of auteurship, as he uses both his physical presence and authorial authority, as well as that of the filmmakers and writers who shaped his perspectives, as a means of drawing attention to competing perspectives and biases. He also highlights the real-world consequences of ignoring the inherent presence of such perspectives and biases in filmmaking.

Whereas "Congo" ranks among the best examples of Bourdain using his biggest influences to express a more nuanced, filmic perspective on auteurship, "Hanoi" serves as an example of his ability to abandon direct references to the authors who shaped him altogether, turning, instead, to his own cinematic style to express what they taught him. The other book (along with *Heart of Darkness*) that dominated Bourdain's youth, and later his television career, was Graham Greene's *The Quiet American* (1955). It shaped how he imagined Việt Nam, his thoughts about the history of US foreign policy, how he reacted to the homogenization, often through colonization, of unique and distinct cultures. He repeatedly referred to it in episodes set in Việt Nam, going so far as to physically carry it around Hanoi in a *No Reservations* episode titled "Vietnam: There's No Place like Home" (NR S5E10), reading it at a café and awkwardly holding it up in front of the Hotel Continental, a haunt of Greene's. In "Hanoi," Bourdain manages to take a single quotation from the novel and express its meaning through some of the most sophisticated cinema of his career, all while using the spectator's awareness of Bourdain's on-screen presence to shape their view of Việt Nam.

The contrast between the Việt Nam Western cinema traditionally depicts versus the Việt Nam Bourdain wishes to convey is embodied by the episode's lone Greene reference and, more importantly, displayed by the filmic contrast Bourdain creates in the episode's opening minutes. "Hanoi" opens with shots of Vietnamese people farming and walking. The shots emulate countless Western depictions of Việt Nam and are set to an original score heavily reminiscent of multiple Hollywood movies that romanticize colonial Việt Nam. The style is so romanticized as to draw attention to the dominant tradition of Western perspectives. The images throughout the sequence, however, become increasingly urban and modern. The episode then switches to the opening credit sequence and returns to a blank, black-filled screen with the quotation from *The Quiet American*, which serves as epigraph: "They say whatever you're looking for, you will find here . . . [ellipses in original] The smell: that's the first thing that hits you, promising everything in exchange for your soul." It is worth noting that the "they" in the first half of the quotation is undeniably those from the outside, the West, and the smell that draws the narrator in, is that of Việt Nam. This is the same contrast Bourdain creates between the before-the-credits sequence and what comes immediately after this epigraph.

The shift to the Việt Nam Bourdain wants to show begins with the use of an avant-garde film choice that actively denies the spectator's ability to see; it also draws the spectator's attention to the impact of that denial. As we leave the epigraph frame, we hear Bourdain ask, "Do you smell that? Motorbike exhaust? Fish sauce? Incense? The faraway smell of . . . something? Is that pork grilling over charcoal? Việt Nam. It could be no place else." Bourdain chooses not to provide images to match this narration—images that could only, like the ones before the title sequence, draw upon a history of the Western gaze. Rather, the screen turns to a series of bright, vibrant colors, matching the emotion Bourdain hopes the description of the smells will spark. This choice draws the spectator's attention to film's limitations; the inability, for instance, to re-create smell, or to physically transport the spectator to the imagined reality film creates. Nothing Bourdain showed could match the potential for what the spectator could imagine. Thus, Bourdain uses film to embody smell, the most evocative yet difficult sense to transmute, rather than represent it.

If, as the American New Wave filmmaker Martin Scorsese claims, "cinema is a matter of what's in the frame and what's out,"[26] then

Bourdain's decision to emphasize what is *left out*, what is (essentially) denied, not only draws attention to film's limitations, but also to cinema as a constructed space, as well as who constructs it—in this case, Bourdain. Further, because of Bourdain's decision, the spectator is left to solely focus on his questions, the degree to which the description sounds foreign, unknowable, all-encompassing. Then, when images return, they return in a three-minute sequence dominated by close-ups of everyday Vietnamese people with Vietnamese folk music as soundtrack. It is the opposite of the Việt Nam typically depicted in Western media. While Bourdain has just reminded his spectator this is a construct, this contrast deconstructs the previous dominant images of Việt Nam and renders the spectator keenly aware of what is different about Bourdain's construction, and what is at stake in such differences.

Bourdain thereby creates a thesis for the episode, born from Greene's impact. Namely, that a place, in this case Việt Nam, can draw you in precisely because (not in spite) of the fact it is foreign, unknowable. Rather than exotic, it is simply different, and the onus is on Bourdain, as filmmaker, to attempt to see, embrace, and express that difference. This is a responsibility he also places on the spectator with the filmic choices I just described in "Hanoi's" opening moments. And this approach stretches across the episode. Bourdain asks for guidance from a guest about drinking a beer from a bottle or glass: "how would you do it if I wasn't here?" He interviews President Barack Obama at a hyper-local restaurant, and orders the US president *bún chả*, a uniquely Hanoi dish, rather than stereotypical dishes such as phở or bánh mí—a decision that inspires Obama to share his own story of a specific dish in a specific region of Indonesia. In an extended, mostly silent tracking shot, the camera moves up a street peeking in open doors as Bourdain narrates, "every doorway, every window, a little slice of life. A story all its own, lives lived, being lived, caught for a second, a moment, then gone." He concludes the episode by reminding us, "General William Westmoreland . . . famously said 'the Oriental doesn't put the same high price on life as does a Westerner. Life is plentiful, life is cheap in the Orient.' It was an extraordinarily grotesque and wrong-headed observation from a guy who—if nothing else—was expected to understand his enemy. He could not, it turned out, do even that." Bourdain's music then returns to that of the opening, and he proclaims, "Maybe, I hope, we are a little bit smarter now," and the episode concludes with a minute-long montage of Việt Nam streetlife. In short, the entire episode asks the spectator to dive headfirst into difference, to be enticed by it, to strive to be aware of it, all through the lens of a filmmaker who also makes it clear none of us, himself included, can ever fully understand it.

Much like "Congo," Bourdain's approach is best embodied in a moment where he performs auteurship on-screen. Immediately after the Greene quotation and denied spectatorship, we find ourselves following Bourdain on a handheld camera as he rides the streets of Hanoi on a scooter. It is, aesthetically speaking, some of the most seamless and beautiful filmmaking I have seen on television. More importantly, more tangibly, it is a prime example of the success of Bourdain's conscious use of authorial voice. The voice-over tells us, in a tone of pressing urgency, "*Listen* to me. Listen *to me*. There is *no* other way to see this city, Hanoi, than from a motorbike or a scooter. To do otherwise would be to miss it *all*. It is one of the great pleasures of my life to join a river of people rushing through the streets." The matching images are tracking shots of Bourdain sliding smoothly in and out of traffic, coupled with point-of-view shots of unromanticized Vietnamese gliding on their own bikes. After about a minute the music slows down, and turns slightly more romantic, and Bourdain's tone mellows, "Việt Nam. It grabs you and doesn't let you go. Once you love it, you love it forever. I've been coming here since 2000 . . . I keep coming back. I have to." In a single sequence, he simultaneously universalizes Việt Nam (as well as difference), and makes it wholly personal, about him.

Bourdain emphasizes the unique, the local, the (too) easily missed, but he also emphasizes how that relates to his own spectatorship, as traveler, and performed auteurship, as filmmaker. His body physically embodies the themes of the entire episode. As such, Bourdain's performance yet again recalls Sayad, who claims these "directors offer not only self-conscious commentaries on the relationship between artists and their works, but also an understanding of the perception of authors by audiences and critics alike. They reclaim a voice in the theoretical articulations of cinematic authorship by inviting us to think of it not as a critical construction, but as a self-construction—not as an artificial attempt to humanize the source of the film's discourse through a reading practice, but as the filmmaker's performance of the processes that lead to the fabrication of meaning."[27] And thus, Bourdain's self-construction of auteurship, which drives his filmmaking approach from the Congo to Hanoi (and beyond), becomes a sophisticated example of an approach to auteurship that has dominated the last half century.

2
CINEMATOGRAPHY

It's very easy to make beautiful pictures. But pictures which mean something, with what's in it, that's a totally different story.

—Vilmos Zsigmond, *Parts Unknown*, "Budapest"[1]

I went to film school. Tony did not go to film school. But the expanse of his knowledge of film was just unreal. Half the directors of the films that he would talk about before we'd go into an episode, that he would want to pay some kind of homage to, half of those directors I'd never even heard of. So, it was almost like I went to graduate school, working with Tony. He would give us a list of films and we would go home and do our homework, and kind of absorb the style or the pacing of certain directors. It was a language that we could communicate with, in an abstract and visual sense. We could talk about certain scenes; we could talk about certain shots within films that we would want to either completely steal from or lean into.

—Nick Brigden, *Bourdain: The Definitive Oral Biography*[2]

Of the many filmic aspects traditionally ascribed to auteurship, cinematography was Anthony Bourdain's primary point of emphasis. Much as the French nouvelle vague critics felt a director's thumbprint could, and should, be best expressed in a filmmaker's visual style, Bourdain's obsession with cinema always seemed connected to cinematography. Bourdain's first concern when hiring crew was that they "love movies," but I find it notable he defines proof of that love as a knowledge of cinematographers, not directors—Vittorio Storaro rather than Francis Ford Coppola or Bernardo Bertolucci.[3] Bourdain's emphasis on cinematography led to innovative, high-quality work that pushed the technical boundaries of what could be filmed in real time. Visually speaking, his shows were trendsetters that were among the first programs to fully embrace the potential of high-definition and widescreen formats, resulting in a much higher visual quality than most of his contemporaries. But the significance of Bourdain's relationship with cinematography is not technical. Robert Bresson famously defined cinematography as "writing with images in movement and with sounds,"[4] and while Bourdain began his artistic career as a traditional writer, Bourdain best expressed himself visually. Unlike most food and travel TV, which embrace beautiful images to chase a romanticized imagination of realism for the spectator to consume, Bourdain *uses* images to open a discussion about cinematography: how cinematography shapes not only how we experience filmic texts, but the world itself. In short, his work answers Vilmos Zsigmond's call for images to "mean something."

For clarity, I often refer to "Bourdain's camera" in this chapter *not* to imply complete control or a romantic imagination of auteurship. Rather, I do so for clarity, to differentiate each episode's own cinematography from that of the cinematographers Bourdain interviews (and invokes) within each episode. In short, I do not simply mean Bourdain, the man, but rather "Bourdain," the collaborative cinematography created by Bourdain and his Zero Point Zero crew.

Bourdain insisted on a different visual style for every episode, typically drawing upon a filmmaker who shaped his worldview, an influence which could then be interrogated, both within Bourdain's narrative and by the way he used, and altered, the borrowed visual style. For instance, "Copenhagen" (PU S2E4) was shot in the style of Terrence Malick's *The Tree of Life* (2011), "Miami" (PU S5E2) mirrors Paolo Sorrentino's *The Great Beauty* (2013), "Paraguay" (PU S4E3) borrows from Steven Soderbergh's *The Limey* (1999), and an entire episode in Rome (NR S6E20) was shot in black and white to invoke Federico Fellini. When Bourdain wanted to explore the impact of overtourism in "Venice" (NR S5E2), he referenced Paul Schrader's *The Comfort of Strangers* (1990), a film that uses cinematography to make a similar indictment in the same location. To quote Todd Liebler, one of his longtime directors of photography, "Tony challenges us a lot. He would say 'I love this film and we're going to Hong Kong. Make sure you watch *Chungking Express*.' Wong Kar Wai is the director. We want to borrow from him."[5] But, Liebler emphasizes, "He did it artfully. It was not random."[6] Or, as Nick Brigden suggests in this chapter's second epigraph, cinematography creates its own "language" that is always, inherently in conversation with the cinematography which comes before it. Thus, much as Robert Altman was defined by his change of genre in almost every film to perpetually make films *about* the deconstruction of genre, the unique visual thumbprint of Bourdain's work manifests itself in a unique willingness to perpetually alter and change the style of cinematography to deconstruct dominant visual images.

As I intend to demonstrate throughout this book, Bourdain's visual choices routinely draw the spectator's attention precisely to how the image is *constructed*, a visual embodiment of Bourdain's persistent, broader intentions to remind us how all perspectives are constructed, thus deconstructing the perception of objectivity inherent in documentary filmmaking. For example, while editing "Madagascar" (PU S5E4), Bourdain wanted to include two distinct camera angles of the same event, drawing attention to the presence of the camera and the constructed image the spectator sees. His producer, Tom Vitale, worried it would "needlessly distract from the very serious issues we bring up in the show and instead call attention to us."[7] Bourdain answered bluntly, without hesitation, "*Exactly* . . . It's about the moral quandary of travel and white privilege. The camera is a liar. Drawing attention to it calls into question our own reliability and shows our hands aren't clean. I want to show how manipulative even 'honest, tell it like it is' TV can be."[8]

This intent exhibits itself in subtle ways throughout Bourdain's filmography as he uses visual references to the films that influenced him precisely because they force the spectator to be aware of how the camera in Bourdain's films is shaped by those influences, much as his camera shapes how they experience the story and the location. Almost every episode's cinematography emphasizes the camera's presence and the effect of the "lies" Bourdain and his crew use that camera to tell. Most every episode becomes a treatise about how *no* depiction of any location, or filmic subject of any kind for that matter, could ever be objective or unshaped by the visual representations which come before them. Similarly, when we travel our experiences are inevitably shaped by how the location matches or denies our preconceived notions of that location, largely shaped by cinema much as Bourdain, in the opening epigraph to this book, imagined the outside world through movies as a boy.

The continual pressure to achieve high-quality cinematography while changing visual style every episode was only sustainable because Bourdain surrounded himself with talented crew and managed to keep the same people for extended periods of time, such as his two primary directors of photography, Todd Liebler and Zach Zamboni, who each worked with Bourdain for over a decade. As Vitale explained, "One of [Bourdain's] most important rules was the shows always had to be different each week. Manic depressively and schizophrenically different. Always pushing forward, doing the hard thing, even the stupid thing, as long as it was the different thing."[9] Liebler proclaimed he was constantly having to "[hold] on for dear life,"[10] Zamboni complained about having to go "into a shoot with 11 different types of cameras"[11] and, in another location, having to limit his options by keeping "the camera on the tripod until it was just painful to do so."[12] In particular, the invocation of predetermined visual styles while shooting documentary-style interviews on location in real time made the efforts even more difficult. Liebler cites "Japan" (PU S8E6) as a specific example, in which, "We look at old Ozu movies . . . black and white and we would try to emulate those. Not everywhere, but where we could set a mood, a theme, color palettes. [But] everything is very much *vérité*. We would go into a location and that's the location we have to use."[13] Because of their experience and long-term investment in Bourdain's vision, however, the camera crew embraced the challenge. For instance, Zamboni's description of the approach claims, "Philosophically, it's very much like travel, where if you want to see something new, it's got to be challenging and scary for you. Otherwise, you're just treading the same territory."[14]

Zamboni, ironically, attributed his ability to meet this pressure to his background in reality TV. They were "terrible shows," Zamboni explained, but they "taught me to be really fast on my feet but also coming from the film world to have a good eye for things."[15] Elsewhere, Zamboni pointed to the way reality TV gave him experience with "walking through a different space all the time, over and over, different conditions and trying to find something beautiful in there."[16] For Zamboni, no matter the genre or the location, "it goes back to story. What's the story in this particular place? First of all, what are my building blocks and how does that become beautiful . . . Blocking: how do I and the camera relate to subject and therefore how does the audience relate to subject. You can't get around that."[17] Thus, a return to the fundamentals of cinematography as a means of achieving beautiful images adhering to a unified style—an approach most typically found in narrative film—captured guerrilla-style while shooting documentary subjects. For Bourdain, that meant documentary subject matter shot with a narrative lens—the cinematography *part* of the story telling.

Vitale emphasized how Bourdain's awareness of, and interest in, cinematography was ever-present. Even early in his career, imagined as on-screen talent, Bourdain regularly complained about tired, genre cinematography, such as when filming walk-in shots in Saint Martin (ACT S2E1), cajoling, "Film the kids playing by the fishing boats, the surf, or even a fucking palm tree. Literally everything else here would make a better and more interesting introduction shot than my bony ass."[18]

Much as Bourdain used his physical body to emphasize his performance of auteurship, he also used the challenges caused by his visual approach to emphasize the presence of the cinematographer and his cinematography. When Bourdain leadingly asks the photographer Roberto Salas in "Cuba" (NR S7E9), "does the camera always tell the truth?" Salas responds "No. The camera is one of the worst liars in the world. Because the mind is behind the instrument, it's what goes into the image." Bourdain emphases such ideas throughout his work, and while I will explore it in each of the episodes in the Dégustation, it is brought to the surface in two episodes where his primary guest is a cinematographer, Vilmos Zsigmond in "Budapest" (PU S5E6) and Christopher Doyle in "Hong Kong" (PU S11E5), as well as an episode in Andalucía (PU S2E2) in which he visits the adopted home of his own cinematographer, Zach Zamboni.

By focusing these three episodes on discussions of cinematography, between Bourdain (as host and as narrator) and cinematographer (as guest), Bourdain forces attention toward what is at stake in *how* something is visually represented. Bourdain draws attention to the differences in approach between the guest and his own work, the influence the guest's cinematography has had upon that of Bourdain's team, the degree to which Bourdain's cinematography (in the episode) draws upon that of his guest's, and the ways in which Bourdain's camera changes or alters that influence. In so doing, Bourdain comments on what all that all has to say about each one's ideas about what the aim of cinematography should be. Bourdain manages to draw attention to the very element of cinema that the spectator most often accepts without question and makes the spectator an active participant in a debate about the nature of cinematography.

Of the three episodes, "Budapest" is the most unabashedly *about* cinematography from start to finish. It opens, before the credits, with footage Zsigmond shot in 1956 of Russian tanks squashing rebellion interspersed with images of Bourdain and Zsigmond walking the same streets six decades later; the sequence ends with the Zsigmond quotation that serves as epigraph for this chapter. Then, immediately after the credits, the camera opens from the back of a movie theater with scenes from Zsigmond's films on-screen as Bourdain narrates:

> You know these images. You grew up with them. They are burned into your brain. They are iconic sequences. Framed and lit and seen through the lens in ways that changed filmmaking forever. All made by the same man. So, who made these beautiful things? Where did he come from? It didn't begin in Hollywood; it began here in the streets of Budapest. What about his life, his past, his upbringing, led him again and again to look through a piece of glass and make images like these? But first, some context.

The episode then seemingly moves on; first to images of Budapest and a discussion of its unique architecture, then to a history lesson, and eventually to schnitzel. Just as the emphasis seems to ignore cinematography, however, the camera turns to art on the wall of a café before switching back to street architecture. Bourdain interjects again, "There is another long tradition of artistry here in Budapest. We grew up with their works. Visual artists. Photographers, filmmakers. Where did they all go?" Zsigmond then returns to the screen for almost the entirety of the last thirty-minutes of the show. With Zsigmond, Bourdain manages to essentialize

Hungarian culture—architecture, food, history, music—via connection to visual culture and relegates everything to context for Zsigmond's art. Cinematography is what matters.

For all of Bourdain's centering his story on cinematography and his admiration for Zsigmond, the point never settles on homage or flattery; rather, Bourdain focuses on the construction of images. The duo watches scenes from Zsigmond's films in a movie theater and discuss visual images as they sit within the space of cinematic spectacle, we see Zsigmond develop his own still images in a dark room, and Bourdain and Zsigmond walk across a bridge where Zsigmond filmed tanks as they talk about *how* he did so. When Bourdain reintroduces Zsigmond after the "context" section, he does so enthusiastically, declaring him a "legendary cinematographer" who "created a whole new palate, took crazy risks, changed film language in ways people still try to imitate," but Bourdain ends by adding, "he's making our camera crew very nervous, I'll tell you," thus breaking the fourth wall and drawing attention to the construction of Bourdain's own cinematography, as well as the fact Bourdain is one of the imitators of whom he speaks. It is not enough for Bourdain to simply show beautiful images from the cinematographer who shot *McCabe & Mrs. Miller* (Robert Altman, 1971), *The Deer Hunter* (Michael Cimino, 1978), *Deliverance* (John Boorman, 1972), and many more. Nor is it enough for those shots to "mean something" in their original context. Bourdain must make sure his film is a treatise on how and why these images were constructed in a way that "meant" something in all contexts.

The most complete amalgamation of these intentions occurs in a scene where the two trespass an abandoned building that served as secret police headquarters in 1956, the sight of a firefight between Russian tanks and Hungarian snipers who were later hanged in front of the building. Bourdain's camera follows Zsigmond as he shoots still images on a digital camera. Zsigmond tells Bourdain "It is probably the first time I have shot this building." We see Zsigmond, from behind, as he frames and chooses his shot. We see what he is looking at in his digital viewfinder. We hear the artificial sound of a camera shutter as Bourdain's frame snaps to the still images Zsigmond is shooting; images that appear more beautiful than the ruins have seemed previously. These choices emphasize the *construction* of both sets of images, Zsigmond's and Bourdain's, as well as the way Zsigmond's serve as examples of poetic realism, the philosophy Zsigmond helped invent. To quote Zsigmond elsewhere in the episode, it was "not realism, we called it poetic realism . . . we emphasize basically the beauty of the things but also I make it more beautiful than it is."

Complicating this dynamic even further, Bourdain's shots of Zsigmond's still images are bookended by multiple shots directly borrowed from *McCabe & Mrs. Miller*, itself one of the defining examples of poetic realism and a film Bourdain has already told his audience represents "absolutely revolutionary work." In fact, Bourdain's assertion about that film had come as he showed one of the very shots from *McCabe* that Bourdain's camera now copies: a shot in which a gunman watches his pursuer through a broken hole in a door window, planning to shoot him sniper-style once he passes. In Bourdain's shot, we see Zsigmond through just such a hole in the building's ruins. As such, Bourdain ensures the spectator is made aware of the reference as he creates a visual dialogue between both filmmaker's lenses that is centered on image as a constructed reality.

"Budapest" concludes with a dialogue between Bourdain and Zsigmond that further emphasizes images as constructed. More to the point, it emphasizes the cinematographer, himself, as a construction, echoing Bourdain's earlier assertion it is the "context" of Budapest that explains what led Zsigmond to "look through a piece of glass and make images like these." Sitting at a family dinner table, Bourdain asks "Why is Hungary so strong on photography?" Zsigmond's wife answers, "I think they are very strong on mathematics which was in the early days connected to photography." Zsigmond confirms this view, "that's what I said, that schools in Hungary are very good." The entire table joins Bourdain in laughter as he responds, "This is no kind of answer to me. You've made some of the most iconically beautiful images that we've known in the modern world and you keep telling me, well, I was smart in school, I was good at math." Zsigmond quips, "well Tony what would you like to hear?" to which Bourdain responds, "I was touched by God [laughs]. I don't know. If you were regularly creating the sublime and looking for a metaphysical answer." The conversation ends as Zsigmond cuts Bourdain off, "We *learn* this. We *learn* to be an artist." The episode's themes are thus reinforced: images can transcend, can shape how we see the world, but they cannot be judged by beauty alone. Much like Bourdain's

Bourdain includes this shot from Robert Altman's *McCabe & Mrs. Miller* (1971), shot by episode guest Vilmos Zsigmond, only to then copy that very image later in the episode. Bourdain draws attention to how all cinematography is built upon a history and language of what comes before it.

performance of auteurship, the images are most powerful when we focus on who made them, how they made them, why they made them.

"Budapest's" overarching theme extends beyond direct conversations about Zsigmond and cinematography. For Bourdain, the discussion is about his own cinematography as much as anyone else's. Early in the episode, during the "context" section, Bourdain visits Pléhcsárda, a local eatery where he eats a pancake covered with chicken liver and bone marrow sauce. Bourdain offers less narration about the dish's history than one might expect from a food show. Instead, the camera focuses on close-ups of the food and, notably, the construction of that food by the proprietor István Bábel, who we see laboring over each stage of the dish's preparation. As the camera cuts to Bourdain, he draws attention to the sparse narration:

> You know, some of you have noticed—and complained—that I don't really *describe* food any more on the show. That's a deliberate strategy on my part, actually. It's really a lot like writing porn. After you've used the same adjectives over and over, like you know the *Penthouse* letters. Look at it. It's chicken livers, it's bone marrow, it's paprika, it's a delicious pancake. Is it going to make your life better at all if I describe exactly how while smacking my lips annoyingly? No. [long pause]. It's good.

This scene is not *just* another example of Bourdain breaking the fourth wall or of drawing attention to the defiance of genre expectations. It is a moment where Bourdain does both of those things while framing them within a conversation about cinematography and narration, and the limits of both. It asserts what are, for Bourdain, obvious—but typically ignored—truths: that neither words nor images can accurately communicate experience, that attempts to do so should focus on their construction, and that, in the end, the best way to come closest to that goal is to let images speak for themselves, so long as the spectator is made aware of the bias inherent in those perspectives and images. This idea is further driven home when, served a giant schnitzel, Bourdain briefly reverts to a food-show aesthetic and snaps a shot of the dish on his phone while being filmed on his own show. Even the schnitzel is more about its own spectacle, massive on the plate, and the spectacle of how it is depicted, than it is about the food itself.

The pattern of approach Bourdain uses for "Budapest" is largely mirrored in "Hong Kong" and "Andalucía." Bourdain's visual style in "Hong Kong" persistently and clearly references the work of his guest, Christopher Doyle, cinematographer for six of Wong Kar Wai's films, including *Chungking Express* (1994) and *In the Mood for Love* (2000). The Wong-Doyle filmography arguably represents the most important Asian cinema of the past thirty years and, much like Bourdain's episode, the themes of these films are largely the inevitability of change, nostalgia for what is lost, and an exploration of what cinema's ethical role in those processes can be. Similarly, Bourdain's visual style in and around the bullfighting sequences in "Andalucía" are direct references to Pedro Almodóvar's *Hable con ella* (*Talk to Her*, 2002), drawing upon *the* dominant voice in post-Franco Spanish cinema to emphasize cinematic spectacle, the theme that drives the episode. For instance, we see the spectacle caused by cameramen walking backward as they shoot Bourdain and Zamboni cutting through a crowd, across another spectacle—a parade of religious effigies. The camera also emphasizes spectacle with how it depicts flamenco and bullfighting, as well as the way it frames *costaleros* presenting their effigy to a crowd on the street with the camera placed behind them, as if backstage at a concert, focusing upon their performance rather than the result the crowd sees. Even what the crowd sees, much like the crowd watching the parade, is defined by the pictures and videos they are taking on their cell phones, a horde of people creating images. Essentially, in both episodes, as in "Budapest," Bourdain's cinematography draws upon filmic influences to guide his own themes which are, in turn, about visual art.

Also, as in "Budapest," Bourdain regularly seeks opportunities to break the fourth wall. In "Hong Kong," Bourdain hands Doyle a camera and lets him shoot a scene. In that scene, we see one of Bourdain's cameramen show Doyle how to close the aperture, and we see the image, now through Doyle's camera, as he slowly corrects the lighting and Bourdain's face goes from washed out to perfectly lit. Doyle proceeds to turn the camera on one of Bourdain's cameramen, and the show cuts back and forth between the two perspectives, Doyle proclaiming, "This is one of the most beautiful shots I've ever made. I don't think I've ever made a shot about cameras before." Later, having made it clear Doyle took over principal photography, we witness Bourdain interrupt an interview to re-set the table to a better angle for Doyle's camera and, in the episode's final sequence, see Doyle and director Asia Argento filming Bourdain on the Star Ferry, revealing their presence, which was hidden from the same scene at the beginning of the episode.

Meanwhile, in "Andalucía," we see Zamboni, camera in hand, shooting Bourdain walking and talking to Zamboni's fiancée. Bourdain pulls out his cell phone and begins to shoot back at Zamboni, proclaiming "I do like the increasingly meta-aspect of this show." Elsewhere, Bourdain switches cameras to show Zamboni, whose camera we had been peering out of as Bourdain toyed with a young bull in a ring, almost getting gored by that very bull. Time and again, Bourdain breaks the fourth wall to emphasize these episodes about cinematography are, themselves, examples of cinematography, constructed by specific people holding a camera who themselves invisibly affect both the creation and depiction of the experience.

Bourdain's imagination of visual culture shaping the real world only to, in turn, have that world shape the visual images that come after it, creating a perpetual cause-and-effect relationship between representation and reality, is a dominant theme in Bourdain's approach to filmmaking. In "Hong Kong," introducing Doyle, Bourdain proclaims Doyle has produced "unspeakably gorgeous images of beautiful people moving through spaces both unfamiliar and yet painfully intimate. Ultimately jagged, frenzied, innovative, languid, composed, chaotic. I *obsessed* over his work. Fetishized it. Longed to see Hong Kong like the characters in so many of his films longed for each other." The juxtaposition between what seem to be oppositional adjectives speaks to the way in which Bourdain's approach to cinematography does not seek an identifiable,

Bourdain's director of photography, Zach Zamboni, is shown walking backward as he films Bourdain with Zamboni's fiancée, Fuen Sanchez. Shortly thereafter, Bourdain takes out his phone and snaps photos back at Zamboni.

traditional endpoint of beauty or truth; rather, it seeks a subjective definition of truth and beauty, with a strong focus on the way the collective weight of visual culture inevitably shapes how the spectator sees the world around them.

Think of this in relation to Bourdain's use of *McCabe & Mrs. Miller* discussed earlier. Several minutes before depicting Zsigmond taking (and later developing) pictures of the building where Hungarian snipers were executed, Bourdain pointedly shows the spectator the relevant shot from *McCabe* so the spectator is more likely to recognize the reference. Thus, when Bourdain frames Zsigmond constructing an image via an overt reference drawn from Zsigmond's own filmography, Bourdain implies Zsigmond's experience watching the snipers hanged at this building in 1956 impacts how he depicts the US West in 1971, which, in turn, shapes how Bourdain imagines and depicts Budapest in 2015. No cinematic shot ever stands alone, in a vacuum; it is built upon everything that comes before, much as Bourdain can never enter Hong Kong blind once he has seen Doyle depict it.

Structuring his episode around an on-the-surface conversation about both the influence the cinematographer has had upon Bourdain and the construction of cinematography that is ongoing in Bourdain's own art allows him to build to a moment where he could have a direct, on-screen conversation with the cinematographer about their philosophy of cinematography. In each episode, this conversation is more focused because Bourdain's approach prepares the spectator to be aware of just how much is at stake in such a conversation. For Zsigmond, the answer was the attempt to make reality more beautiful, but in a way that emphasized the fact he was doing so. To Zsigmond, settling for beauty, which he considered "easy," was not enough, he wanted his poetic images to "mean something." Meanwhile, Doyle's perspective is similar but more precise. Bourdain asks Doyle if there is "value in just beautiful people and objects moving through space in beautiful ways?" Doyle responds incredulously, "Is there a value to the color of a pomegranate?" Bourdain immediately agrees there is, prompting Doyle to surmise, "Exactly. This is our challenge to celebrate that. So-called beauty is not 'my makeup is so good' and 'I lifted my face a bit.' No. Beauty is the darkness and the pleasure of embracing that and that giving you something more of your experience of life." Thus, Doyle's imagination of beauty is not about aesthetic perfection, but rather a beauty which adds something to the life of both filmmaker and spectator. To quote Doyle, you "have a movie" when you can "tune into the energy," when the filmmaker and subject are collectively "doing something which all of those energies focus in a way that somehow connects with other people."

While I have argued Bourdain interrogates these ideas within his own cinematography in both "Budapest" and "Hong Kong," the moment Bourdain verbalizes his response to this dialogue actually predates them. As Zamboni and Bourdain tour the Alhambra at the conclusion of "Andalucía," Bourdain ruminates on cinematography in a manner that relates in uncanny ways to what Zsigmond and Doyle articulate in those later episodes. It is worth noting Bourdain rarely visited major tourist sites, making the decision to conclude the episode at the Alhambra almost inexplicable outside of this context. Introducing the location, Bourdain claims "Zamboni has gone . . . a bit mad about the place. . . . He's a cinematographer so you can understand, once you start to really look around, how that might get a grip on a guy whose profession is the intricate play between light and darkness." Bourdain further emphasizes this connection between visual cultures—design and cinematography—inside the palace. Zamboni comments, "I think the best assumption is nothing is random. They came here and laid out everything according to a plan . . . Everything is about light and math. Obviously, they weren't cinematographers, but everything is framing for them." Bourdain interjects his own narration right in the middle of Zamboni's conversation, proclaiming, "This was a place for reflection. Each element of design presumably intended to have effects both psychological and religious." The dialogue, edited together, points to the tensions at stake in the conversations with Zsigmond and Doyle: beauty and meaning, intentionality and connection, mathematic and metaphysical, science and art.

As Bourdain strives for resolution, the sense of uncanny conversation with the later episodes is strengthened. Bourdain asks Zamboni if the Alhambra's builders "want[ed] to contemplate nature or [did] they want to conquer it, control it?" Zamboni responds, "they were certainly trying to emulate it. You know all their mathematics were really trying to figure out how nature worked." At this point, Bourdain's voice-over takes over and bridges to the episode's end, "They saw mathematical patterns in the sky and on earth. The way water moved and rippled, the way things grew, a simple pine cone, a fern, a pomegranate. And they thought about the basic truths these things might represent." While Bourdain is literally talking about the Alhambra, he has framed the conversation to equally apply to cinematography, which he, as filmmaker, routinely emphasizes as the center of everything. Much as Doyle finds intrinsic value in the beauty of a pomegranate, and takes it to be the cinematographer's duty and challenge to express that pomegranate in a way that connects to the spectator, and much as Zsigmond thought the path to metaphysical expression was through preparation and mathematics, Bourdain expresses his view of visual art as an attempt to understand nature by controlling it through the cinematographer's lens; the pomegranate is beautiful precisely because *how* it is depicted means something.

3
ETHNOGRAPHIC FILMMAKING

> Food experts can assess how Bourdain brought a personable edge to highbrow cuisine and pushed beyond fine-dining formulas to explore the value of food at every level of society. However, what defines his legacy may have more to do with his capacity to deconstruct the Western gaze. By sharing a meal, he could go anywhere in the world and make the people look just like us, and us like them. He was a hero we needed in divided times, when the specter of bigotry looms large and ugly, and perhaps our world was too good for him. I wish I had asked him if that was true. . . . Bourdain had more in common with ethnographic filmmaker Jean Rouch than any contemporary celebrity chef. Both men positioned their cameras around faces we often don't see represented in mainstream media, then provided space for their subjects to drive the narrative.
>
> —Erik Kohn, *IndieWire*[1]

Questions pertaining to the importance and relevance of how the world is depicted are hardly limited to cinematography. One of the most pressing areas of such debate is that of genre. What added meaning can a filmmaker create by using camera, sound, editing, or narrative choices to invoke a specific genre? What expectations does the spectator place upon a film based on their perception of genre and the degree to which a filmmaker chooses to meet or deny those expectations? What ethical questions are at stake within a given genre, especially inside the confines of documentary filmmaking or journalism, both of which invoke a history of debate about authenticity and subjectivity? Such questions seem particularly pertinent when one considers Anthony Bourdain, a filmmaker whom critics and audiences intermittently pigeonhole into competing genres. Is his work best understood as food TV, in conversation with the likes of Gordon Ramsey and Andrew Zimmern? Or is it travel TV, building upon Rick Steves and Samantha Brown? After his association with CNN, is it possible he is best understood as a journalist, à la Christiane Amanpour? The reality, I argue, is that Bourdain actively *used* disparate genres, drawing upon them to invoke and create meaning as he forged his own distinctive approach to documentary filmmaking, one rooted in New Wave film tendencies that actively emphasize the construction of reality.

While I will return to what Bourdain's filmmaking has to say about each of these genres in the "Genre" section of this book, I believe one first must consider Bourdain's approach within the context of ethnographic filmmaking, which has its own contested past, and one in which I argue Bourdain is best understood. One of the few consistencies across Bourdain's filmography is an ethnographer's perspective, but because he perpetually blended and borrowed from so many disparate genres, he cannot be limited even to that. Therefore, this chapter contextualizes Bourdain's work within the history of ethnographic documentary filmmaking, ranging from Timothy Asch to Jean Rouch, but it also complicates that relationship within larger contexts that blur the line between documentary and narrative film, paying particular attention to Werner Herzog's *Grizzly Man* (2005),[2] a film which sheds much light on Bourdain and serves as one of the few outside examples of filmmaking similar to what he aimed to achieve. In short, Bourdain forged a distinctive approach to interrogating (rather than depicting) authenticity and subjectivity, as he simultaneously engaged in and launched an all-out critique of ethnographic filmmaking.

From the invention of the motion-picture camera, one of cinema's primary questions has centered on the divide between seeing film as an impartial, objective reflection of an authentic reality versus seeing it as a subjective expression of the imagination of its maker. Nowhere has this debate been more contentious and omnipresent than in the world of documentary filmmaking, a branch of filmmaking that, by its very name, promises the spectator an objective "document" of presumed reality. This promise was reinforced by the aesthetic choices of most documentary filmmakers from the first half of the twentieth century (as well as many today), who sought to do as much as they could to hide their presence within their films, utilizing long shots with subtle editing techniques, relying upon talking-head interviews, and providing a sense of cohesion for these images via omniscient, and typically white male, narrators. As Cecilia Sayad points out, however, "Irrespective of how much emphasis documentarians may place on the tedious line separating the real from their filmic renditions of it, the documentary mode inevitably addresses the tensions between subjectivity and objectivity."[3]

Whereas the response to these tensions for most early documentarians was to disguise the tensions, in the second half of the twentieth century, documentarians began to emphasize their own subjectivity. Such emphasis of the director's presence only widened contentious divides about authorship precisely because of the (documentary) form in which it now occurred. Bourdain therefore serves as a compelling point of discussion precisely because he bridged multiple types of filmmaking approaches, including ethnographic documentaries, while developing and asserting a type of filmmaking that owes much of its intellectual underpinnings to narrative film.

Unsurprising, given the context of Bourdain, some of the most influential examples of the turn toward emphasizing the documentarian's presence were spawned by the nouvelle vague. For example, Alain Resnais's 1956 *Nuit et brouillard* (*Night and Fog*), controversially, but effectively, pairs horrific images of Nazi concentration camps with a carefree, counterpoint soundtrack and a narrative structure borrowed from the travelogue genre. The juxtaposition serves to make the images, and the Holocaust itself, seem more horrific within the context of Nazi indifference, an indifference at times shared, and thus highlighted, by the camera, music, and mood of the film. This drive to borrow from narrative film strategies eventually became the dominant trend within documentary filmmaking. Directors like Errol Morris established a sense of auteurship by repeating themes and style choices across their films. Further, Morris, in films such as *The Thin Blue Line* (1988), included narrative scenes portrayed by actors depicting conflicting versions of the film's central event and then used found footage from detective-TV shows to comically comment upon the interviewees. By the end of the century, filmmakers like Michael Moore and Morgan Spurlock normalized the insertion of their voices and bodies into their work, in some cases, such as in Moore's *Roger & Me* (1989) and *Bowling for Columbine* (2002), actively instigating events. Sarah Polley's *Stories We Tell* (2012) renders her own life the subject of her documentary, a film largely *about* how conflicting perspectives and biases render all familial memories about her conception and upbringing suspect, thereby highlighting the subjective nature of both truth and documentary filmmaking.

Bourdain's reflexive approach to documentary filmmaking participates in this tradition, even as his subject matter and genre stem from a subgenre, ethnographic filmmaking, that has, for most of its history, largely existed in counterpoint to such trends. Originating in the first half of the twentieth century with filmmakers like Robert J. Flaherty, the subgenre typically walks a line between anthropology and filmmaking. In fact, one could argue that one of the genre's central problems is that many of its creators deny or ignore the very medium in which they partake, imagining themselves only as anthropologists, not filmmakers, thereby denying the realities of how film makes meaning. This insistence is what leads to it being controversial in some circles to even say it constitutes a "genre," and, in part, why this chapter comes in this book's first section rather than its section about genre (part II). The prevailing aesthetic of ethnographies is that of realism, with a goal of achieving authenticity. Further, traditionally, ethnographic films predominantly consist of Western men filming non-Western subjects to present those subjects back to a Western audience, and, given the genre's colonialist history, it has often faced criticism for exoticizing its subjects.

A classic example is Timothy Asch and Napoleon Chagnon's *The Ax Fight* (1975), in which the two anthropologists go to great lengths to objectively depict a fight between Yanomami villagers. Asch and Chagnon divide the film into four parts; an unedited eleven-minute shot of the fight, an edited version in which Asch narrates an explanation of what occurred, a series of kinship diagrams in which Asch explains his understanding of the complex familial and political relationships within the Amazonian tribe, and a final, edited replay of the main events without narration. As such, the filmmakers provide the audience with what they see as the necessary details while trying to remain wholly objective, like the proverbial fly on the wall.

The Ax Fight serves as a near-perfect example of the way that no matter how hard documentarians work to separate themselves from the world they depict, the tensions between subjectivity and objectivity are inevitably brought to the forefront by virtue of both the genre and the medium in which they partake. For all the extreme lengths Asch and Chagnon take to objectively depict a fight in a Venezuelan village, for all the ways *The Ax Fight* embodies one of the purest examples of ethnographic filmmaking's quest for objectivity, the dominant discourse surrounding the film has always been about the film's subjectivity. The spectator can easily notice that members of the tribe smile back at the camera, that Asch's version of events contradicts itself, that, miraculously, no one gets hit by the blade of the ax, and that there are nine additional minutes of the fight left unfilmed. Meanwhile, later work by the anthropologist Brian Ferguson indicates the fight began because of disagreements between villagers over possession of the goods the film crew had introduced to the tribe, including the ax used in the fight.[4] In a 2007 BBC Two documentary, the filmmaker Adam Curtis famously presents Ferguson's findings to Chagnon. The latter adamantly insists, "No, I don't think the ax fight happened because I was there . . . I think it would be a reasonable presumption that this ax fight would have happened whether or not I was there. And the very fact that I was there and documented it was not the cause of it."[5] Curtis responds in an exasperated tone, "You don't think a film crew in the middle of a fight in a village has an effect?" causing Chagnon to stand up and walk out of the interview, declaring "No, I don't, that's the end of my interview."[6]

The shift in Bourdain's aesthetic between *A Cook's Tour* and *No Reservations* demonstrates that he realized quite early in his career that both food and travel genres share similar subject matter to ethnographies, promising to provide the spectator with an understanding of a foreign culture. Unlike travel and food television, however, Bourdain was not interested in dissecting isolated elements of a foreign culture in ways that make the spectator more comfortable, all for the spectator's visual consumption, be they tourist or foodie. Instead, drawing from ethnography, Bourdain uses cultural artifacts—food, architecture, music, sport, popular culture, ritual—as means of constructing a holistic understanding of the culture that produced them. Further, his interests were drawn to taking an ethnographic approach to such artifacts as a means of understanding and embracing difference, rather than objectifying or exploiting it. For example, in "Cajun Country" (NR S7E16), Bourdain prominently features a quotation by food writer Lolis Elie, who answers Bourdain's query of why someone should "care" about New Orleans by claiming,

> If you think about what this represents, New Orleans still has a regional culture. In much of the rest of the country, you ask them what kind of food they eat, they say McDonalds or Burger King. You ask them what kind of music they listen to, whatever's top 40. In New Orleans we get emblematic food, emblematic music, emblematic architecture. And we are an example for the rest of the country to rediscover those things about themselves. Because I don't believe that the people in Ohio didn't have anything to eat before they got McDonald's.

The passage serves as the thesis for Bourdain as he leaves New Orleans and spends the rest of the episode in Acadiana. Bourdain was interested in understanding unique cultures through an ethnographic lens, but he did so to encourage his spectator to embrace difference, not objectify it—an idea to which I will return in later chapters.

The other thing Bourdain did not share with much of ethnographic filmmaking is an imagination, such as the one expressed by Chagnon, that any type of filmmaking, ethnographic or otherwise, could be void of subjectivity, could manage to not impact the subjects it records. Think of the statement I have quoted from the conclusion of his final complete episode, "Kenya" (PU S12E1), "In the end, I know it's my story—not Kamau's, not Kenya's, or Kenyans.' Those stories are yet to be heard." Or, as he claims in "Madagascar" (PU S5E4), "The camera is a liar. It shows everything. It shows nothing. It reveals only what we want. Often what we see is seen only from a *window*. Moving past, then gone. One window. My window. If you'd been here, chances are, you would have seen things differently."

It is for precisely these reasons Bourdain's films draw the spectator's attention to his presence, his bias, and the impact it has on his subject(s). Unlike Chagnon, Bourdain thinks it is impossible to be a fly on the wall. In the words of Zach Zamboni, one of Bourdain's directors of photography, "Light affects people. You go into a dark bar, supposed to be a *vérité* scene, put up a bunch of lights, you can't tell me that doesn't change things. Cameras affect people, lights affect people, anytime you introduce something to the environment, you are affecting people."[7]

To be clear, such a perspective is not without precedence within ethnographic filmmaking. In fact, some of these concerns are partially raised by one of the genre's most influential filmmakers, Jean Rouch. Claimed by nouvelle vague critics as one of their own,[8] lauded by some as the father of Nigerian cinema,[9] and attacked by others as representing a colonialist lens,[10] the Frenchman dedicated most of his life's work to making ethnographic films across the African continent. His 1961 documentary about Paris, co-directed with the sociologist Edgar Morin, *Chronique d'un été* (*Chronicle of a Summer*), coined the term *cinéma vérité*. Translating to "cinema of truth," the concept gave birth to Direct Cinema, one of the purest, most traditional approaches to documentary filmmaking, which primarily concerns itself with recording and presenting events in ways that imagine the subject and spectator are unaware of the camera's presence.

But that was never the type of "truth" Rouch imagined. Rouch was aware the ethnographer "stimulates, modifies, accelerates, catalyzes, opens a window" and that "people respond by revealing themselves, and meanings emerge in that revelation."[11] Thus, Rouch emphasized subjectivity and performance, and was careful to expose the fact that a director often serves not only as mediator, but also as catalyst. Yes, Rouch's films set out to represent truth and authenticity, but they never imagine that truth could be achieved by ignoring the filmmaker's presence. As Rouch's obituary notes, Rouch (much like Bourdain) "aimed for the immediacy of television, without its superficiality. He believed that the camera's intervention stimulated people to greater spontaneity, expression and truth without asking them, as in the American Direct Cinema, to act as though the camera was not there."[12]

Rouch's attempt to arrive at a truth was therefore typically connected to decisions that make the spectator more aware of his presence, not less. Rouch not only includes his voice, as narration, but, quite often, his body. *Chronique d'un été* opens with Rouch and his co-director on-screen discussing if it is possible to act sincerely on camera. At the film's end, they join a roundtable panel with their subjects discussing the film and how they all feel about it. As such, Rouch achieves a "shared anthropology"[13] in which he becomes a subject of his own film and his methodology interrogated. In other films, such as 1958's *Moi, un noir* (*I, a Negro*) and 1967's *Jaguar*, Rouch goes further, asking his subjects to dramatically re-create realities from their lives, and, in the case of *Moi, un noir*, giving them a voice in directorial decisions.

All in all, Rouch sought to distance himself from approaches (like Asch's) that forefront perceived objectivity because Rouch felt objectivity stood in the way of depicting reality. For example, rather than clarifying images, Rouch thought traditional voice-over narration, descriptive and neutral in tone, "obscures [images], masking them until it finally substitutes itself for them. And so, the film ceases to be a film and becomes a lecture, a demonstration."[14] For Rouch, truth can only be achieved by drawing attention to the filmmaker's influence, not denying it.

Thus, comparisons between Bourdain and Rouch are compelling. I would posit, however, that the fundamental difference that separates the two lies in the fact Rouch still believes he is achieving "a" truth, even if it is a truth far removed from the type imagined by ethnographic filmmakers like Asch or the proponents of Direct Cinema. Rouch thinks that by acknowledging the artificiality of film, by emphasizing spectacle, he can achieve authenticity. In Rouch's own words, "It is due to this equipment and the new behavior (which has nothing to do with the observable behavior of the same person when he is not filming) that the filmmaker can throw himself into a ritual, integrate himself with it, and follow it step by step."[15] Rouch imagines himself part of the construction of an authentic moment of truth simply because he does not deny that his presence has altered said truth.

Contrast this to Bourdain, who the camera shows sitting alone in "Kenya," off by himself, removed from the spectacle, Bourdain's own narration reminding the spectator the ritual he depicts can never be his. And I argue it is precisely this difference of perspective and approach that opens Rouch to the criticisms of demonstrating a Western gaze. Just because Rouch offers his subjects agency in the type of spectacle they serve does not, in fact, mean they are not rendered spectacle. Similarly, just because Rouch emphasizes the impact of his presence does not mean he has "integrated" himself with his subjects. As the Burkina Faso director Gaston Kaboré states, referencing colonialist critiques of

Rouch, "It is because there is a lot of confusion in some minds about whether to treat Rouch as an African filmmaker. I disagree; not because I am ostracizing him. No. Only because, even if I stay in France for four decades making films, I never become French. In my culture, it is said that the piece of wood does not become a crocodile because it has stayed long in the water."[16]

This difference of perspectives also serves to largely define Bourdain's cinema; the reason his approach constantly reinforces the inevitable distance between filmmaker and subject, between films and objective reality. Two key moments in the two Bourdain episodes most directly *about* film as an art form help drive this point home. First, Bourdain's assertion in "Hong Kong's" introduction (PU S11E5), "All of us when we travel look at the places we go, the things we see, through different eyes. And how we see them is shaped by our previous lives. The books we've read, the films we've seen, the baggage we carry." Second, his questions that conclude "Budapest" (PU S5E6), "Do we emerge fully formed with a God-given eye, for pictures, images that can move people? Or are we the end result of all the things we've seen, all the things we've done, the places we've been? The places, the people we've had to leave behind? All that's happened in our life? Is it those things that bring the light or the darkness to the blank screen?" Bourdain thus suggests a filmmaker should not "throw himself" into what he observes and literally cannot "integrate" himself into what his camera depicts. The filmmaker always remains on the outside, in the periphery—his perspective wholly subjective as it is influenced by his life, his experience, his training; and the depiction of his subject is equally subjective because of the presence of the camera and the filmmaker himself.

What Bourdain thus leaves us with is the power of film to affect the world rather than represent it. To quote Bourdain, sitting in a Budapest theater next to Vilmos Zsigmond, reminiscing about the films of his youth, "Films could be inspiring. They could be dangerous. It was magic to me. I mean they still are. To go to a film, especially a dangerous one, where the subject matter and the content was different, and to see that, it was just, ah, oh my God. What do I do with my life now, after seeing it?" The duty to his subjects, Bourdain infers, is not to declare that he, an outsider, can present them authentically; rather, the duty is to take an ethical approach to deciding *how* he re-presents them. As Bourdain's film shows him walking streets and bridges with Zsigmond, intercutting to Zsigmond's documentary footage of Russian tanks in 1956, the famed cinematographer talks about feeling scared because they were killing photographers, but simply asserts, "But I felt that I had to photograph it." Zsigmond then turns to the quotation I have discussed at length about how it is "easy" to make "beautiful pictures," but how the important, more difficult thing is for them to "mean something." All this serves as context for the closing questions of Bourdain's episode, when he asks, "And what about the faces of those we capture in our magic lenses for a minute or a second or an hour? Afterwards, should we think about them and where they might be now?" Such questions haunt Bourdain across multiple episodes, multiple seasons. The answer, for Christopher Doyle in "Hong Kong," is, "The only function of what we do of art or of anything is to give voice to the unspoken, to give it a form it's never been perceived in before." Bourdain thus returns all such questions, all such ethical debates, back to questions about film. It is not that the filmmaker does not have an obligation to his subjects, it is that he can never meet that obligation if he worries about objective truth. Cinema, as a constructed fallacy, is the only truth available to him.

While Bourdain's shift in interests toward ethnographic content is first recognizable in the changes between *A Cook's Tour* and *No Reservations*, the groundwork for where Bourdain's approach ultimately arrived in *Parts Unknown* was largely laid down in the much maligned, even by Bourdain, *The Layover*. The short-lived show, which ran for two seasons between 2011 and 2013, was structured around Bourdain offering food and travel advice about what to do in a single destination during an arbitrary, thirty-six-hour layover. Handcuffed by a format that owed more to the genres from which he had worked to distance himself, and limited by the short timeframe he was available in each city to appear on camera, Bourdain inserted man-on-the-street interviews in which his physical presence was unnecessary, locals offering insider insight into the city. For instance, in the introduction to "New Orleans" (TL S2E9), Bourdain cuts to a talking-head shot of an anonymous local man asserting "the proper way to say the name of my city is 'New Orleans.'" Bourdain quickly cuts to a series of locals from a variety of ethnic and social backgrounds providing their own pronunciations, culminating with a woman, standing in front of her house, proclaiming, "The only time you ever hear someone say, 'New Or-Leans' is if they are not from here or if they are trying to rhyme in a song." As the woman speaks, Bourdain switches to a split-screen format with the woman filling half the screen and images of Bourbon Street tourists and a musician sharing the other half. Elsewhere, such as in "Miami" (TL S1E4), the talking heads give advice on what to "do" or where to "eat," often offering advice pointedly different from what Bourdain has just recommended. In each case, Bourdain's presence is limited to juxtapositions via camerawork (e.g., the New Orleanian sharing the screen with tourists and a musician) and editing (e.g., the conflicting advice in Miami). Essentially, to return to this chapter's epigraph, "position[ing] [his] camera around faces we often don't see represented in mainstream media, then provid[ing] space for [his] subjects to drive the narrative."

Bourdain continued the man-on-the-street montages in a few early episodes of *Parts Unknown*, but, more importantly, Bourdain's interest in juxtaposing his perspective with shots and sound that do not fit into the narrative structure of his own activities became commonplace throughout that series, fostering a type of free, indirect subjectivity meant to both express and complicate his own perspective. I will return to this use of free, indirect subjectivity throughout the book, particularly in chapters 5 and 10.

Bourdain also increasingly became drawn to topics and content from the realm of ethnography and anthropology. As I have already implied, he began to use cultural markers, particularly visual ones, almost exclusively as a means of analyzing and understanding the culture he depicted, rather than exoticizing food, film, music, or politics as a means of codifying what the spectator might want to visit or eat. Unlike food TV, which sees a dish as the endpoint, Bourdain viewed it as a starting point, one additional text to analyze.

His interests also continued to shift toward micro-communities, exploring regions and cities who define their cultural identity in opposition to larger, national narratives, such as episodes set in Kurdistan (NR S7E15), Okinawa (PU S6E3), Basque Country (PU S9E3), and Hawai'i (PU S5E7)—where he focuses on the island of Moloka'i. Or, when turning to national identities, choosing the ones not commonly depicted (or visited), such as Bhutan (PU S11E8), Congo (PU S1E8), or even Antarctica (PU S9E5)—where he defies the expectation his interest would be nature, instead focusing on the subculture that has developed among the scientists who live there and their varied and esoteric research interests.

The result was a filmmaker increasingly focused and dedicated to ethnographic concerns simultaneously approaching that subject matter from New Wave perspectives that emphasize film's (and Bourdain's) subjectivity, and the manner with which everything he sees and depicts is shaped by the weight of film history. Even the remote examples listed above, Bhutan, Congo, and Antarctica, actively invoke visual styles borrowed from Darren Aronofsky, Francis Ford Coppola, and Werner Herzog, respectively. Meanwhile, the man-on-the-street interviews pointedly juxtapose the subjects' perspective against Bourdain's via image and editing, utilizing camera angles and editing choices to emphasize the performative nature of interviewees talking to a camera.

Other moments, where Bourdain inserts narrative scenes, such as the opening of *Parts Unknown* "Miami" (S5E2), when he reconstructs a party scene from by Paolo Sorrentino's *The Great Beauty* (2013), may seem to invoke Rouch's ethno-fictions, but are used for entirely different aims. Whereas Rouch encouraged his subjects to act out scenes as part of his storytelling, the goal was still to depict a type of truth about them. Conversely, while it is likely Bourdain's "actors" are actual Miami partiers, they are positioned identically to the characters in Sorrentino's film; depicted by the same, highly stylized camera angle, slow motion, and lighting, and; asked to perform in ways reminiscent of Sorrentino's partygoers. Meanwhile, the shot's final emphasis is on Bourdain standing at the end of the row of partiers, clearly out of place based on his suit, age, and the fact he is breaking the fourth wall, staring directly back at the camera. Bourdain wants his spectator to be aware that this is an image stolen from a film and meant to emphasize the stereotypical depiction that shapes his (and likely the spectator's) imagination of Miami. The documentary film that follows will, almost by definition, be in conversation with these filmic images, and whatever Bourdain depicts will still only be his view, the view of a dedicated and enthusiastic outsider, but an outsider all the same.

But for all the obvious comparisons to Rouch, the best context for Bourdain's approach to documentary filmmaking may come from one of his narrative film heroes, Werner Herzog, which is, itself, quite telling. Partially a product of New Wave movements, the German filmmaker's early narrative films *Aguirre, the Wrath of God* (1972) and *Fitzcarraldo* (1982), are frequent reference points for Bourdain, particularly his episode in the Brazilian Amazon (NR S7E6). Both films follow maniacally obsessive protagonists as they venture up a river on fool's errands against nature's will. For Herzog, the concept of a pristine, virginal "nature" with redemptive qualities is a social construct propagated by nineteenth-century Romantics; the only "harmony" that can be found in nature, he once claimed, "is the harmony of overwhelming and collective murder" existing in an "overwhelming lack of order" because "there is no real harmony as we have conceived it."[17]

For Herzog, how we imagine nature, how we anthropomorphize it, and how we depict those imaginations, say far more about us as humans than nature itself. Thus, much like Bourdain's relationship with food, Herzog's approach to nature becomes almost anthropologic, as his films "explore central issues in our understanding of the relationship between nature and culture."[18] Later in his career, when Herzog became better known for documentaries, his interest in interrogating nature as a social construct rooted in artistic images of nature remained central. For example, *Encounters at the End of the World* (2007), which Bourdain visually references in "Antarctica," and *Grizzly Man*, which asks questions about cinema (both narrative and documentary), nature, and art in ways that seem to embody Bourdain's approach more clearly than any other single text. My claim that Bourdain's approach to documentary filmmaking is nearly unique is only strengthened by the idea the closest example that I can offer is a feature-length documentary, made by a narrative director, ostensibly about *nature*.

To understand *Grizzly Man*'s relevance to Bourdain, one must first understand Herzog's understanding of documentary film, the problems he sees as inherent within ideas of objective truth in cinema, and the nuanced but essential differentiation he makes between fact and truth. In a 1999 interview, Roger Ebert asked Herzog to define "ecstatic truth," a term he had used to refer to his cinematic goals. Herzog responded by issuing what came to be known as the Minnesota Declaration. Herzog begins his manifesto by attacking *cinéma vérité*, which he asserts as "devoid of *vérité*" because "it reaches a merely superficial truth, the truth of accountants."[19] Offering the example of a "representative of *cinéma vérité* [who] declared publicly that truth can be easily found by taking a camera and trying to be honest," Herzog claims "*cinema vérité* confounds fact and truth, and thus plows only stones."[20] Drawing upon a conceptualization similar to Jean-Luc Godard's intent when he declared "film is truth,"[21] Herzog draws a stark distinction between "fact," which "creates norms," and "truth," which "illuminates."[22] For Herzog, "there are deeper strata of truth in cinema, and there is such a thing as poetic, ecstatic truth. It is mysterious and elusive, and can be reached only through fabrication and imagination and stylization."[23]

Such a definition of "ecstatic truth" is not, intellectually speaking, far removed from Vilmos Zsigmond's idea, explored in Bourdain's "Budapest," of "poetic realism," a type of realism or truth defined by subjectivity, in Zsigmond's case by making images "more beautiful," rather than depicting objective fact. Such an approach has much in common with broader tendencies across New Wave traditions. Take, for instance, the claim by Walter Murch, the sound editor who worked on eight Francis Ford Coppola films:

> The danger of present-day cinema is that it can suffocate its subjects by its very ability to represent them: it doesn't possess the built-in escape valves of ambiguity that painting, music, literature, radio drama and black-and-white silent film automatically have simply by virtue of their sensory incompleteness—an incompleteness that engages the imagination of the viewer as compensation for what is only evoked by the artist. By comparison, film seems to be "all there" (It isn't, but it seems to be), and thus the responsibility of filmmakers is to find ways within that completeness to refrain from achieving it.[24]

I have argued this conceptualization is central to the entirety of Bourdain's approach, and it is almost uncannily reminiscent of the claim made by Bourdain's longtime director Tom Vitale, "Tony viewed an end-of-the-episode conclusion as a betrayal of what was inevitably a much bigger and more complex subject. He'd always rather leave the audience thinking, keep them guessing, wondering."[25] If a filmmaker wants to illuminate truth, they must consciously deny their spectator the illusion of reality achieved.

While Herzog employs such an approach across his filmography, *Grizzly Man* is its literal embodiment. On its surface, the documentary is an investigation into the life and death of Timothy Treadwell, a grizzly bear activist who was eventually eaten by the bears he lived with for thirteen summers in the Alaskan wilderness, trying to promote protections for said bears via his homemade movies and celebrity. In truth, however, *Grizzly Man* is a depiction of a man who lives in an altered reality of his own making, which he imagines as authentic based upon a constructed imagination of nature.

For Herzog, the only true way to depict that kind of subject is by using film to deconstruct how Treadwell constructed such an imagination in his own filmmaking. Most of Herzog's images are taken directly from the over one-hundred hours of video Treadwell recorded over his last five summers, but for every moment when he lets Treadwell speak for himself, trying to shape how the spectator imagines reality, Herzog uses facts interjected from his own narration or comments from talking-head interviews to question that reality. For instance, experts deny Treadwell's claims of active poachers, Herzog informs us Treadwell often had female companions present whom he hid from his camera because it did not match his self-narrative, and a helicopter pilot proclaims Treadwell was negatively impacting wildlife, anthropomorphizing bears, and "got what he deserved." Even those counter-perspectives are themselves problematized, however, as, for instance, the pilot anthropomorphizes the bear himself, claiming the bear killed Treadwell because "the bear thought there was something wrong with him, like he was mentally retarded or something. That day the bear thought he'd had enough of Timothy Treadwell." Every perspective is exposed, questioned, problematized. In the opening sequence, Herzog proclaims, "I found that beyond a wildlife film, in his material lay dormant a story of astonishing beauty and depth. I discovered a film of human ecstasies and darkest inner turmoil." In short, while the footage is mostly made about Treadwell's view of nature, the film Herzog constructs is entirely about Herzog's view of Treadwell; or, more to the point, it is about the fact it is about that.

The duality between these perspectives drives the film, and Herzog constantly emphasizes both his own presence and the way in which both he and Treadwell create an illusion that their biases are indicative of reality. For example, the film opens with Treadwell in front of the camera, posed to the side of the shot, framed by a classic nature shot of grizzlies in idyllic fields with snowcapped mountains in the distance. Treadwell expounds on his own virtues, as well as the risks he takes to "preserve" this image of nature, but Herzog uses the blank canvas created by Treadwell's framing to impose the title of his film on Treadwell's world. Next, at the height of Treadwell's monologue, the grizzly bear, staged center-screen, defecates a large amount of excrement. It is important to note Treadwell has multiple takes of similar dialogue, yet Herzog opens his film with *this* one, letting the bear serve as a metaphor for Herzog's perspective much as Treadwell intended a pristine nature shot as a metaphor for his own. Separately, Herzog exposes and emphasizes the fact most of his talking-head interviews are rehearsed, placing the camera uncomfortably close to some subjects, and always emphasizing performativity—particularly in the scenes where the coroner gives a watch to Treadwell's ex-girlfriend and later describes the autopsy. Herzog not only believes that the presence of the camera affects his subjects, he actively draws attention to it. Where Rouch wanted scripted scenes to give a sense of authenticity, Herzog wants the opposite as both his and Treadwell's films try to shape reality rather than depict it.

That emphasis upon cinema is related to the way it quickly becomes clear Herzog has more respect for Treadwell as a filmmaker than as an environmentalist. Specifically, in one moment, Herzog interjects, "I too would like to step in here in his defense, not as an ecologist, but as a filmmaker. He captured such glorious, improvised moments the likes of which the studio directors with their union crews can never dream of." Elsewhere, discussing Treadwell's filmmaking approach, and his willingness to let the camera keep rolling after he is done talking, Herzog adds, "Now the scene seems to be over, but as a filmmaker sometimes things fall into your lap which you couldn't expect, never even dream of. There is something like an inexplicable magic of cinema." Herzog is not implying Treadwell's success is accidental. In fact, Herzog means it as high praise, because "ecstatic truth" is partially linked to the ability to know how to recognize happenstance, as Zsigmond says on *Parts Unknown*, "the difficult part" is to recognize "the right moment you have to capture." For Herzog, Treadwell's instincts equate with great skill, skill that creates the magic of cinema: "Timothy used his camera as a tool to get his message across. Sometimes his approach was very playful. But as a filmmaker he was methodical, often repeating takes fifteen times." Herzog inserts specific examples from Treadwell's films amid this analysis to illustrate his claims.

Just as Herzog's primary interest is to bring awareness of film as medium to the forefront of his documentary, he emphasizes the ethical questions inherent in the genre, calling to mind the end of Bourdain's "Budapest," when Bourdain asks, "What about the faces of those we capture in our magic lenses . . . should we think about them and where they might be?" As hard as Herzog works to deconstruct Treadwell's narratives, he spends equal time drawing attention to his own biases, and the degree to which he can manipulate Treadwell's story at least as much as he accuses his subject of manipulating nature. As I have already noted, we see this in the way Herzog consistently draws attention to his presence throughout the film, but we also see it as he draws attention to his decisions about what to put in or leave out. For instance, Herzog does not simply omit the audio track of Treadwell's death (accidentally recorded by Treadwell), his narration *tells* the audience he is omitting it; instead, Herzog includes his facial reactions as he listens to the tape via headphones, as well as his telling Treadwell's ex-girlfriend she should destroy the tapes. Herzog continues his pattern of paralleling his filmmaking with Treadwell's by asking similar ethical questions, such as his discussion of Treadwell hiding the presence of his girlfriend(s) from the camera, and his query, upon finding footage of Treadwell's final partner, "Did Treadwell wait till his last tape to put her in his film?" Herzog persistently returns to questions of intentionality, perspective, and bias—and always those of Herzog and Treadwell as filmmaker, not as untrained anthropologist or ecologist.

Again, because Herzog considers nature to be a human construct, how we imagine nature, as well as how we depict it, says more about humankind than nature itself. Thus, much as how we imagine food is, for Bourdain, a lens with which to understand culture, how one imagines nature is a similar lens for Herzog. Herzog returns, throughout the film, to the idea that what is most essential is to expose and interrogate *how* we represent nature. First, trying to explain Treadwell's tirade against the park authorities, Herzog declares, "His rage is almost incandescent, artistic. The actor in his film has taken over from the filmmaker . . . But Treadwell is not an actor in opposition to a director or a producer. He is fighting civilization itself. It is the same civilization that cast Thoreau out of Walden and John Muir into the wild." Elsewhere, Herzog claims, "Beyond his poses the camera was his omnipresent companion. It was his instrument to explore the wilderness around him. But increasingly it became something more. He started to scrutinize his innermost being, his demons, his exhilarations. Facing the lens of a camera took on the quality of a confessional." Even more directly, in the film's conclusion, Herzog asserts, "Treadwell is gone. The argument how wrong or how right he was disappears into a distance, into a fog. What remains is his footage. And while we watch the animals . . . a thought becomes more and more clear that it is not so much a look at wild nature as it is an insight into ourselves, our nature. And that, for me, beyond his mission, gives meaning to his life and to his death." The meaning is thus created by *how* Treadwell depicts himself and *how* Herzog, in turn, depicts Treadwell—not by *what* is depicted.

Herzog's approach to documentary subject matter contains revealing parallels to the way Bourdain uses food, film, architecture, and countless other artifacts as ways of understanding culture. In fact, the attempt to see cultural artifacts (similar to Herzog's depictions of nature) as a construction that tell us something important about the culture that constructed it, paired with the idea that the truest way to understand that culture is by exposing how and why it was constructed in film, almost completely embodies Bourdain's approach to documentary filmmaking. Within his Minnesota Manifesto, Herzog proclaims, "Filmmakers of *cinéma vérité* resemble tourists who take pictures amid ancient ruins of facts. Tourism is sin, and travel on foot a virtue."[26] The distinction between tourist and traveler, fact and truth, embody the tensions, as well as the great achievements, displayed in Bourdain's filmmaking. In "Hong Kong," Bourdain admits he believes filmmakers "chang[e] the world by looking at it through cameras as happens every time you look at real people, the real world, real places." Bourdain's episodes are almost always at least as much about *how* he constructs his subjects as they are the subjects themselves.

Herzog's traveler-tourist dichotomy echoes Travel Channel's efforts to market *No Reservations* with ads that sometimes included an image of Bourdain in front of a sign stating, "Be a traveler not a tourist!" Despite his bosses and fans equating him with this almost mythic traveler, it is unclear if Bourdain ever actually uttered the phrase. More to the point, over time, it *is* clear he grew wary of the ways this distinction was applied, as he became increasingly aware of the ways it, in practice, creates a false dichotomy; too often, tourists imagining themselves as "travelers" prove to be just another, more conceited subgenre of tourism. I think Bourdain's growing ambivalence about tourism at large, awareness that his shows had inspired many people to travel, and the realization there were real-world consequences as hordes of fans flocked to the next "undiscovered" bar, restaurant, or town, informs the themes and perspectives to which I return in chapter 4. But, at its philosophical heart, I think the tourist-traveler distinction, as expressed by Herzog, is essential to understanding Bourdain's *filmmaking*.

The distinction is meant ontologically. It imagines subject matter as something to be explored, challenged, affirmed, and resisted all at the same time. Even more, it encompasses an endless journey that assumes truth as an objective goal is unachievable; at best, truth is a subjective idea for which one should perpetually strive. His fans may be able to visit and see the places Bourdain went, but they will never experience it or see it like he did, and his shows progressively wanted to make sure they realized that.

Bourdain used ethnographic approaches to make a new type of documentary, a type that merges and blends genres as it teaches us to learn from those who are different from us rather than objectify them, and to do so by consistently exposing the manner in which how we see them is a social construct that says at least as much about us as it does those we gaze upon. Thus, by making shows that are about *both* his subjects *and* how and why we construct our imaginations of those subjects, Bourdain attempts to free himself from the constraints of his medium. To quote Éric Ripert, the celebrity chef and repeat guest on *No Reservations* and *Parts Unknown*, Bourdain "changed the way we see the world. He has changed the way television covers travel shows and food shows . . . Who would have known what happened in Congo or in Libya except through his eyes? He was giving a voice to people. His show was not a food show. It was not a travel show. It was much bigger than that."[27] More than anything, Bourdain's shows attempted an understanding of their subjects reminiscent of the aims of an ethnographic filmmaker, created from the perspective of a New Wave narrative filmmaker—a perspective nearly unique within the world of documentary film.

II
GENRE

4
TRAVELOGUES

> That's the problem in making travel television. When we succeed, we inspire others to travel to the places we care about, and in a sense, we help kill what we love.
>
> —Anthony Bourdain, *No Reservations*, "Laos"[1]

> People who grow up adjacent to water, to idyllic views, lovely beaches, traditional architecture can no longer afford to live there. Their homes, their neighborhoods are, in the modern economy, in the harsh reality of the present day, undervalued. Traditional ways of life, like fishing, seem quaint anachronisms when the simple fact is that you can make a lot more money carrying a golf bag for a tourist or making blender drinks at Margaritaville.
>
> —Anthony Bourdain, Field Notes for "Jamaica"[2]

Travelogue is a term broadly applied to forms of expression in which the primary purpose is to relate a traveler's experience to an audience that has likely never been to the destination described. A popular form of writing since the nineteenth century (and before), travelogues manifested themselves most popularly in visual culture in the twentieth century—in the form of published collections of travel photographs, and in a subgenre of documentary films present from the birth of cinema and reaching an apex of popularity in the 1940s and '50s.[3] Travelogues tend to romanticize both the experience of travel and the destination, and one of the vicarious thrills they offer their audience is the imagination they are experiencing the vacation depicted, maybe even cataloging advice about where to go and how to act upon arrival. Aesthetically, travelogues strive for cohesion, the impression they have depicted the relevant aspects of their subject in their entirety. Contemporary travel TV is a manifestation of this genre with *Rick Steve's Europe* (syndicated, 2000–present), Samantha Brown's *Passport to Europe* (Travel Channel, 2004–6), and *Passport to Latin America* (Travel Channel, 2007) serving as foundational examples.

Without a doubt, this is the genre to which both Food Network and Travel Channel imagined *A Cook's Tour* and *No Reservations* as belonging to, and large swaths of Bourdain's audience believed the same. Yet, except for *The Layover*, none of Bourdain's programs neatly fit into most conceits of the genre; rather, Bourdain typically thwarted those aims altogether. For instance, while Bourdain typically relates his experiences, his point almost never has to do with the spectator imagining (or planning) their own travel; in fact, Bourdain often tells his spectators *not* to go to the places he visits.[4] Further, with some regularity, Bourdain visually mocks tourists and vocally discusses the idea that tourism might do harm. This chapter's epigraphs are only two of many such examples. Occasionally Bourdain even indirectly likens mass tourism to colonialism. In the case of "Madagascar" (PU S5E4), he bluntly states it outright. More than anything, Bourdain emphasizes how both cultures and films are constructions, and he therefore never offers the illusion of a complete depiction. Rather than providing his spectator with the illusion of a whole, complete representation of a place, Bourdain emphasizes the space between filmic representation and reality, typically offering more questions than answers. Two episodes, "French Polynesia" (NR S3E10) and "Jamaica" (PU S4E8), are particularly useful for understanding Bourdain's deconstruction of the aims of travelogues.

The episodes in French Polynesia and Jamaica are separated by seven years, two networks, and over five thousand miles. Yet, a thorough comparison reveals stark similarities in their approach to exposing cinema's complicity in the construction of romantic notions of "paradise." Defying all expectations of the travel-TV genre, both episodes invoke examples of popular art—particularly Paul Gauguin's paintings and James Bond narratives—to interrogate how these texts moved into the realm of popular culture and helped shape tourist culture. Bourdain then uses his own close readings of those texts to create a dialectic on the costs of tourist culture, and the way visual art is partially responsible for destroying local landscapes and cultures, as Bourdain suggests tourism is a new type of colonialism.

While the later episode, "Jamaica," is the more sophisticated, both are complex in their own right, and examining the two side by side illustrates how Bourdain's evolution as a filmmaker was a natural progression rooted in a perspective that had been dominant from the beginning. To quote Bourdain's field notes about "Jamaica," the island "has a harsh past and an uncomfortable present, in spite of its spectacular and captivating beauty. It is a place that's easy to romanticize. But one shouldn't do that. Like a lot of our shows, we come to no neat conclusions, only more questions. Which is, I suppose, conclusion enough."[5] Bourdain uses his filmmaking approach to invoke the real-world consequences of romanticism in all modes of visual culture, particularly travelogues.

While it is certainly true the primary connection between these two cultures is that Bourdain, a Western filmmaker, chooses to depict them similarly, that should not serve as critique. In fact, it is entirely appropriate because it is precisely Bourdain's point: both cultures have largely been defined, dominated, and shaped by how the West has imagined them at least since the colonial period. As I detail particularly in the final third of this book, Bourdain's work demonstrates a deep, recurring desire to embrace local differences, and one means of achieving this desire is to draw attention to the way the world, assisted by film form, homogenizes difference via allegiance to a Western gaze. By using a self-reflexive documentary film approach to deconstruct film form, as well as genre (such as the travelogue), Bourdain often achieves a deconstruction of that very gaze.

While I return to "Jamaica" later in the chapter, there are few places better to begin an exploration of Bourdain's approach than understanding his depiction of Gauguin's work and its impact upon Polynesia. Born in Paris, Gauguin is an influential post-impressionist painter renowned for his distinctive style and experimental use of bold color. Gauguin traveled first to Brittany, a Celtic region on the west coast of France, then to Martinique, located in the French Caribbean, and finally to Tahiti and the Marquesas, in French Polynesia, in search of increasingly exotic subject matter. As such, Gauguin was at the forefront of the late-nineteenth-century turn toward nostalgia embodied in "primitivism," a mode of aesthetic idealization that seeks to re-create experience it sees as authentic because Western artists imagine it as pre-social, pre-civilization. While Gauguin's manifestation belongs to modernist tradition, primitivism has roots both in the Enlightenment (think Jean-Jacques Rousseau's *Confessions*) and Romanticism (think Henry David Thoreau's *Walden* and Caspar David Friedrich's *Wanderer Above the Sea of Fog*), all of which idealize a pre-social autonomy within nature. As such, primitivism is hard to pin down because it "was neither an eternal Idea nor a thing to be touched, but rather a *discourse*, and one that traversed the boundaries of culture, language, and genre."[6] Not *just* an artistic genre, it is part of a conversation about how the West reimagines the Other in written and visual culture, including travelogues.

Gauguin's most famous paintings from his period in Polynesia embody this romanticism and helped shape the conversations that determined how the West imagined the Pacific; an imagination that, in turn, shaped twentieth and twenty-first century tourist culture and the travel-TV genre to which Bourdain responds. Gauguin's paintings "have played a significant role in shaping the discourse of 'Polynesianism,' a global imaginary of Polynesia . . . that constructs the people and places of this region as desirable for the Euro-American viewer."[7] This notion is embodied in two of his most representative paintings, *D'où venons-nous? Que sommes-nous? Où allons-nous?* (*Where Do We Come From? What Are We? Where Are We Going?*, 1897)[8] and *Contes barbares* (*Primitive Tales*, 1902).[9] Painted in his signature bold style, the paintings depict young, Polynesian women lounging in a virginal paradise in various states of dress. In the case of *Where Do We Come From?*, most are topless, a few are clothed, and two are nude. The women are grouped in three categories metaphorically depicting a Western conceptualization of the life cycle. In *Primitive Tales*, two topless women sit facing one another, with a self-reflective depiction of the Dutch painter Meijer de Haan, a deceased friend of Gauguin's, staring lecherously from behind. While both paintings depict their "primitive" subjects in a positive manner, as something to aspire to, they imagine them as pre-social. Even as Gauguin goes to great lengths to accurately depict Polynesian dress, the paintings allow, for the Western eye, an idealization that, because most are topless, they are somehow outside of society's "bounds" of dress, rather than dressed in the societal trappings of a *different* society. Meanwhile, one painting makes its meaning via a Garden of Eden metaphor and the other through self-reflective modernist commentary. The painting's audience and meaning are thus fully intended for the West, no matter how much Polynesia enchants Gauguin.

Primitivism's participation in a broader discourse is what allowed it, by Bourdain's century, to enter the popular consciousness in means quite unrelated to its original context. As Heather Waldroup explains, Gauguin's "body of artwork is firmly based in European art, and he saw himself as an heir to, rather than a rebel against, this tradition. Still, his work has taken on important roles that move beyond the significance of his work as a revered object in a museum. As an index of the tourist fantasy of Tahiti, adorning postcards and advertisements for cruise ships, Gauguin's paintings in a popular context underscore the intertwined histories of colonialism and exoticism."[10]

Gauguin was attracted to Tahiti and the Marquesas, in part, by the written genre of travel writing, a genre in which he, in turn, eventually partook. More to the point, his paintings *also* enter the same discourse even if they are imagined in a different genre, setting the stage for their meaning to morph into the postmodern images that end up on postcards and travel guides. To quote Alison Nordström, "Travel photographs serve to define, value, commodify and validate the travel experience; their organization into books fixed, cohered and materialized it. Once made, these complex photographic objects constructed the journey that should have been, one without boring moments, bad weather, late trains, pickpockets or lost luggage. The foreign worlds depicted were composed only of significant moments, sublime views, and picturesque or exotic inhabitants."[11] In my opinion, the same could equally be said of the inevitable spawn of collections of travel photography: filmic travelogues and travel TV.

It is therefore within this discourse the average spectator and television executive imagines a show like *No Reservations*, and Bourdain intentionally invokes those genre expectations before thwarting them. While it is true Bourdain frames his episode with six epigraphs taken from Gauguin, the episode is more clearly structured around the context of a popular imagination of primitive paradise. For instance, while the editing follows Gauguin's biography, beginning with Bourdain's arrival in Tahiti, continuing with his journey to the Marquesas, and ending beside Gauguin's grave, the artist is primarily used as a vessel to explore the West's romanticized imaginations of the South Pacific and their often-destructive results. Such a focus is clear from Bourdain's opening voice-over after the opening credits:

> French Polynesia. Just the name evokes images of South Sea adventure and romance and another time. When the first French sailors arrived, their ships boarded by bronzed skinned, bare-breasted women, the myth of French Polynesia as a savage but beautiful Garden of Eden was born. Of subsequent visitors perhaps no one planted the dream of French Polynesia as an exotic wonderland filled with mystery, symbolism, and uninhibited savages more deeply into popular consciousness than famed post-impressionist artist Paul Gauguin. Gauguin abandoned the trappings of his former life in Paris and immersed himself in what he considered a primitive but more spiritual culture. Like any young boy who grew up reading adventure stories, I too saw his paintings and dreamed of faraway islands surrounded by blue where *anything* was possible. I wanted to find out for myself what Gauguin saw in French Polynesia, and I did find faraway islands. Tiny dots of outrageously vibrant green surrounded by gin clear blue and more blue water. Verdant valleys. Cloud topped peaks. Majestic cliffs. Deserted beaches. I went. I found them. They exist.

The camera rotates between idealized, touristic images of Polynesia, close-ups of Gauguin's paintings, screenshots of romantic exploration maps, and shots of Bourdain riding in a boat. Immediately after, however, the camera totally washes out to white and then slowly fades back into modern images of Western-dressed locals paddling a boat with Bourdain. The soundtrack becomes stark, bare, naturalistic. Bourdain continues, "I found, sort of, the fiercely tattooed warriors, the beautiful people who once ruled these seas. These navigators and cannibals of whom Herman Melville wrote." Bourdain thus immediately creates a visual and narrative contrast between Gauguin's imagination and a more modern reality; a reality that does not match the image, which is, again, pointedly linked to a Western gaze (this time Melville), and something Bourdain can only "sort of" experience.

Bourdain continues to emphasize this dialectic throughout the episode as he repeatedly destabilizes the idea any place could be filled exclusively with Nordström's "significant moments, sublime views, and picturesque or exotic inhabitants." Between bursts of Eden-like images, island meals, and tours of historic sights, we see a series of insignificant moments and failures. Bourdain swings on a hammock in boredom. He attempts to paint "like Gauguin," but abandons the project when he realizes his crew forgot turpentine. He goes on a fishing expedition that the editing emphasizes is constructed for television. He hunts sea urchins on a surface that is both dangerous and uncomfortable, comparing it to a "cheese-grater," he also admits that the guides catch most of the urchins. He subsequently sleeps in a hammock while his guides hunt coconut crabs to cook for his pleasure. Even before the opening credits, Bourdain inserts a fictional scene in which he naively, like a tourist, swims and is eaten by reef sharks he has mistaken for dolphins, as the cinematography and the soundtrack invoke Steven Spielberg's *Jaws* (1975). On the surface, these scenes are played for comedy in line with the travelogue genre. Collectively, however, it becomes apparent the awkward, gimmicky, genre-driven scenes disassemble the image of paradise constructed by Gauguin, the spectator, and Bourdain's camera in the more polished scenes. This anti-travelogue approach is mirrored by Bourdain's willingness to bluntly tell his Western audience that the West's first "gifts" were "shame, typhoid, and syphilis" and that, "European explorers brought diseases that eventually wiped out 98 percent of the population and the missionaries who followed systematically destroyed or obliterated their culture."

The history of colonization is a narrative Bourdain never lets slip far from his spectator's mind, and he works hard to make it feel contemporary, setting the table for its connection to tourism. When Bourdain first lands in Papeete, which he calls "very far from paradise," he asserts, "French Polynesia is officially French overseas territory, but it felt like a colony to me. Now, there's nothing wrong with a fresh baguette in a foreign land, but this is Tahiti, the supposed Garden of Eden of the Pacific.

It looks a lot like St. Barthes. Or the Southwest of France. Or anywhere the French go for *les vacances*. Similar architecture. Same cars. God, they love their boulevards and planting trees." Interviewing a French expat chef, Patrick Brunelle, who runs a French bakery staffed by Polynesian employees in postcard-worthy "native" garb, Bourdain asks, "Are there French people who just refuse to eat anything local?" Later, after eating a Polynesian-French fusion meal at Brunelle's new restaurant, Bourdain concludes the Papeete portion of the episode, "Who will eat there, at that stark temple to fusion on the other side of the world from Paris? Well, surely not the tattooed warriors and dark maidens of lore. There will be drinking of cosmos at this bar by now. And blender drinks with umbrellas in them I suspect. And lovers from worlds other than this one will gaze at each other from across the room and the past, and all that ever happened here will be scenery. Another holiday in the sun." The restaurant represents a tourist economy in which locals must perform a Western imagination of their culture to survive, a type of cultural colonialism.

Much as many episodes draw the spectator's attention to the construction of cinema, Bourdain continually draws attention to the degree to which his experience in Polynesia is that of a tourist, and, more pointedly, a tourist with a camera crew. Pampered and catered to at every turn, Bourdain reminds us his Polynesia is more about him, and Western tourist imaginations, than it is Polynesia; that "those who come here looking for a savage past look really for themselves. An aspect in the mirror." Both the camera and his voice-over remind the viewer he cannot bridge the gap to any authentic Polynesian experience, to the degree Bourdain believes authenticity exists to begin with. He claims one of his best moments is watching a family sing post-dinner entertainment, but the camera shows him sitting apart, separate, an invitee because he is staying at the resort bungalow on their property. He enjoys watching a performance troupe reenact Polynesian drums and dance, but he explicitly reminds us they are performing for the cameras. He rides with guides through the jungles showing Māʻohi ruins and talking about the impact the West had on their culture, but he makes jokes that mirrors himself with Westerners in the history, not the locals. He has a touching conversation in French about a meal with the grandmother who cooked it for him, but he pointedly tells the spectator there is "nothing French here but the common language."

The way Bourdain's approach emphasizes the multiple discourses inherent in all representations of paradise, and the degree to which he admits his own work is part of that construction, renders him a type of mediator. We see this role made concrete at episode's end when, sitting next to Gauguin's grave, Bourdain reads the Samoan word, "*Oviri*," etched upon it. Rather than translating it directly to English, Bourdain first translates it to French, "*Sauvage*," and only then to English, "Wild." The articulation mirrors the change of audience across the history of the gravesite, from Mā'ohi to French colonizer to English-speaking tourist. Bourdain then personifies his role as mediator as he points out two conflicting ways of understanding Gauguin and arrives, instead, at a nuanced middle ground: "The more I read about Paul Gauguin, the less I liked him. He was a cranky contrarian, egotistical, sponger, a dope fiend I believe, a pederast and a syphilitic . . . But at least he recognized the people here and the culture here and this place as something beautiful when the rest of the Western world seemed to be working very hard to willfully obliterate it." While Bourdain participates in the discourse about paradise I have thus far explored, the impact of his constant awareness of his participation in that construction is how he manages to carve this middle ground. By becoming an active mediator for an audience that is aware both of his bias and of the fact he is mediating, suddenly he can subvert the tendencies of the genre.

In this context, one can see the radical nature of Bourdain's filmmaking as his deconstruction of tourist culture has far-reaching consequences. Lori Kido Lopez's "Eating a Meal with the Other: The Ethical Challenges of Travel Food Shows" articulates problems many see in travel TV, claiming, "The unequal power dynamic between the white American television crew and the individuals who are being interviewed is often troubling, and the question of whether or not we actually want these communities to be swamped by American tourists eager to experience 'authentic' cultures and cuisines is left unanswered."[12] What such critiques miss, however, is that these are Bourdain's concerns as well, that he makes his spectator aware of these problems at every turn. In fairness, Lopez admits Bourdain is "able to distance himself from the outward goal of travel shows" because his discomfort with the power dynamics leads to self-reflexive language.[13] Still, Lopez insists "it cannot be forgotten that this is a travel show, and that an important aspect of such shows is to effectively advertise for the locale that is being presented [as] Travel shows are inextricably entwined with the tourism industry."[14]

I would argue Bourdain's work is, at best, difficult to place within the bounds of normative travel TV. Meanwhile, the idea that his show is "inextricably entwined with the tourism industry" seems almost antithetical to Bourdain's open mockery of the industry and the tourists who fund it. Bourdain does not simply "complicate what would otherwise be seen as a colonialist intrusion into third-world countries."[15] He makes such colonialist intrusion his central point and disrupts the simplistic view any location could be authentically represented by an image. While Lopez chides, "a simple interest in sampling ethnic food rarely carries the potential for any power structures to be disrupted, or for the subjects of fascination to demonstrate agency or resistance,"[16] I argue Bourdain actively disrupts said power structure via filmmaking that reveals the genre's colonialist lens.

Lopez's ambivalence is not unique. In fact, ambivalence highlights most of the (limited) academic writing on Bourdain and postcolonialism, most of which focuses on Africa, most of which focuses more on representation than film theory.[17] For instance, Casey Ryan Kelly, in his book *Food Television and Otherness in the Age of Globalization*, is drawn to the possibilities posed by Bourdain, claiming, "I find *No Reservations* to be an invective against global tourist culture, a program structured like a long-form argument against close-minded ethnocentric forms of food tourism."[18] Still, Kelly, like Lopez, is hesitant because "the show's emphasis on 'going native,' or living like the locals, is also premised on a fixed and binary notion of culture, that behind the smokescreen of staged tourism is an authentic and knowable Other."[19] This, to me, is the central misreading. Over the course of his career Bourdain came to see both the Other and the Western spectator as constructed. More to the point, he increasingly made his films *about* those constructions, making it clear we can never tangibly understand what we see, that parts will remain unknown. I therefore think it is no coincidence that Kelly limits his discussion almost exclusively to *No Reservations*, thereby avoiding the best examples of how Bourdain uses cinema to make films *about* cinema, not travel.

If Bourdain's deconstruction is not clear enough in the body of "Polynesia," it is certainly driven home at its end, as he connects Gauguin and himself to the tourist industry, ties that awareness to his critiques of colonialism, and hints at the spectator's complicit participation in all of it. Walking away from the artist's grave, Bourdain begins, "Like many travelers who the farther from home they venture find themselves turning inwards, Gauguin's paintings were more about himself. The colors and images eerily free of the troublesome details of reality were in fact, a superimposed version of the world as he perhaps wanted it to be." The camera then returns to the scene on the beach where the traditional dancers performed, contrasting Gauguin's Polynesia to a local depiction, but one Bourdain has already shown to be inauthentic, performed for cameras. The soundtrack fills with drums. Bourdain continues, "Though he heard the spirits and gods of these islands and recognized their beauty, their sensual pull, they never spoke to him. We smash a bit of the world beneath our feet as we travel through it, in footprints large and small. However heavily, like the soldiers and missionaries who came here, or lightly, like Gauguin, we tread. Gauguin's Tahiti and Marquesas Islands were already a vanished dream when he arrived." Thus, Bourdain links the colonist, the missionary, the tourist, and the filmmaker. All are culpable to varying degrees. All exploit a "power dynamic" between themselves and the culture they impact. All exist in counterpoint to the efforts of travelogues to "define, value, commodify and validate the travel experience."

These ideas remain at the center of *Parts Unknown*'s "Jamaica," one of Bourdain's most nuanced, articulate, and masterfully constructed episodes. Bourdain's interests, namely the deconstruction of paradise and concerns about the connections he draws between colonial and tourist economies, remain the same. So do most of his strategies of approach, such as highlighting a discourse between multiple images of paradise and using them to destabilize ideas of authenticity, eventually using his own close reading of those texts to mediate the discourse.

A comparison of "French Polynesia" and "Jamaica" demonstrates how the seeds for the endpoint of Bourdain's filmmaking in *Parts Unknown* were present at least as soon as the early seasons of *No Reservations*, while it simultaneously establishes the way budget, freedom, and experience afforded *Parts Unknown* a level of polish and complexity unavailable at Travel Channel. The differences are evident on multiple levels: (1) the access Bourdain gets in Jamaica, including lengthy interviews with two of the country's richest men and free use of their resorts, (2) production values that are superior at almost every level, and a budget to shoot narrative scenes that feel as if they could be from a Hollywood movie rather than the awkward joke sequences in Polynesia, and (3) a more complex and confident narrative structure that, rather than framing the episode around a single influence (Gauguin), complicates the discourse by using multiple texts in conversation with each other; specifically Ian Fleming's Bond novels, the Bond film franchise, Alexander Payne's *The Descendants* (2011), and Bourdain's construction of a filmic image I call "American Tourist," who serves as a composite of all of the discourses on primitivism and paradise that came before him.

Of the four framing devices, *The Descendants* is the least overt, but it is a good starting point precisely because its subtle, quiet presence informs the episode in ways that could easily be missed. *The Descendants* entered mainstream culture with strong box office sales and five Academy Award nominations, and Bourdain visually references it twice—in "Jamaica" and in "Hawai'i" (PU S5E7). Payne's protagonist, Matt King (George Clooney), is a self-admitted whitewashed descendant of Hawai'ian royalty whose heritage makes him the head of a trust that owns the last untouched real estate on Kaua'i's coast. Tax laws force the family to entertain offers from a variety of resort developers; something King ultimately resolves to fight. Two scenes are of particular significance for "Jamaica." The first is split before and after King takes his daughters to visit the property a final time. Riding in an open-air jeep, the first half shows beautiful landscape set to the upbeat soundtrack of Dennis Kamakahi's "'Ūlili Ē." The second half stands in contrast as Kamakahi's lament, "Pua Hone," is paired with an increasingly aseptic, corporate landscape of golf courses and resort homes where only the street names resemble Hawai'i. The other scene is King's opening monologue, when he asserts, "My friends on the mainland think just because I live in Hawai'i, I live in paradise. Like a permanent vacation. We're all just out here sipping mai tais, shaking our hips, and catching waves. Are they insane? Do they think we are immune to life? How can they possibly think our families are less screwed up, our cancers less fatal, our heartaches less painful? Hell, I haven't been on a surfboard in fifteen years. . . . Paradise? Paradise can go fuck itself." The images progress from romantic, sweeping views to close-ups of the impoverished and, finally, King's wife on a ventilator.

In short, the scenes use juxtaposition to deconstruct paradise in a manner similar to Bourdain's "Polynesia" and provide a visual reference point for Bourdain's approach to Jamaica.

While the relationship between the multiple framing devices is complex, Bourdain is more direct about introducing the others. The minute-long scene that precedes the opening credits is an overt reference to the famous openings of every Bond movie. Bourdain's sequence opens with an iris shot that is a direct copy of the first shot of *Dr. No* (Terrence Young, 1962), the first film in the Bond franchise and the only one set and shot in Jamaica, home of the author of the Bond series of books, Ian Fleming. The music for the opening sequence is evocative of Bond music, the subject matter—a nude woman swimming in silhouette underwater—is typical for the Bond series, and the water-filled screen even turns red from top to bottom, just as in *Dr. No*'s iris shot. The title credits make Bond-era jokes, such as titling the episode "Rum Lives Forever" and a title card declaring the episode is filmed in "ZamboniVision," referencing Bourdain's director of photography, Zach Zamboni, and the 1950s widescreen formats Panavision and VistaVision. The significant difference, however, is that the subject of Bourdain's iris shot is not Bond (Sean Connery) breaking the fourth wall and firing a gun directly into the iris. Instead, what slides down the iris is an overweight, American tourist wearing a yellow "Jamaica Crazy" T-shirt complete with racially questionable caricatures. He holds a straw hat and a strawberry daiquiri. He proceeds, in silhouette and daiquiri still in hand, to swim after the nude woman. Unlike the awkward *Jaws* gag before "Polynesia's" opening credits, the humor sets up an intricate interplay between images that dominate the episode's discourse: (a) Bond films, which Bourdain's narration close reads later in the episode, (b) by extension, Ian Fleming, whose home Bourdain visits, and (c) American Tourist, whom Bourdain jarringly inserts at key points throughout the episode, always running at the camera, drink in hand.

If one accepts the tacit connection between colonialism and tourism Bourdain explored in Polynesia, Bond can serve as a natural bridge between the two, rendering Bourdain's coupling of images of Bond and American Tourist not *just* a stark juxtaposition played for kicks, but also a nuanced exposition of a multifaceted discourse about colonialism and tourism, the discourse around which Bourdain centers his episode. As Anna Christoffersen asserts, aside from Bond's well-documented sexism,

"Bond is, at his core, an escapist, misogynist, *imperialist* fantasy, and has been since Ian Fleming's very first conception of him. He must have women for toys, and non-Western countries for a playground."[20]

I find *Dr. No* to be a particularly good example. Shot largely on location in Jamaica, which is rare for its era, the movie does little with the setting. Jamaica serves mostly as backdrop, and often not even impressive backdrop at that, as it avoids Jamaica's beauty much as it avoids Jamaicans and their culture. We are told the food is good at a barbecue joint, but we never see the food. The only real nod to Jamaican music is the opening "Three Blind Mice" sequence, which is a Western nursery rhyme simply sung in Jamaican style and used in a sequence that essentializes stereotypes. There are few Jamaican characters besides Quarrel, a cardboard cut-out of a Jamaican fisherman-turned-spy, who also stereotypically dies unceremoniously so that Bond and the object of his sexual desire may live. Bond's sexual conquests are British, Chinese (played by a white actress in yellow face to sidestep Hays Code rules about miscegenation), and Dutch (altered from the book where she is Jamaican), respectively. Even the "enemy" is not Jamaican, rather a Chinese evil-mastermind, himself a stereotype, and represents a threat of world domination that has little to do with local culture. The entire second half of the film on Dr. No's Island could have been filmed almost anywhere. To return to Christoffersen, "Bond's hallmark is to wreak spectacular infrastructural havoc on Central American, South American, African, and Middle Eastern countries with impunity and in the name of England, leaving behind a repair bill that must total in the millions (billions, sometimes). His treatment of women must always be remembered in this light. All too often, Bond's targets are not only reduced to a sex object, but to an exoticized, fetishized one at that; another piece of a foreign nation that Bond 'conquers.'"[21] Viewed in this context, American Tourist is not Bond's counterpoint, but, rather, his progeny; both are a threat to local culture because both seek to conquer paradise.

Bourdain's more formal opening, immediately after the credits, is as subtle as the pre-credit sequence is overt. It is beautiful, emblematic Bourdain filmmaking: pointed visual references, nuanced narrative discourse, masterful use of juxtaposition both within and between the visuals and the audio, and the personalization and personification of Bourdain's experience. Before we hear Bourdain, we hear and see a mento band, the Jolly Boys, sitting on a porch performing "Iron Bar" in Patois, a language rarely heard by outsiders, especially tourists. The music remains the dominant soundtrack for most of the sequence. Bourdain drives an open-top jeep, cracking jokes about being on the left side of the road, thus emphasizing both the jeep, which is one of the episode's many references to *The Descendants*, as well as traffic laws left over from colonization. Bourdain's voice-over begins:

> Nearly a year on the road. All those miles. All those airports. *Infinite* variety of *awful* plumbing. It was time for something low impact. So, off to Jamaica. . . . But this time a different angle. You probably know of Jamaica as a vacation paradise. But it's worth mentioning this is a divided country and has been in one form or another since the days of slavery. There's a small minority who control most everything, and then there's the poorer, generally darker-skinned majority. Less connected, left out. Jamaican cuisine, a lot of it, still reflects this conflicted history. Breadfruit, salt fish. This was slave food. Cheap, long lasting, filling. Introduced, basically, as *feed*.

As Bourdain emphasizes "feed," the mento music comes to a halt, the camera snapping back to the Jolly Boys as they stop playing, reminding the spectator that the upbeat music comes from this very history. Throughout the sequence, to this point, most of the images are of the mento band and other locals, occasionally juxtaposed against the *Descendants*-like vistas Bourdain drives past, wealthy estates, and a tourist postcard in which American Tourist makes an appearance. But the juxtapositions are not polemic, they are embodiments of a multilayered discourse as Bourdain's personal search for "low impact" escapism is fundamentally separated not only from the local and the authentic, but also from the wealthy landowners and American Tourist. It is a multitude of perspectives in conversation with one another.

After quickly eating at a jerk hut, Bourdain's narration picks back up: "And there are still, all these years later, *two* Jamaicas. There's the Jamaica that most Jamaicans live in, cook in, struggle to survive in. The real Jamaica." The soundtrack is sparse, Jamaican music playing softly in the background. The images are close-ups of a fishmonger and his son waiting for business. Suddenly, we hear an original score evocative of the Beach Boys, American Tourist appears on-screen, and Bourdain concludes, "Then there's the Jamaica which you are probably more familiar with." American Tourist runs straight toward the camera, coming out of the surf as if invading the island, a daiquiri in one hand and a margarita in the other, a direct threat to what Bourdain had just previously shown. Even as the voice-over connects the spectator to American Tourist by invoking "you," the camera positions the spectator on land, positioned with the Jamaicans, facing the assault, thereby positioning the spectator with the Other. The music abruptly stops and the audio and visual cut to an outdated bus honking as it passes; the markings of a different tourist past that serve as yet another layer of discourse.

With a history of slavery and colonialism, and his own desire for low impact escape as preamble, Bourdain sets into a brief history of tourism on the island, rolling through a series of tourist stills and films from the 1940s and '50s as Bourdain ties colonialism to tourism even more bluntly than in Polynesia. Laying out Jamaican history as "An empire of bananas, a huge industry that later became United Fruit," Bourdain concludes, "Bananas went out, tourists came in." In short, American Tourist is simply the modern iteration of the United Fruit Company.

"American Tourist" appears throughout "Jamaica" (PU S4E8). Bourdain uses this image as a short-hand metaphor for the damage mass tourism causes to locations that the West deems "paradise."

The remainder of the episode can be split into two sections differentiated by the high-end resorts that host Bourdain, as he uses his digs as a means of creating a contrast between the type of Jamaica billionaire investors envision and the Jamaica their visions would destroy. Michael Lee-Chin, the owner of the first hotel, the Trident in Port Antonio, is given the full-on Bond treatment as he arrives at what Bourdain describes as "a castle." First, the resort is shown in all its luxuriousness in shots (and set to music) directly evocative of Bond. Next, Lee-Chin arrives by helicopter, as Bourdain asks, "What kind of person would own a building like that? Who? Why?" Bourdain tells us Lee-Chin has invited him for dinner, but the music turns ominous and the camera cuts to a night sequence in which Bourdain goes crab hunting with the resort chefs for said dinner.

Much as Bourdain emphasized the performative nature of his pampered stay in the Marquesas in which he slept while his hosts caught and prepared his dinner, Bourdain depicts the usually unseen work that enables escapism. Here, however, Bourdain is more biting. The crab hunting scene is longer than the dinner scene that follows, the music out of a scary movie. Bourdain stresses the intense heat, the darkness, fire ants, and the fact the crabs are dangerous, that the chefs are being asked to "willingly risk dismemberment for the sake of procuring a tasty dinner." Both Bourdain and the camera make clear just how uncomfortable he is, and the degree to which the chefs are doing most of the real work. Then, when the episode snaps to the fancy dinner, and a shot of a prepared crab on a fancy plate, Bourdain emphasizes the wealth and privilege present at a table that even includes Errol Flynn's grandson. Lee-Chen explains his plans, "Great things will happen when you romanticize, you dream, you aspire, you see a vision, and you settle to achieve that vision. Trident is here to catalyze people to come to Port Antonio and discover, wow, wow, and wow again." Lee-Chin's economic vision is thus described in romantic terms that blend a discourse as diverse as Rousseau's essentialism, Emerson's self-determination, and Gauguin's imagination of paradise, and a discourse that Bourdain displays as repositioned in wholly economic terms.

While Bourdain, as filmmaker, allows Lee-Chin space and time to have his say, Bourdain's immediate response to the first part of Lee-Chin's explanation coupled with subsequent cinematic choices makes

Bourdain's indictment clear. The table, dress, and camerawork all invoke the glamour and mystique of Bond. As we are shown a series of close-ups of high-end food served by white-gloved waiters, Bourdain responds with a telling question: "Where does it cross over, where all of the things you love about this area, where all of the villas are spanking new, and people are building 400 room hotels, is there a threshold where things start to not be the things that you loved about the place in the first place, and how do you guard against that?" Lee-Chin mostly dodges the question at first, then, after the conversation turns toward questions about why tourists are drawn, in the words of Errol Flynn's grandson, to "lame" resort versions of Jamaica rather than places with the "real feeling," Lee-Chin attempts to clarify his vision: "You can't go many places in the world and find *natural* beauty, people who are genuinely warm, where there's a strong culture of food, strong culture in terms of music, and at the same time be able to be part of a community, and you can be a visitor without being part of a tourist industry."

The camera, however, leaves the dinner table before Lee-Chin even *begins* speaking. The background music again turns ominous and creates an off-putting counterpoint sound; through sound editing, Lee-Chin's voice is given an eerie echo; and, immediately after Lee-Chin finishes, we enter a lengthy sequence of over a minute in which a multitude of dancers, fire-eaters, and drummers offer a highly performative display of Jamaican culture in front of wealthy dinner guests who snap images on their cell phones, and then a cut straight to commercial. Without saying a word, Bourdain deconstructs Lee-Chin's claims. This is not the world of jerk chicken and mento music on a ramshackle front porch Bourdain so happily partook in at the beginning of the episode; it is not about "natural beauty," and it is very much "part of a tourist industry."

The second resort, Golden Eye, is owned by Chris Blackwell, founder of Island Records and credited by Bourdain as having "discovered" Bob Marley for a Western audience. At the time of filming, the hotel was expanding outward from Ian Fleming's house, which sits at the center of the property. We are introduced to the hotel with an over-the-shoulder shot of Bourdain as he tours Fleming's cottage and stares out a rectangle window, framed to emphasize its widescreen nature. With Bond-style music playing, Bourdain tells us Blackwell has "big plans for the area," implies those plans may come at the expense of the fishing village next door, Oracabessa, and cuts to a model he finds in Blackwell's offices depicting their expansive vision. The model is displayed almost identically to a model in *The Descendants*, and Bourdain returns to this shot multiple times in the episode. Several shots of the still untouched beach next to Golden Eye are also framed similarly to how *The Descendants* frames the beach its protagonist takes his daughters to see one final time.

Immediately after identifying the potential expansion and the threat to the fishermen, the audio reverts to mento music, and the camera cuts to Bourdain at a hyper-local eatery eating oxtail, callaloo, curried goat, and rice and pigeon peas. The contrast between resort and local is further accentuated when Bourdain emphasizes the diverse nature of the culture, claiming "God, I love the food in this country . . . it's so diverse." The restaurant's proprietor alerts Bourdain to worries the area's last public beach is also under threat, leading Bourdain to assert, "It's expanding fast in the town. They are going to be building all around. So that's thousands of tourists." Instantly, the camera and audio cut to another American Tourist insert, then back to silence and a local cutting a coconut with a machete, continuing to use the filmic lens to emphasize the two Jamaicas articulated in the introduction.

The following scene, an impromptu visit to a rum bar at James Bond Beach, serves as a microcosm of the varying discourses that drive the episode, as well as Bourdain's ability as guest and filmmaker to shape that discourse. Bourdain pointedly informs us Blackwell, upon hearing he wanted to go to the fisherman's beach, insisted his "good friend Carl accompany [him]." After taking lessons from Carl on how to mix beer and rum, Bourdain asks the group if there is a realistic "future for the traditional fishing industry in Jamaica" given the threat of "end[ing] up an entirely tourist economy." One fisherman answers, "This is going to be to the tourists. This place here. . . . I live right up the road, lovely spot, which is on the coast, just like Chris Blackwell. And they're going to tell me that I cannot fish in there." As the fisherman compares himself to Blackwell, a multi-millionaire, and expresses concerns for his future, Blackwell's employee, Carl, tries to interrupt. Bourdain inserts himself quickly to avoid it, summarizing, "Rich people want to live what they see as a simple life. In their minds they want to live the life of a Jamaican fisherman, they want to live the life of somebody who doesn't have a lot of money. But the people who actually do that now are giving up their living and essentially entering the tourist sector. There's a certain amount of irony at work here. Who gets to live in paradise?" Carl quickly answers before the others have a chance, "nobody," but the others start to vocally agree with Bourdain. When the fisherman who compared himself to Blackwell tries to speak again, Carl physically inserts his body between the man and Bourdain, tells him in Patois to stop talking, and eventually drags him away. Bourdain decides to use the audio caught on microphone seemingly unbeknownst to Carl and the fisherman, as well as to subtitle it, something he has not heretofore done. Carl tells the man, "To order the program to work, assuming, you just kick back and be cool . . . You can't expose yourself." The camera cuts back to the model at Blackwell's office and then to a chain-link fence being locked while the audience hears an off-putting sound. Bourdain thus highlights a myriad of voices while the filmic choices make clear Bourdain is mediating how we interpret those voices.

In typical Bourdain fashion, he is most willing to overtly assert his voice via narration (rather than through filmic decisions) when he can personalize the perspective. In the case of "Jamaica," he also does just as he promises in the field notes, providing "no neat conclusions, only more questions," albeit questions that make his bias clear. First, as the camera returns to the model of the proposed expansion, Bourdain asks, "Which is better? To be your own man, uphold family tradition in a dangerous, ever shrinking, ever more difficult business, trying to catch fish in the sea, or carry a *golf* bag for a wealthy tourist? I couldn't tell you. I was in the service industry cooking people's food for most of my working life so it's not like I have anything against it. But I don't know." The camera returns to the fishermen, but nothing is resolved. Next, we find Bourdain sitting at the end of a private pier, downbeat music in the background. Bourdain begins with declarations before returning to pointed questions:

> Who gets to live in paradise? It's Jamaica. Let's accept as a basic premise that this is about as close to paradise as it gets, right? This place I'm staying was built by a guy who lived here two months out of the year. That place down there, probably the same, two months a year. Sad to say, I think it's unlikely that fifty years from now anyone but the extraordinarily fortunate, the extraordinarily connected, and the

> extraordinarily rich will be able to even look at a vista like this. That is my personal theory. Look, here I am. Fully aware of the irony of the situation. It's like the whole preservation thing. Preserve for who? Save the reef for who? Save the beach, for whom?

Bourdain pauses, the camera cuts to an even tighter close-up, and Bourdain breaks the fourth wall, turns directly toward the camera, and declares, "Not you, probably." Suddenly, in a single moment, Bourdain repositions the threat posed by American Tourist. It is not *just* a threat to the imagined, Jamaican Other, but a threat to the spectator as well.

When Bourdain finally sits down with Blackwell, the conversation is framed in a manner that mirrors his interview with Lee-Chin, but with heightened awareness of what is at stake. It therefore serves as an example of the increased complexity and nuance Bourdain builds in ways he could not in "Polynesia," because of the multiple visual lenses and perspectives, as well as his own filmic confidence to let juxtapositions and camera angles make much of his argument.

Sitting at Blackwell's private bar overlooking the ocean on Golden Eye property, Bourdain and Blackwell share a table, the camera cutting back and forth between them. But we are also shown Carl sitting at the bar watching the pair, depicted in an over-the-shoulder point-of-view shot emphasizing his quiet gaze. We have seen, shortly before this, the fishermen at James Bond Beach, and in the middle of this interview Bourdain interjects yet another shot of the model for the proposed expansion and yet another American Tourist moment. Bourdain thus, without a word, invokes a multitude of looks, a multitude of perspectives. Bourdain asks Blackwell if it is, "an inevitability that basically all of the Caribbean [is] essentially going to end up as a service economy?" Blackwell replies, "Yes . . . It's based on tourism." Bourdain tries to shape the conversation to steer the spectator back to the rhetorical questions Bourdain had just asked on the pier. Of Blackwell, Bourdain asks, "It's a tough balance. The engine that's going to preserve or save is often dependent on who's coming to look, and what they are willing to pay to come and look. Can there be a balance, do you think?" The camera highlights Blackwell's sense of discomfort via a close-up of him fidgeting and twisting a straw. Bourdain's face looks crushed when Blackwell's only response is "I think there can be a couple hundred places like this in Jamaica." There is nothing left to be said. Instead, Bourdain reverts to Bond as a lens for framing Jamaica, asking Blackwell what character he would be in a Bond movie. Blackwell asserts he would "have to be" Bond himself, because he is "the only hero in a Bond film." Bourdain, always the filmmaker, always the mediator, responds that he would not see himself as the hero or the villain, but another character altogether.

"Jamaica's" final juxtaposition is Bourdain's final interview, conducted with local women who run restaurants on the endangered beach, and the scene allows Bourdain to synthesize his perspective one final time, and move away from the confines of the resort, which have been depicted in a sinister manner. By this point, Bourdain seems to hope he has the spectator fully on the side of the locals. Bourdain introduces the beach, proclaiming, "What we are all looking for, isn't it? The perfect beach. Remote. Uncluttered by douchery. Cold, local beer." I think it is not a coincidence that the introductory shot of the beach is framed by a tree branch that creates an almost perfect, filmic, widescreen shot. Eating the women's food, listening to their stories of their fight to keep the beach public, Bourdain claims, "That would be sort of ridiculous, if Jamaicans can't go to the beach in Jamaica. . . . Let's face it, there are only so many beaches in this world. Even fewer unspoiled beaches. And even fewer beaches like this." Moved by both the experience and the food, Bourdain declares he is going to make an impromptu return for breakfast the next morning on his way to the airport. He does so, he says, "Because it may not be here that much longer. Not like this anyway . . . The way the world turns, the inevitable grind of history seems to indicate that places like this and people like this get plowed under, pushed aside, paved over. Who owns paradise after all? Who in the end gets to own paradise, use paradise, or even visit it? That's a question that's probably worth paying attention to before there's none left at all." Bourdain's summation thus provides us with the questions he promised to end upon all along, as he depicts an island, a culture, a population, in danger of facing the same fate depicted in "Polynesia."

Bourdain's ability to reposition discourse to such a degree that he feels he can assume the spectator is actively on the side of the locals, rather than simply conflicted as at the end of "Polynesia," may be the ultimate testament to his growth as filmmaker. As I will explore in more detail in my final four chapters (and the conclusion), Bourdain seeks to depict difference without essentializing it, to deconstruct the Western gaze via a self-reflexive brand of filmmaking that habitually draws attention to how we are all constructed; to question authenticity, both filmic and cultural, in a way that denies binaries. In so doing, he comes close to manifesting bell hooks's desire for "mutual exchange"[22] that defies Self-Other dichotomies, a type of mediation made possible precisely because he makes films *about* those dichotomies. To quote Claire Johnson, writing about attempts to thwart a male gaze, "Any revolutionary strategy must challenge the depiction of reality: it is not enough to discuss oppression . . . within the text of the film, the language of the cinema/the depiction of reality must also be interrogated, so that a break between ideology and text is effected."[23] As example, she points to a scene in Dorothy Arzner's *Dance, Girl, Dance* (1940), in which the object of the gaze breaks the fourth wall and "turns on the audience and tells them *how she sees them*."[24] Bourdain's American Tourist comes to mind, and it is Bourdain's embrace of New Wave film techniques and willingness to expose the construction of cinema that allow him to draw attention to a touristic gaze as a means of challenging it, to use travel TV to attack travelogues.

Bourdain's reliance on filmic choices to make his argument, his breaking the fourth wall to tell the spectator they, too, will be denied his privileged view, his repeated merging of the spectator with the object of the gaze rather than their assumed screen surrogate, American Tourist running at the camera, are all examples of the challenge Bourdain poses to a Western gaze. His subversion of that gaze becomes complete in a ninety-second coda that plays as the credits roll. Sitting in a hammock on a private beach, rum drink in hand, Bourdain breaks the fourth wall yet again to completely reposition Bond as a tool of a colonialist machine. It is a repositioning that would have been unthinkable in "Polynesia," and only works because of the way Bourdain has used film to interrogate a multitude of constructed images throughout "Jamaica." Bourdain begins, drinking leisurely in his hammock:

> How do you do this and be a good person? I don't think you can. Like, if you wanted to do this regularly, for the rest of your life. 'I would like to spend three months of the year in a

> hammock looking out at the Caribbean on a secluded beach like this?' You'd have to do bad things to do this, right? James Bond doesn't get this. James Bond is a hustler. He gets this for a couple days before he moves on to the next location. The guy who lives here is the Bond villain, not James Bond. It is much closer to Blofeld or Hugo Drax. You know *those* guys had lots of leisure time, sitting around in hammocks figuring out how to take over the fucking world. A lot of downtime in world domination. Bond was a working-class motherfucker. *That's* what I've been missing.

The episode thus ends on Bourdain actively reframing one of film history's most famous protagonists—who had a formative impact on Bourdain and whom he used as a framing device the entire episode. That re-reading allows Bourdain to refashion Bond in a way that mirrors how he reframes paradise and travel in both "Jamaica" and "Polynesia."

Much as travelogues and Bond films ask spectators to imagine themselves visually consuming their screen surrogate's experiences, Bourdain's repositioning asserts both are simply tools for larger forces that want to consume culture altogether, and which offer their protagonists and spectators only the *illusion* of authenticity or pleasure. As the screen goes black, we hear Bourdain tell the camera crew, "OK, go wide," invoking the construction of film form, which, yet again, allows Bourdain to interrogate and indict the very idea of paradise itself and unravels the aims of almost every travelogue before him by exposing their construction.

5
PERSONAL CINEMA

Autobiography becomes ethnographic at the point where the film—or video—maker understands his or her personal history to be implicated in larger social formations and historical processes. Identity is no longer a transcendental or essential self that is revealed, but a "staging of subjectivity"—a representation of the self as a performance.

—Catherine Russell, *Experimental Ethnography*[1]

Defined by Francis Vanoye as the work of filmmakers who consistently foreground autobiographical elements "implicitly, to varying degrees, through the entirety of their works, in the eyes of the spectator,"[2] personal cinema loosely encompasses a wide variety of films, both narrative and documentary. Examples date to the birth of cinema, but the idea a film should not only bear its auteur's thumbprint but actively draw the spectator's attention to the creation of that thumbprint—Jean-Luc Godard's desire "to show myself showing"[3]—was central to the New Wave. Thus, the term is widely used to refer to the work of the European filmmakers who most influenced Bourdain, as well as US cinema from late 1960s through the '70s, often collectively referred to as the era of personal cinema. By the turn of the twenty-first century, personal cinema became *the* dominant mode of documentary film as filmmakers like Michael Moore, Ross McElwee, and Sarah Polley made autobiography central to their films and their filmmaking identities. In the case of *Les plages d'Agnès* (2008),[4] Agnès Varda went so far as to make a film explicitly about her own auteurship. Similarly, Bourdain foregrounds his biography (and his presence as filmmaker) throughout his filmography, but a comparison of three episodes taken from early seasons of his major programs, set in locations Bourdain chose because they are central to his biography, are particularly pertinent to understanding his progression as a filmmaker. Specifically, "Childhood Flavors: Southwest France" (ACT S1E9), "New Jersey" (NR S1E3), and "Massachusetts" (PU S4E7) illustrate Bourdain's use of film to show all identity as constructed, including his own, in ways that allow him to reveal central truths not just about himself, but society at large.

Writing about trends in French cinema since 1950, Emma Wilson points to the way the question of "history itself, public and private, documentary or home movie"[5] became central to French filmmaking, and, subsequently, the ways that interest in history caused narrative and documentary filmmakers to use autobiography as a means of exposing and exploring those blurred lines. In Wilson's words, "Film as a photographic art-form appears ideally suited to offering true evidence and literal images of past events. Film can be seen as a faithful record. Yet, ironically . . . cinema questions precisely this belief," as postwar French films "repeatedly reveal the ways in which any history, and any cinematic representation of history is both partial and personal."[6] To me, it is impossible for Wilson's idea not to draw to mind Walter Murch's articulation, discussed in chapter 3, that a filmmaker has a responsibility to "refrain from achieving" a sense of "completeness" precisely because film, as an art form, offers a dangerous and false pretext that it can faithfully depict reality.[7]

Personal cinema is thus part of a larger trend to refrain from that completeness, and filmmakers like Bourdain use the construction of their own identity to deconstruct realism in film and the concrete imagination of social identity it could otherwise pretend to provide. Film offers a way of showing how identity is formed and constructed artificially because, while it "may provide us with identity images, yet it can also remind us that identities are unstable, change through time, location, and encounters, have many facets and are inherently unknowable."[8] As such, identities represent a "parts unknown" much like civilizations, and it is the filmmakers' responsibility to both mediate those identities *and* draw the spectator's awareness to the fact any explanation is mediated, that the identities will always remain unknown.

In interviews, Bourdain repeatedly stated he imagined *Parts Unknown* episodes as extended, visual essays,[9] terminology parroted by members of his team, such as director Tom Vitale[10] and cinematographer Zach Zamboni.[11] This term invokes a specific subset of personal documentary filmmaking, the essay film, that uses autobiography to support a thesis about a broader, social subject, while still highlighting how that autobiography shapes the filmmaker's inability to effectively and impartially mediate that subject. To quote Laura Rascaroli's *The Personal Camera: Subjective Cinema and the Essay Film*, "metalinguistic, autobiographical, and reflective, they all posit a well-defined, extra-textual authorial figure as their point of origin and of constant reference; they strongly articulate a subjective, personal point of view; and they set up a particular communicative structure, largely based . . . on the address to the spectator, or interpellation."[12] Such a description is an apt description of Bourdain's entire filmography. When applied to his *most* autobiographical episodes, however, it becomes clear that they may have the *most* to say about the world that constructed that autobiography; such are the aims of personal cinema.

The episodes I examine in this chapter are far from the only examples of Bourdain partaking in personal cinema. Not only do I argue Bourdain used biographical elements to highlight his subjectivity in nearly every episode he made, but these three episodes were also not the only locations specifically chosen because of autobiography; there are episodes in St. Martin (ACT S2E1), where Bourdain and his first wife had a home, the Hudson River Valley (NR S6E5), where Bourdain visits his alma mater, the Culinary Institute of America, a return to Brasserie Les Halles (NR S4E10), the restaurant Bourdain helmed before his television career, a variety of episodes set in and around his adopted hometown of New York, and another episode in New Jersey (PU S5E5). I chose "Southwest France," "New Jersey," and "Massachusetts," however, because they are pointed, self-conscious returns to the places that most constructed Bourdain's identity. As Cecilia Sayad says, writing of Varda's *Les plages d'Agnès*, "With [a] promise to 'open' and fully reveal herself . . . the director hints at . . . personal biography and full access to the author's subjectivity. . . . The film's emphasis, however, is less on the events of Varda's life than on the construction of her story. *New York Times* critic A. O. Scott rightly noted that 'the tone of the film is personal, but not confessional. It is more of an essay in memory than a memoire.'"[13] Viewed in a similar light, the three Bourdain episodes I focus upon are key examples of "essays on memory" and what subjective memory can teach us about the world in which we live.

At first glance, *A Cook's Tour*'s Southwest France episode seems a straightforward approach to the travelogue genre Food Network imagined Bourdain's program to be. Like most of the series, Bourdain and his Zero Point Zero crew were still in the early stages of developing strategies to challenge normative television genres, and the episode follows a relatively straightforward, chronological structure around Bourdain's return to his father's hometown of Arcachon, a formative location in Bourdain's youth, as he spent at least four summers there at the ages of nine, eleven, twelve, and seventeen,[14] and developed his first serious interest in food.[15] The episode even goes to great lengths to fit itself neatly within the chronological context of *A Cook's Tour*'s first season, situating Bourdain on a platform waiting for a French SNCF train to Arcachon at the Hendaia train station, the spot where one would transfer from the Spanish-Basque Euskotren Bourdain boarded in the final scene of the previous episode in Donostia–San Sebastián (ACT S1E8). Near the opening, Bourdain declares, "I haven't been here in *twenty* years . . . Hopefully there'll be some reminisces and maybe we'll discover some things along the way. I'm really looking forward to it. Of all the places I'm going, of all the places I've been, I'm really excited about this one." In short, Bourdain's introduction promises lighthearted reminiscences of childhood flavors fitting neatly into a travelogue of a chef's well-organized trip in search of the perfect meal.

For all these straightforward indications, however, even Bourdain's saccharin introduction provides clues he wants something more complex; it is *his* story, *his* interests that determine the setting and spark his excitement. This tension is highlighted in a brief sequence squeezed between the opening credits and the introduction at the train station, in which Bourdain walks the streets of Paris. For all the effort in the shots immediately following to situate the episode within the narrative arc of Bourdain's diegetic journey from the Spanish border to Arcachon, *these* shots are awkwardly stuck in from a city (Paris) that Bourdain does not even visit in *A Cook's Tour*. The shots are paired with off-putting, atonal music, and Bourdain's assertion, "Now, a sensible chef doing a world tour would probably go straight to Paris, hugely popular center of great food, but *my* center of food has always been Arcachon." The music turns upbeat only when the camera situates him under signage pointing to his father's hometown. As Bourdain rides the train, a black-and-white image of his father is superimposed upon the window, followed by flash-forward shots of the flavors Bourdain describes as memories but consumes later in the episode, all while Bourdain's narration assists:

> My father loved this town. It's where he spent much of his youth. He imparted the spirit of this place to my brother and me, and it's where we spent many happy summers as a family. It's where I crept on adolescence, where I had my first and most important food experience. I have powerful memories of the taste of murky brown fish soup at the local joint, the taste of *saucisson a l'ail*, the smell of Gitanes cigarettes. Those summers played an important part of who I am today. So, I want to go back and try all of those things. I want to re-live those moments. My father's long since passed away, so it's my way of reconnecting with whatever sense of family and tradition I have.

But the episode is not just a thinly veiled search for connection with Bourdain's deceased father, it quickly becomes a search for understanding how Bourdain's romantic imagination of that connection is linked to a specific place, and the tastes, smells, and memories embodied by that place. It is a treatise on how location forms (and constructs) identity.

Throughout the episode, Bourdain obsesses about what has and has not changed since childhood, such as how he notices the water is deeper in the oyster beds, wonders aloud if the oysters will taste the same, and hopes the fish soup has not "lost its authenticity" despite "the local joint" having a new, fancier decor. At every stage, however, Bourdain deconstructs generic, romanticized imaginations of France, calling Arcachon Bay "the Jersey Shore of France where working families vacation," and mediating the brasserie where he eats steak frites as "the French version of Joe's Diner." It is Bourdain's memories of his boyhood that imply romance, and it is a romanticization Bourdain wants his spectator to remain keenly aware of, because it is that very attachment to memory that is universal, not France. For instance, the first thing Bourdain wants is a street waffle, but he insists he must wait for his brother, Chris, a guest on the episode, to arrive. When the brothers finally eat waffles, Bourdain mockingly sings and hums the chorus of Barbra Streisand's "Memory," drawing attention to the performative nature of their endeavor and the way the insistence things remain unchanged matters more to Bourdain than to Arcachon. Even of the waffle, Bourdain freely admits, "it's magic, but, you know, that's because I have happy memories of long ago, far away, exotic places in my mind, when I bite into one." The waffles offer magic because they elicit innate connection to memory and romantic imagination, themselves childhood constructions of exoticism, not something innate within a simple *gaufre*.

Because of this interest in the constructed nature of memory, Bourdain emphasizes not just the recreations of his childhood but also the fact his endeavors are indeed re-creations. Walking across town to their boyhood home, the brothers stop to take photographs, which Bourdain shows first in black and white, slowly changing into color, and then moving back to real time. Reminiscent of a sequence in Stanley Donen's *Funny Face* (1957), in which photographs Fred Astaire takes of Audrey Hepburn in and around Paris are presented in the same pattern, the shift from still black and white to color and then back to live action emphasizes the filmic construction of shot and image. In the case of Bourdain, however, it *also* emphasizes the way the brothers' return to Arcachon alters their memories, and therefore the way memory is *also* constructed. As they approach the house, Bourdain draws attention to the fact he is visibly anxious, stating that he is "nervous" and "getting chills." Upon arrival, Bourdain's primary desire is to identify where a childhood photo was taken, despite the gate and sidewalk having been rendered unrecognizable. Elsewhere, he pokes fun at himself for insisting on riding a scooter in winter in a vain attempt to fulfill a childhood desire. Similarly, while he excitedly declares the diploid oysters taste the "same," he makes sure to say no oyster could ever truly re-create what had been a defining moment for him within the construction of his own identity, his own self-mythologization, the moment that made him "start to think about food as something with power." The weight of history, memory, and nostalgia is far greater than the reality of any oyster, be it 1967 or 2001. Essentially, Bourdain over-emphasizes the emulative nature of his re-creations to draw attention to the fact they are just that, an emulation of memories which are, themselves, partially fiction.

The climax is a picnic of their fathers' favorite foods at the local beach, where the brothers eat, drink, and shoot firecrackers around an abandoned Nazi bunker, reliving their childhood in a spot chosen because Bourdain "remember[s] the look of my father's look of perfect happiness on the beach." Much as the filmic representation of Bourdain's journey creates a mere image of his experiences, Bourdain chases an image of an image of his father in his mind; it is layers of constructed identity and perception upon constructed identity and perception. Closing the sequence (and the episode), Bourdain confides:

> I know that my brother and I are old now, that things can't be the same. That it's been thirty years, things change, things move on, one can't recapture the past. So, one can go through the motions, and one can *feel* it, but no matter how wonderful, one cannot revisit the past, one cannot be nine years old again. Later, talking about it with Chris, we realized that perhaps we were looking for my father the whole time. We had a nice moment of realization. You know, how badly we missed my dad and how much he would have loved the idea of us throwing firecrackers inside a blockhouse at Cap Ferret.

Just as Bourdain earlier admitted "eating these oysters is as close as I'll get to stepping into a time machine," Bourdain thus confesses the entire filmic endeavor is really about chasing a nostalgic image that can never be fulfilled, much as film itself can never achieve realism; memory, like film, is a construction that changes based upon perspective, both the perspective of the person who creates it and the perspective of the person for whom it was created. Even in a rudimentary, twenty-one-minute episode from Bourdain's first season of television, the prescient attempt to use autobiography to mediate something far larger is already present.

Three years after the trip to his father's hometown, Bourdain set an episode of *No Reservations*' first season in his own home state of New Jersey. The episode shares interests with "Southwest France" in terms of repositioning memory, deconstructing stereotypes of locations and impressions of the past, and exploring the influence film and photography have upon all those things. With more experience, a bigger budget, and twice the runtime, however, "New Jersey" comes closer to the style of approach that eventually defined Bourdain's filmmaking. Namely, Bourdain connects the influences which shaped his upbringing to that of other individuals, such as Bruce Springsteen, and cultures, such as New Jersey's thriving Korean population. Further, he filters his experiences through his repositioning of well-known filmic lenses, such as *The Sopranos* (HBO, 1999–2007), which he parrots and makes reference to throughout the episode, and Francis Ford Coppola's *The Godfather* (1972), which he invokes in the episode's final sequence when chef Mario Batali and a baker from Giancarlo's pretend to kill Bourdain in the back of a car; the shot an exact mirror of the scene where Peter Clemenza has Paulie Gatto murdered on an abandoned stretch of road in front of New Jersey marshland, ending, in both texts, with the catchline "leave the gun, take the cannoli." Thus, even in a return to his home state, Bourdain mediates his subject matter through a repositioning of the filmic lens, emphasizing how popular culture constructs the dominant, popular imaginations of every location.

Bourdain's repositioning of *The Sopranos* is foregrounded from the episode's first moments. Reminiscent of several canted angles that appear in *The Sopranos*' opening sequence, the first shot after Bourdain's opening credits is canted, as is at least one more soon after. Quickly, we see Bourdain driving the streets of his hometown, as well as New Jersey's expressways. Bourdain passes many of the same cityscapes as Tony Soprano in that series' opening, and, more important, the camera angles, the editing, and the rhythm of the music are all also similar; in fact, shots of Manhattan out a car window, Bourdain's hand changing the music, Bourdain's eyes in the rearview mirror, are all *exact* matches from *The Sopranos*. In voice-over, Bourdain alternatively confirms and debunks stereotypes about the state, before drawing attention to the *Sopranos* references, as he jocularly declares, "if Jersey is famous worldwide for anything, it's our very own first family, the Sopranos. What Sam Houston is to Texas, Paul Revere to Massachusetts, Tony Soprano is to New Jersey." First, this implies popular culture constructs fictional images of historical figures (Revere and Houston) to explain and represent cultural identity, and that the way their personal identities are constructed says more about the larger culture than the historical figures themselves. Second, it ensures the spectator does not miss the filmic *Sopranos* references so Bourdain can successfully reposition them, claiming, "while

I was technically raised in a town called Leonia, really, I was raised in cars. Cars that were usually on their way to, or from, getting food." Thus, Tony Soprano is a metaphor for New Jersey identity not because he is a mobster, but, rather, because his cultural identity is constructed in much the same way as Bourdain's—in a car, in transit to and from hyper-local, all-American eateries.

As such, Bourdain uses *The Sopranos* much like the generic New Jersey stereotypes with which he begins his introduction, a construction to be confirmed *and* denied. Yes, he jokes about the Bada Bing! strip club as New Jersey's equivalent to the Eiffel Tower, Big Ben, and the pyramids, but he also tells us to judge a restaurant's quality by the presence of autographed photos of *Sopranos* cast members on the wall. Yes, we laugh at a tour bus guide for calling a street "downtown Sopranoland," but we also hear the Giancarlo's baker tell Bourdain Sundays are busy because actual Jerseyites want Italian pastry for *Sopranos* watch parties. Yes, Tony Soprano is a construction, and imitations of him performative, just like the *Sopranos* tour Bourdain mocks, but, for Bourdain, so is identity in general, and therefore the character of Tony Soprano can be illustrative of how Bourdain imagines his own youth, and the impact location had upon it. Similarly, Bourdain refers to his time in New Jersey as his "wonder years," the place he spent his "glory days," invoking the CBS television show and Springsteen song of the same names, both about nostalgia for one's boyhood. But he also conducts a semi-serious interview with a stripper at Satin Dolls (the real-life Bada Bing!) and semi-seriously deconstructs their chicken wings much as he would any other restaurant, exploring it just like any other text that might help explain a location or subject. As with Arcachon, the space between how we popularly imagine cultural identity and real life is analogous to how we construct our personal identity and nostalgia for the places that formed it. For these reasons, Bourdain explores both.

This idea that we are formed not just by the locations we call home, but also by how we re-remember them, is equally present from "New Jersey's" onset. The short intro before the credits begin with a white screen slowly focusing to reveal a shot out the front window of a car crossing the George Washington Bridge. The sequence then cuts to images taken inside Bourdain's high school, in which current students slowly fade into, and back out of, dingy hallways. The awkward cinematography reinforces how memory and nostalgia are constructed, not innate. Meanwhile, Bourdain's voice-over imagines New Jersey from an outsider's perspective, interested in what formed his identity, but also as a place to be studied, dissected, discovered, with much still to teach him:

> We all grow up somewhere. It isn't so much the place where we're born as it is the place we come of age. The place where our strengths and weaknesses are first exposed, our interests and prejudices get discovered and developed. A series of small worlds we used to live in that brought us to where and who we are today. Worlds for the most part we couldn't wait to be done with and move on from. In my case, I got out and went a lot farther than a lot of people figured I would. I've traveled to a lot of interesting places in my life. Recently, I've started wondering whether I grew up in one. Oh yeah, I'm Tony, and I grew up in New Jersey.

Much as this chapter's epigraph claims autobiography becomes ethnographic when the filmmaker forgoes notions of an "essential self" and, instead, "understands his or her personal history to be implicated in larger social formations and historical processes," Bourdain thus deromanticizes his youth and uses his experiences to find what is interesting and unique about the construction of the identity of the place he grew up, a construction he shares with Springsteen and Soprano. In so doing, Bourdain not only takes a nonessentialist perspective of "his" New Jersey, but, by implication, hometowns everywhere—as his narration asserts, "we all grow up somewhere."

While Bourdain's approach to Arcachon was to first chase and then explore the impossibility of recapturing the nostalgic memories of childhood, marked by an obsession with his desire for nothing to change, his approach to New Jersey highlights change as both good *and* bad, and, more than anything, inevitable. Bourdain walks the ruins of Asbury Park, where he again invokes Springsteen, calls it the "archetype of *all* seaside resorts gone bust," and strolls a deserted shoreline he says, "was always *my* idea of a beach." Despite the change and decay, Bourdain is thrilled to eat fried seafood, claiming, "I should be cynical about this dining experience, but I'm strangely not. Fried clams, the taste of childhood, some things never change." Much like Arcachon's fish soup, flavors take one back in meaningful ways. Yet, Bourdain is also careful to avoid romanticism, highlighting a bad grilled cheese sandwich at a dilapidated, seaside Howard Johnson's, and admitting, "fond recollections of childhood aside, the food options I grew up with were limited in both quality and quantity. Mediocre spaghetti and meatballs was passed off as Italian food, and the Americanized version of Chinese food consisted mostly of dishes that had never existed in China." Instead, he interviews a Korean American he pointedly describes as a "Jersey Girl" to discuss kimchi, and visits the favorite soda shop of his youth, Baumgard's, which now sells sushi alongside chocolate egg creams. Walking through a Korean market, Bourdain proclaims, "I can't tell you how happy I am right now, ok? Look at this. It's an entire counter of completely unidentifiable stuff that I have no idea what it is. It's beautiful, what is it?" Early in the episode, he says "New Jersey has many lessons to teach" him, and the one he seems to want to impart is that his New Jersey, Springsteen's New Jersey, Tony Soprano's New Jersey, are all constructions, and it therefore matters not that they are constructed, but, rather, *how* they are constructed, and what our attempts to organize memory into nostalgia reveal about ourselves.

If the difference between *A Cook's Tour* and *No Reservations* is a shift from organizing episodes around personal narrative to using autobiography with the intent of mediating culture, then *Parts Unknown*'s "Massachusetts" represents the powerful, nuanced, complex work of a mature filmmaker "performing" his autobiography to reveal "larger social formations and historical processes." One of Bourdain's primary filmic influences, the Italian filmmaker and theorist Pier Paolo Pasolini, whose impact upon Bourdain I examine in chapter 10, thought one should achieve a "cinema of poetry" via "free indirect subjectivity"[16] that merges the filmmaker's point of view with that of the screen surrogate. In the words of Laura Rascaroli, such a process constitutes "a stylistic operation—because the cinema, lacking a *langue*, is not capable of effecting a naturalistic, mimetic reproduction of a character's vision (in the way in which literature is able to reproduce a character's speech). It is through a radical display of his idiosyncratic style that the director can fully embrace a character's vision of the world and make it manifest."[17] As such, Pasolini's cinema of poetry represents a first-person filmic practice that places authorial subjectivity at the discourse's forefront.[18] I argue Bourdain's performance of auteurship mirrors this approach across his filmography, but "Massachusetts" is a particularly useful lens because it pairs idiosyncratic and free indirect cinematography with autobiography, and then uses that autobiography to investigate outward.

"Massachusetts" is divided in two halves: a visit to Provincetown, where Bourdain first worked restaurant summer jobs and experimented with drugs, and Franklin County, somewhere Bourdain had never been, and, at the time of the show's airing, an epicenter of the heroin epidemic. The halves are united not *just* in the way Bourdain's personal perspective directs how we perceive drug addicts in Franklin County, but also by how idiosyncratic cinematography and editing draw attention to how Bourdain's perspective does so, as well as the way Bourdain's perspective is, again, a construct in and of itself. The only time the halves are placed in *direct* conversation is in the sequence before the opening credits, in which Bourdain opens with discordant music and a blurry screen that slowly fades into a black-and-white close-up of street graffiti on a brick wall. Only then does Bourdain cut to an establishing shot, still in black and white, situating the location as a storefront on Manhattan's Lower East Side, Bourdain telling us, "This is where I bought my first bag of heroin. It was 1980, I was twenty-four years old. But in a lot of ways my whole life up until that point was leading to this address." As Bourdain states the age and year, we are shown a strip of photograph negatives of a young Bourdain, the key code complete with notations visible above and below the images; rather than a concrete depiction of Bourdain at twenty-four, Bourdain thus emphasizes the *construction* of his image. The episode then cuts to Greenville, referencing the heroin epidemic and drawing a sharp, visual contrast between the black-and-white past and the colorful western Massachusetts present.

This approach of contrasting black and white with color, motion images with still, is repeated throughout the episode, both in Provincetown and Franklin County, and not only shapes Bourdain's idiosyncratic, free indirect subjectivity, but also draws the spectator's attention to it. Time and again, particularly when Bourdain introduces characters who represent some type of change, the person is first depicted in a black-and-white still image, where they typically break the fourth wall, and typically with their narration (rather than Bourdain's) as accompaniment; as the people speak, the cinematography typically switches between multiple images, at varying speeds, while the camera sometimes slowly zooms in or out, collectively creating a sense of motion in spite of the still nature of the images. The episode eventually switches to color, motion images set in the present, thereby creating a contrast like the one I discussed in the opening sequence. This approach is reminiscent of how *A Cook's Tour* treats the photographs Bourdain and his brother take upon arriving in Arcachon, but the approach here is more foregrounded because these moments are prolonged, repeated, and often come at the beginning of a sequence, before Bourdain even introduces his subject. Essentially, where "Southwest France" and "New Jersey" primarily rely on Bourdain's narration to deconstruct the concrete and nostalgic nature of images, such as the childhood shot of him and his brother in front of the family home in Arcachon and a young Bourdain enjoying Asbury Park, *Parts Unknown* allows an unusual, distinctive approach to cinematography and editing do the heavy lifting. The cinematography quite literally evokes nostalgia (via black and white) only to deconstruct it, and Bourdain's perspective presents itself at the level of cinema.

The interplay between personal and collective memory is the dominant theme of "Massachusetts," not just in terms of structure, divided between personal and global halves, but within each individual sequence as well. For instance, Bourdain returns from the credits to beautiful, widescreen shots of an untamed shoreline, paired with a voice-over in which he declares, "There's nothing like the North Atlantic. It's majestic. Yeah, I love the beach. Pretty much had my first everything on a beach. You name it, first time I did it, beach." The assertion of a highly personal connection to a North Atlantic beach is reminiscent of Arcachon and Asbury Park, and, as the episode cuts to a boarded-up house overlooking the dunes, Bourdain's narration makes it clear this is indeed not just *a* beach, but, rather, *his* beach, where he first "washed into town with a head full of orange sunshine."

Bourdain constructs that romantic memory, however, within its context of the culture at large. First, he tells us "If you put on Marvin Gaye right now, I'd burst into tears." Then, he visually situates those memories within a global context, cutting to home videos of Bourdain and his friends playing in the surf in what he calls "happier, stupider times," then to a tourist-map of the state as he provides historic and cultural context dating to the Pilgrims, all before reverting to home videos in which he points out, in immediate succession, the global (filmmaker John Waters), the personal (Nancy Putkoski, his first wife), and the space between (John Yingling, owner of Spiritus Pizza, a friend of Bourdain's in that era, but also "a central figure in all of our lives"). In short, the construction of memory and identity are inextricably linked both to the public *and* the personal.

Meanwhile, the idea that public and personal identity are constructed remains near the surface, directly in the spectator's vision, throughout Bourdain's time in Provincetown; for all his stated desire to "go back to that summer," that "golden time," the episode repeatedly denies easy acceptance of that construction. First, immediately upon calling the nostalgic home videos "golden," Bourdain adds, "I look back on those fuzzy memories and they *seem* golden anyway," calling into question the validity of memory. Next, he tells Yingling, "I cannot tell you how frequently I dream about Spiritus Pizza. I'm walking down Commercial Street . . . and there's this sense of dislocation and loss as I stumble around this sort of Provincetown dreamscape of *forty* years ago." The camerawork in this sequence is handheld and unstable, with quick cuts between shots, rendering the spectator as discombobulated by Bourdain's misremembering and obsession with lost youth as he is. Third, waxing nostalgic about how the seafood at the Lobster Pot remains unchanged, Bourdain riffs on how great those times were, when he could "get all I wanted" in terms of sex, drugs, and fun, but the music cuts off and Yingling reminds Bourdain of how many friends did not live long. Bourdain agrees, "yeah, many of my friends are dead," and the soundtrack turns to awkward silence as the two stare at each other with an awareness Bourdain can only afford to be nostalgic about those times because he managed to survive them. Finally, as the duo leave, the camera pulls back, revealing a throng of fans who have been watching the scene, now clapping and cheering for Bourdain as he interacts with them on the way out, effectively disclosing how the conversation was as constructed and performed for film as memories are for ourselves.

Having foregrounded these conflicting realities, Bourdain shifts to personifying memory via a series of fishermen in one of the most complete examples of the idiosyncratic black-and-white still progressions discussed previously, infusing his own free indirect subjectivity while emphasizing that these fishermen's individual stories are interconnected with changes in the collective culture. Bourdain returns from commercial with limited narration offering only brief maritime history context, primarily yielding the narrative to the fishermen who talk about their own biographies and perspectives. The fishermen's articulations of self in relation to their profession, as structured by Bourdain, emphasize certain commonalities: (a) individualism in a profession that embodied the qualities of "a cowboy, a pioneer . . . fiercely independent"; (b) the collective, the fisherman forming "part of [a] heritage"; (c) nostalgia, a past when "it was cool" and "there was like 70 or 80 boats"; and (d) change and loss, "two out of three families in this town, in this community, were fishing families, most of them are now gone and we are really like a minority." On the surface, Bourdain distances himself, both with his physical and vocal absence and, when he *is* on-screen, jokes about learning what to do from *The Deadliest Catch* (Discovery Channel, 2005–present); yet, we easily see how the filmic depiction emphasizes Bourdain's themes, Bourdain's perspectives. Meanwhile, lest the spectator retreat to nostalgia as Bourdain and the fishermen drink at Old Colony Tap, we are told multiple times it is the only fisherman's bar left in town. The sequence then ends with a fisherman bluntly declaring, "It's going to die. . . . This is the end: fishing is going to die." The table sits in stunned silence, raises a toast, the camera focuses on a nostalgic nautical painting on the wall, and then returns to the images of the beach that opened the episode; nostalgia is a construction, and, in this case, Bourdain's construction.

Having crushed any hopes of simple nostalgia for the fishing community, Bourdain ends the Provincetown section by returning to the scene from the beach outside his old house, completing the deconstruction of his own nostalgia for the site of those "fuzzy memories" he previously admitted may only have "*seemed* golden." The camerawork remains as beautiful and romantic as the section's opening shots, but the depiction is quite different. Bourdain begins by pointing to the spot where his narrative had earlier attempted to concretize his identity, "It's a nice house. I mean it just feels like I never left in a lot of ways." Immediately, however, Bourdain draws a distance between present-day images and the realities of what occurred, adding, "of course, it's forty years later almost." Bourdain then points his arm up the coast, the camera following, declaring, "And that was the Sodom and Gomorrah by the sea over there. You know a big candy store for a horny, stupid 17-year-old with a taste for chemicals. You know I was an angry young man. What the hell was I so angry about?" As Bourdain repositions the happy home videos with an angry and self-destructive reality, the camera cuts to a perfectly framed, highly cinematic close-up of a rusted-out beer can half-buried in the sand; much like Bourdain's construction of identity, how something is perceived is altered by how (and by whom) it is depicted, and much like memory, it decays over time. Bourdain then concludes, "It came as a rude surprise to me when I turned thirty, 'cause I always sort of figured I'd be dead by then. I was still quite some time away from my first bag of heroin, but, you know, in a lot of ways it was a foregone conclusion. My whole life was kind of leading up to that point." Rather than a golden moment one should long to recapture, the house was a mere stop on a journey of self-destruction.

Bourdain mediates the shift to Franklin County by merging the personal narrative he just delivered with global narratives we already know, all with the intention of exposing rural New England identity as just as constructed as any other. The opening shots are idyllic images of farmland, reminiscent of the style of beach shots that opened the episode's first half. We soon see Bourdain driving a station wagon, his narration informing us,

> I left Provincetown with restaurant experience, a suntan, and an ever-deepening experience with recreational drugs. I went to culinary school, then to New York, and never returned. Today, however, I'm *staying* in Massachusetts. Heading over to the western part of the state, one of the most beautiful areas of the country. The gorgeous mill towns, Victorian houses, deeply felt, famously uptight New England values. Norman Rockwell America. Where something really inexplicable and unexpected has happened.

Letting media—first the radio and later a pharmaceutical commercial—introduce us to America's growing rural heroin epidemic, Bourdain embraces the rural image, showing great admiration for Greenville, where he bases himself. He repeatedly, fondly refers to it as "Mayberry," referencing *The Andy Griffith Show* (CBS, 1960–68), visits diners and coffee shops, and says a candlepin bowling alley feels like "the good old days that everybody used to talk about back when I was a kid. . . . Where time *seems anyway* to have stopped."

Even as his narration increasingly renders the epidemic omnipresent, negatively impacting every single location and conversation, sometimes in unexpected ways, Bourdain's admiration for rural Massachusetts identity remains. The episode's most optimistic moments occur when he attends a group therapy session for addicts and a clam bake, both sponsored by community-based organizations. In both cases he argues just such an approach, inextricably linked to regional identity, may be the path forward. Yet, while he admires the constructed identity, he never lets us forget how that image shields reality. For instance, juxtaposing idyllic images of Greenville with blurry videos of 1970s New York, he claims, "back then heroin was mostly seen as a poor people problem. Somebody *else's* problem. . . . Marginal people far from the white main streets of Mayberry USA. What *those* people did to themselves, well it was unfortunate, but not *our* problem . . . today it's the absolute reverse. The new addicts are almost entirely white, middle class, and from areas like this."

As in Provincetown, Bourdain personifies memory via individuals who share their narratives, introduced in the idiosyncratic pattern used throughout the episode: we meet an addict who lost custody of her three young children for two years, a doctor who over-prescribed oxycodone, a drug dealer cooperating undercover with the police, the county's lone drug enforcement officer, and a chef who returned home to open a diner only to be repeatedly robbed. However, Bourdain emphasizes how these individual struggles are set amid a larger context of changes to the community, which shaped the construction of their identities.

Walking around the ruins of local mills with the photographer Ed Gregory, himself first depicted in a black-and-white still image progression, Bourdain asserts, "It used to be a very different world, towns like this one, and there were many. But like *every*where else it seems the mills, the factories closed-down. And with them a certain kind of social contract with the people who worked there." Bourdain depicts the decaying ruins of the mills in beautifully framed, still shots that are almost identical to those used in episodes exploring similar ruins and similar themes in places like Detroit (PU S2E8), the Rust Belt (NR S5E13), Pittsburgh (PU

S10E4), and Butte, Montana (PU S7E4); as such, Bourdain universalizes individual struggle within the culture that constructed those struggles. Bourdain tells Gregory, "Again and again, all over the country, I keep running into situations like *this* where industry has died or fled or simply relocated." Unlike an era where one could "work in a mill, live in a nice home, send your kids to school, make a living all on a mill salary, it's unthinkable now, almost."

The ultimate interplay between individual and collective comes in the juxtaposition between a group therapy session Bourdain attends late in the episode and the episode's formal conclusion. After several participants tell their stories, depicted in close-ups, the camera moves out of the room, to the hallway, Bourdain's back awkwardly framed, and partially blocked by the door, as he tells *his* story: "I'll tell you something really shameful about myself. The first time I shot up I looked at myself in the mirror with a big grin. You know something was missing in me. Whether it was a self-image situation, whether it was a character flaw . . . there was some dark genie in me . . . that led me to dope." Even as the camera returns to the room, it focuses on others' reactions, not Bourdain, a sharp contrast to the other stories. Having linked his "genie," in part, to the construction of a dope identity in front of a mirror, Bourdain offers hope via a shift to another image of another mirror in which he constructs a different identity: "I have a seven-year-old daughter now who I never would have had. I looked in a mirror and I saw somebody worth saving, or that I wanted to at least try real hard and save. *Any*body can find themselves very easily in this situation." Moments later, Bourdain concludes the episode:

> As a nation, for decades, we were perfectly happy to write off whole neighborhoods, whole cities, whole generations of young men and women. As long as it was an inner-city problem, an urban problem, which is to say a Black people problem, a brown people problem. . . . Maybe now that it's really come home to roost, now that it's the high school quarterback, your next-door neighbor, your son, your daughter, now that grandma's as likely to be a junkie as anyone else, we'll accept that there's never been a real war on drugs. 'War' on 'drugs' implies an 'us' versus 'them,' and all over this part of

> America people are learning there is no them, there is only us, and we're going to have to figure this out together.

Much as the images that mattered when Bourdain told his story were the reactions of the community around him, and much as the abandoned social contract between industry and worker altered Greenville's identity, the construction of personal and communal identity are imagined as inextricable, and rather than autobiography, Bourdain achieves ethnography.

In *Les plages d'Agnès*, Agnès Varda uses beaches, her "favorite landscape," to explore the construction of her own identity as a metaphor for how she constructs others in her films. For instance, she says the identity assigned to her at birth, Arlette, was determined by location, the town in which she was conceived, Arles, but she later constructed her own identity, Agnès. As she makes this declaration, the surf wipes away the name "Arlette" written in the sand. Of others, Varda declares, "In my mirrors I met others, *the* others. I filmed them, or not. Understood them, or not. Admired them." Ostensibly a film about her own auteurship, the film is more about the people she filmed, how she constructed them, and how doing so, in turn, constructed her own identity.

Bourdain shares his story during a group therapy session for drug addicts. Unlike the other speakers, whose faces are shown in close-up, Bourdain is depicted from behind, the doorframe creating a distancing effect, and the reactions of his audience are the focus of the shot.

The three Bourdain episodes I discuss also use beaches as metaphors—Arcachon Bay, Asbury Park, and the beach outside Bourdain's Provincetown house. Just as for Varda, what matters to Bourdain are others, the people in his films. Yet, Bourdain's films are less about how his construction of those people impacts him, but, rather, what similarities between his construction of them and his own construction of Self tell us about the world that constructs us all. Denying an "us" or a "them," Bourdain chooses, instead, to explore how personal history is always implicated in larger social formations and historical practices. The beaches of Agnès reveal individuality—constructed individuality, but individuality, nonetheless. The beaches of Tony reveal truths about culture, both political and social.

6
POLITICAL DOCUMENTARIES

I never make an overt decision to make a show political. In fact, I try to avoid it . . . But there is nothing more political than food. If I'm there shoveling food in my face, it's worth mentioning who's not eating. If my host is missing three limbs, it's worth asking "Hey, how'd ya lose them?"

—Anthony Bourdain, *Variety*[1]

The TV shows to me were journalism. And incredibly political without being didactic or ideological. But there was a general ideology, one that was very humanistic and very anti-hierarchical. I remember this image: he's in some urban center in South America. I want to say Montevideo but maybe it was Buenos Aires. He's sitting against the wall of an alley, gangly and tall. He's got his arms wrapped around his knees, and they're all drinking the *siete y tres*, seven and three, and the kids are kicking some sort of ersatz soccer ball. And he's sitting there, and the footage of kids, and the men drinking, and him, and there's this look of incredible sadness and love. It was a moment of *duende* for me. It's like this guy loves people. He's trying desperately to connect in ways that great journalists and great writers connect. And, also, the writing is so good, the narration so well written.

—David Simon, *Bourdain: The Definitive Oral Biography*[2]

Walking Miami Beach (PU S5E2), the musician Iggy Pop tells Bourdain that he "seems like a curious person," to which the latter responds, "It's my only virtue." That curiosity seems intrinsically connected to a deep sense of empathy, remarked upon by many after his death,[3] and defined in Bourdain's own words as his ability to be "good at looking at things from the other guy's point of view. I can put myself in their shoes. I'm willing to reach out. I'm a good listener."[4]

In July 2006, a sudden outbreak of war stranded Bourdain and his crew in Beirut for nine days until the US Navy could evacuate them. The resulting *No Reservations* special edition (NR S2 Special Episode) garnered Zero Point Zero their first Emmy nomination and is popularly accredited as the beginning of the increasingly serious, political nature of Bourdain's work.[5] While his experience in Lebanon, as well as his return four years later (NR S6E21), clearly had a profound impact upon Bourdain, helping him gain confidence in depicting political matters, the reality is the cross section of Bourdain's curiosity and empathy led him to realize as early as his time at Food Network that food—who gets to eat and what they choose to eat—is inherently political. In Bourdain's words, "very early on I came to realize that everything, particularly something intimate as a meal, is a reflection of both a place's history and its present political and military circumstances."[6] Therefore, Bourdain's unified political perspective, which typically defies partisan ideology, was present well before "Lebanon," but became more difficult to ignore as his filmmaking talents and confidence grew.

In the opening monologue for "Lebanon," Bourdain speaks of attempts to make "a happy food and travel show [about] food and people and faraway places and how those subjects intersect." Those attempts were thwarted, however, not just by the physical realities of war, but by his experience of what he later called a "complete disconnect between what [he] was seeing and hearing on the ground from Beirutis of all stripes and what was being reported." That disconnect, that space between, eventually became part and parcel with how he saw food, a complex discourse that sheds light on a not so bright and cheery world. For instance, Bourdain ends "Lebanon" admitting he had once hoped to see the dinner table as "the great leveler where people from opposite sides of the world could sit down and talk and eat and drink and . . . at least find, for a time, common ground," but that he had come to fear the "*real* world, the one without cameras and happy food and travel shows," is one where "everybody, the good and the bad together, are crushed under the same terrible wheel."

Despite his experience, training, and love of the kitchen, food, for Bourdain, came to be less about pleasure, and more a means of understanding a complex world. A meal was, he once claimed, "where you can least escape the realities of a nation's situation. People tend to be less guarded and more frank," and "what you are eating is always the end of a very long story—and often an ingenious but delicious answer to some very complicated problems."[7] As example, Bourdain often spoke of the great lengths his handlers in pre-Revolutionary Egypt (NR S4E18) went to prevent him filming *ful*, a common street food. Bourdain later discovered the military had been hoarding stocks of flour, thus sparking riots; *how* one depicts food, Bourdain realized, actively reinforces, or deconstructs, the political status quo.[8]

Therefore, it is not so much that Bourdain's shows became increasingly political as that they embraced the political nature already present. Bourdain no longer hid behind food or travel to introduce the political situations he wished to mediate. A *No Reservations* episode in Laos (S4E11) inspired Ben Rhodes, deputy national security advisor to US President Barack Obama, to push for ninety million dollars in aid to clear land mines,[9] and later to arrange for Obama to appear on *Parts Unknown*'s "Hanoi" (S8E1).[10] "Mozambique" (NR S8E1) so deftly contextualized the complicated political situation in the East African country that CNN cited it as the example of what they wanted Bourdain to do for them.[11] His frank discussion of the Armenian holocaust (PU S11E4) garnered Bourdain a permanent ban from Azerbaijan.[12] He traveled to Cuba twice (NR S7E9 and PU S6E1), Iran (PU S4E6), Kurdistan (NR S7E15), Palestine (PU S2E1), Haiti (NR S7E1) just months after the 2010 earthquake, West Virginia (PU S11E1) immediately after the election of US President Donald Trump, and set his very first episode of *Parts Unknown* in Myanmar (S1E1), a country just opening from a military dictatorship that no outside film crew had yet visited. Bourdain never tried to provide all the answers nor to hide his biases, but he grew comfortable mediating complex situations through personal experience, and comfortable leaving his audience with more questions than answers.

It is precisely because Bourdain saw the world—and pretty much all social issues within it—as complex that he abandoned simple, genre-based television. In a 2014 interview about politics, Bourdain asserted "I like grey areas, obviously. I like ambiguity . . . and tend to enjoy the company of people who deal in ambiguity."[13] For this reason, Bourdain's views, much like his experiences, cut across party lines. In Bourdain's words, "I don't have to agree with a guy to enjoy their company. As a political ideology and as a practical matter, I loathe communism. However, I often find myself getting along very well with communists. I feel the same way about Red State America."[14] Or, as he stated a month later, "I've never minded pissing people off. I'm perfectly happy to be in communist China or Saudi Arabia one week, and the next week be hanging out with Ted Nugent."[15]

Bourdain took on the responsibilities of a journalist, going to great lengths to acknowledge and represent multiple sides of controversial issues, while simultaneously refusing to shy away from using personal experience as a means of telling the story. More to the point, while he began to spend more time providing political context to the cultures he visited, the center of his story always remained the people he interviewed, the culture he experienced, and the faces his cameras captured. Crucially, it was exceedingly rare that he or his camera negatively commented upon anything or anybody he encountered. Instead, Bourdain used personal cinema as a means of emphasizing connections to individuals, giving a face to an idea, and pointing to the limitations of his own experience; as Bourdain admits in "Lebanon," sitting at a hotel overlooking the war, "I wasn't in Haifa, I wasn't in the north of Israel. I don't know what that was like. I was in Beirut." Bourdain did not try to teach his audience about other cultures, but, rather, make them question their preconceived notions about what they thought they knew about those cultures.

Bourdain's relationship to politics is reminiscent of my description of his relationship to filmmaking—a quest for truth foregrounded in the belief absolute truth is unattainable, but that the way to get closest to truth is to foreground one's inability to achieve it. As Lucia Ricciardelli writes of one of the most influential political documentarians, Errol Morris, he "attacks *cinema vérité* for the manner in which it conceals its construction of truth under the banner of 'objectivity'" because "truth can be found only by means of a laborious process."[16]

Morris, whose *The Thin Blue Line* (1988) I refer to as an example of reflexive documentary in chapter 3, and whose *The Fog of War* (2003) Bourdain visually references in *Parts Unknown* "Laos" (S9E3), may seem a surprising comparison because Morris rarely allows his image or voice to be seen or heard on-screen, whereas Bourdain's centering of his autobiography and physical presence is a hallmark of his work. Despite this surface contrast, the filmmakers have much in common. First, a central tenant of Morris's films is that, visible or not, Morris persistently makes his implied presence visible in subtle but unmistakable ways.[17] Second, he "challenge[s] the conventions of realism, inviting the viewer to question the idea that certain documentary techniques provide unproblematic access to the world."[18] Third, as Ricciardelli asserts, "Morris's documentary films are disturbing . . . because they undermine our certainties, because they make us wonder about the reasons for our behaviors."[19]

Such embrace of uncertainty, manifested in an empathetic depiction of diverse subject matter, filtered through a lens that rejects realism, is a commonality between both filmmakers and is clearly illustrated in three of Bourdain's most overtly political episodes—*No Reservations*' "Laos" and *Parts Unknown*'s "Jerusalem" (S2E1) and "London" (S8E4). Like Morris, Bourdain asks us not to "see *through* documentaries to the world beyond them," but, rather, "to *see documentary* for what it is: a construction of representation."[20]

Appearing in *No Reservations*' fourth season, Bourdain's first Laotian visit illustrates a filmmaker clearly choosing a location to explore political questions, while feeling the need to satisfy genre demands by situating that location within a travel context. At its core, however, "Laos" exhibits a confidence in its holistic approach that makes it, at least arguably, a stronger episode than even his *Parts Unknown* return to Laos nine years later, and it embodies all the nuance, empathy, and curiosity that inform his worldview and his filmmaking.

Bourdain begins by asking and answering a rhetorical question, "Why Laos? Why now?" Bourdain's answer positions Laos within a traveler's desire, linked to Bourdain's own biography, to consume parts unknown: "Because I've *always* wanted to come here. This is, in many ways, kind of the last unexplored frontier in Southeast Asia. The word 'mysterious' was practically created for this place, and, of course, there's all of that amazing, secret history about which few Americans are, sadly, even aware."

The theme of Laos as a "mysterious . . . as of yet industrialized . . . sought after, exotic travel destination" permeates the episode as Bourdain comes and goes from commercials. Yet, between those framing references, Bourdain spends far more time exploring and depicting the dark political history glossed over in the opening, as well as the ongoing costs of how that past shapes the present; by episode's end, he goes so far as to suggest maybe we should not travel to Laos at all, lest we do more damage.

Bourdain is neither slow nor coy about revealing the "empty page" he intends to fill is political. His first, brief, location is an open-air food market where he shows and discusses exotic foods before transitioning to a plain of giant jars laid out in the megalithic. For all his excitement about the food and the (yet again) "mysterious" cultural site he says has long fascinated him, the conversation, music, tone, and focus abruptly shift to "what you begin to notice about [the capital province] Phonsavan. The presence *every*where of twisted, rusting pieces of metal in curious shapes. Used as support structures, building materials, as fencing, as decoration." Bourdain's camera provides image after image of shell casings as his narration further overwhelms us with the sheer magnitude of their omnipresence, telling us, "The US dropped more bombs on this relatively tiny and neutral country than we dropped on Germany and Japan in all of World War II. The equivalent of a bombing run every nine-minutes, twenty-four-hours a day, for *ten* years." Bourdain emphasizes the covert nature of the illegal war, uses found footage and narration to provide comprehensive historical context, and follows a detection team whose job is to detonate the seventy million unexploded bombs, of which Bourdain tells us less than one-half of 1 percent have been cleared. It is this "largest covert operation in history," its cultural impact, and its historical and ongoing effects, that dominates the spectator: surreal images of bombs, not romantic images of *jaew bong* or *khao niew*.

In fact, nowhere is Bourdain's use of food as vehicle for the artifice of cinema to achieve political truth clearer than his Laotian visit to the home of Puvian, a man who lost a leg to a land mine. Arriving for a meal, Bourdain emphasizes both the performative and uncomfortable nature of the visit. His narration points out just how rare meat and fish are when a TV crew is not present and presumably paying; his editing retains long, uneasy silences within the conversation; his camera remains in constant motion, underscoring the visit's awkward nature; he forgoes subtitles, emphasizing the distance between host and guest. At one point, Puvian interrupts Bourdain, offers to show him his leg, and asks if he is "afraid of seeing the reality." This comes only moments after we have been told the land mine was the result of what "your countrymen left behind," laying bare Bourdain's complicity, as well as the spectator's. In trademark fashion, Bourdain's response simultaneously invokes cinema and uses his own physical presence to personify his broader point: "Afraid? Um, no. It *hurts*, but I think that's appropriate, you know, it *should*. I think Americans, *every* American, should see the results of war. You know, it's not a movie. I think it's the least I can do to see the world with open eyes." Bourdain's statement does not change anything, nor even stabilize the camera; it simply draws everyone's attention to the point of the scene—a missing limb rather than a bowl of food.

The filmic depiction only stabilizes when the host says, through the translator, "Please eat, in Lao it means we eat together, don't be shy." Even then, however, Bourdain's narration draws attention to the cinematic nature of such acceptance, "This is something I have seen a fair amount of over time, acts of kindness, generosity, from strangers who have no reason at all to be nice to me. [The camera cuts to a shot that distances Bourdain from his host.] Quite frankly it kicks the hell out of me." In later scenes, Bourdain smiles while eating birds he describes as bringing him close to vomit because his host calls them culturally important and breaks the fourth wall to pass liquor to cameramen because another host was uncomfortable not offering them some. In all things, he is not only a gracious guest, but trying, as this chapter's second epigraph claims, to "connect to people" through cinema.

The attempt to connect is not limited to Bourdain and his subject; rather, Bourdain uses his on-screen physical presence to forge a connection between spectator and subject, deflating perceived political differences by fostering empathy and genuine curiosity rather than a need to consume a culture, or its food, for touristic aims. I just discussed how this works in scenes like the visit/meal, but Bourdain ends "Laos" by rendering the distinction overt. Observing a ritual in which neighbors hand small bits of rice and candy to a procession of fasting monks, Bourdain narrates, "It's a hauntingly quiet affair, the only sounds the patting of bare feet and the occasional passing motor bike. Lately though? A new sound. The clicking of cameras." Bourdain disrupts his own verisimilitude to switch to close-ups of tourists taking photographs, with the sounds of their cameras overwhelming his soundtrack. The moment the procession finishes, Bourdain turns to his host and apologetically states, "If you are from this neighborhood, lived here either all your life or most of your life, this is very much a community, neighborhood thing. We're here because it's beautiful and because we are fascinated by traditional Lao culture. I'm *afraid* sometimes that because we take pleasure in showing people with these cameras how beautiful the place is that we help to destroy it." The local guide does not deny the fear, answering he is "very afraid of globalization of everything. It's not a *show*, it's their land, it's a real ritual each morning. So, help us, help me, to show what the local people think."

Bourdain made a career out of doing just that, using cinema to show the beauties of distinct cultures, fostering empathy and understanding of how and why we all think differently. While his filmmaking talents and confidence continued to grow—his return to Laos, for instance, exhibits superior cinematography, direct visual references to Errol Morris, a willingness to *begin* with politics, and ends on a five-and-a-half-minute sequence with no narration of any kind—the approach and intent had always been central to his work.

By the time of his 2013 move to CNN, Bourdain was emboldened, regularly choosing political hotspots for destinations and not disguising his intentions. After the *Parts Unknown* premier in Myanmar, Bourdain visited Colombia (PU S1E3), Libya (PU S1E6), and Congo (PU S1E8) in just his first season. For the season two premiere, Bourdain set his sights on "Jerusalem," including lengthy visits to the West Bank and Gaza Strip. Rather than hiding behind touristic aims as he had in "Laos," Bourdain cuts straight to the chase, making it clear food would be a means of understanding his subject, but had little to do with *why* he was there. In an opening monologue, Bourdain asserts,

> It's easily the most contentious piece of real estate in the world. And there's no hope, none, of ever talking about it without pissing somebody, if not everybody, off. Maybe that's

> why it's taken me so long to come here. A place where even the names of ordinary things are ferociously disputed. Where does falafel come from? Who makes the best hummus? Is it a fence or a wall? By the end of this hour, I'll be seen by many as a terrorist sympathizer, a Zionist tool, a self-hating Jew, an apologist for American imperialism, an orientalist, socialist, fascist, CIA agent, and worse. So here goes nothing.

Bourdain pairs the monologue with matching images displayed via rhythmic montage increasing in velocity as his speech patterns cut to shorter descriptors. Most of the images emphasize political divides, such as a teenage Palestinian girl darting to the opposite side of a walkway to avoid eye contact with a Jewish man. Bourdain's overt statement of a political justification for his visit is personified by his assertion of his status as a Jew and a subsequent visit to the Wailing Wall. Further, within the first five minutes, Bourdain tours the Old City, emphasizing the city's division into four quarters, which function individually but exist in a contentious relationship that permeates even his discussions about falafel.

Despite the direct nature of his narration and on-screen conversations, Bourdain lets visuals do the heavy lifting, embodying a central theme of the episode: that images, how they are depicted and by whom, have real-world consequences. For example, touring a Palestinian refugee camp, Bourdain points to graffiti depicting martyrs, and asks his host, Abed Abusrour, "In America kids grow up with pop stars, sports players, *never* a politician. I mean it's unthinkable for a child to look up to a politician or a military figure . . . Here, kids four or five years old, every day, they're looking at somebody who brought down a plane. I'm not questioning *why* that is. Do you think that's helpful?" Abusrour's answer is nuanced and multifaceted. He begins by contextualizing Bourdain's framing, claiming, "We have a history. We are people who are under occupation. People honor their heroes, and their heroes are those who resist occupation." Abusrour goes on, however, to talk about how his community work provides those same children with alternative images, how he has argued with street artists about how they imagine martyrs, and ends by pointing to Mohammed Assaf, "a young man from Gaza who is on *Arab Idol*," who "becomes more famous than Abu Mazen and Arafat and everybody else. This is *another* image of

Palestine." The lesson is twofold: every image deserves context, and every image has power.

This idea is reiterated throughout the episode, from Bourdain pressing an Israeli security guard about his failure to remove violent, anti-Palestinian graffiti to Bourdain's own cinematography, such as the opening montage, which alternates depictions of the "wall" between attractive and ugly, innocuous and sinister, all as the narration lays bare the stakes of such depictions. Bourdain's camera also subtly provides broader context, lingering on, and later returning to, pro-Palestinian graffiti that draws parallels to Basque struggles, a recurring political topic explored across his filmography.

The exploration of disparate images and their cultural impact is also fundamental to the way Bourdain uses food as a tool for understanding politics. During his initial tour of Jerusalem's Old City, Bourdain follows up his initial reference to the disputed cultural history of falafel and hummus with a tense conversation with Israeli chef Yotam Ottolenghi that renders the spectator abundantly aware of the politically charged nature of any discussion about the cultural history of such dishes. Later, visiting a Jewish suburb, Bourdain pointedly asks his host if he has ever sat down at the table of one of his nearby Muslim neighbors, revealing he has not. When Bourdain visits Majda, a restaurant owned by a married couple, one Jewish and the other Muslim, whose food reflects their different backgrounds and their commonalities, Bourdain treats the restaurant more like a happy oasis of culinary fusion than a realistic political reality, highlighting the isolated nature of their daily life and struggles to exist together. At episode's end, Jewish chef Gatan Galkowitz, whose daughter was killed by a mortar, expresses pessimism about the ability to reconcile political opponents via discourse, culinary or otherwise, despite the fact he now makes it his life's work to *try* to do just that. Bourdain, in his final narration, just before the Galkowitz interview, himself claims, "One can be forgiven when thinking—when you see how *similar* they are—that two peoples, both of whom cook with pride, eat with passion, love their kids, love the land . . . might somehow, someday, figure out how to live with each other. But that would be very mushy thinking indeed. Those things, in the end, probably don't count for much." Rather than his expressed desire in "Lebanon" to imagine the dinner table as a space to "sit down and talk and eat and drink and . . . at least find, for a time, common ground," Bourdain's tour of Israeli and Palestinian tables is a story about how culinary history is representative of political division, not unity.

Bourdain's exploration of images, and his interest in using his camera to reposition them in a way that elicits empathy extends to cuisine. When asked what drew her to food, cookbook author Laila El-Haddad, Bourdain's guide in Gaza, answers it was, in part, her way to "tell the Palestinian story" as a "child of diaspora," but, more specifically,

> It was also important to be able to provide Palestinians an image of themselves that they recognize, a very humane image, because all they're seeing in the media, whether here or there, rather on Arabic channels or abroad, is you know this kind of very caricatured images of gunmen and wailing women and this kind of grim cinderblock landscape. You're not entering into the private homes. What does a kitchen look like? Or, what does a family, you know, you see here [El-Haddad stops mid-sentence and gestures at the family hosting Bourdain].

Thus, for El-Haddad, it is not only about providing alternative images to outsiders, but, almost more importantly, to Palestinians themselves. What images we see determines, or at least affects, behavior and reality, and, much as El-Haddad stops mid-sentence to simply gesture at the scene Bourdain has crafted, images are often more powerful than words. Rather than food transcending divides, it is images of people, often crafted and always containing elements of bias, which impact how we imagine ourselves and others, that thereby shape the world. Such a worldview seems a near-perfect articulation of Bourdain's approach, and it may be the most political act of all: Bourdain asks us to look at images of people from all political, social, ethnic, and class backgrounds, and think about them as constructed by media, politicians, and filmmakers like himself, and to maybe, just maybe, feel a bit of empathy and kinship.

Bourdain uses this approach not just as a means of deconstructing how mass media determines how we imagine social and political Others, but also how the bombardment of media images controls how the West imagines itself. Appearing in *Parts Unknown*'s eighth season,

Bourdain's final "London" episode is one of his most cohesive in terms of using constructed images of food, and images of the construction of that food, to invert the mind-numbing, sense-overwhelming depictions of geopolitical events present across mass media, instead fostering empathy for everyday individuals depicted on-screen. Bourdain developed similar themes and approaches a year earlier, intentionally visiting Glasgow (PU S5E3) shortly after Scotland's failed independence vote, an episode that draws upon David Fincher's *Fight Club* (1999), but it was happenstance that led Bourdain to arrive in London the night of the Brexit vote and commence filming its immediate aftermath.[21]

Bourdain's deconstruction of the images mass media seeks to manifest is multifaced. Throughout "London," Bourdain repeatedly pairs destabilizing cinematography with a hurried soundtrack of media coverage, such as an audio clip early in the episode in which Christiane Amanpour declares, "It turns out it *was* about immigration, but more than *half* of Britain's immigration comes from *outside* the EU, and the young are very, very anxious about what's happened and the gamble that's been taken with their future." That said, Bourdain *opens* his episode, before the credits, not with media, or even his own voice; rather, he begins with a montage of street interviews, using an approach first developed on *The Layover*, in which unidentified Britons break the fourth wall and talk of "shock" and "uncertainty." The sequence ends with a sudden absence of non-diegetic sound, and a single, unseen voice claiming, "I think human beings are still stupid, and *ego* gets in the way." Thus, Bourdain's episode is *about* politics, but in a way that allows individual voices to cut through the noise.

From its narration to its mise-en-scène, "London" emphasizes a contrast between uncertainty, a "moronic inferno blazing outside," on the macro, political level, and stability, a feeling of "insulation," on the micro, personal level, the stability linked to individuals, primarily friends, with whom Bourdain shares a meal. Each gets an opportunity to voice anger and uncertainty at the global factors, while establishing a sense of normalcy at a shared dinner table, an experience Bourdain uses his physical presence to mediate. As Bourdain declares early in the episode, "In uncertain times, I always look for the comforting and the familiar, the things that always, for me, made England great."

But two things are clear about these moments, and each serve as an example of how Bourdain's romantic vision, expressed in "Lebanon," of the dinner table as equalizer, shifted over time. Here, in post-Brexit London, the table offers an important sense of normalcy that fosters empathy, but it does not bring together opposing viewpoints; every interviewee shares dismay about Brexit and the inability to reconcile their new reality. Also, the table, and food in general, is depicted as constructed rather than an innate expression of culture or individuality. For instance, Bourdain's discussion of "the comforting and the familiar" ends on a close-up of chef Fergus Henderson's hands as he completes his mise en place rather than a dish, and the restaurant, St. JOHN, is clearly closed, upside down chairs sitting atop the tables, a private dining experience in a constructed space specially tailored to Bourdain and his crew. The cinematography even uses those chairs as blocking devices to further accentuate this point.

Bourdain uses these shared moments to depict an alternative reading of England that stands in sharp contrast to the xenophobic, insular imagination his interviewees express fear about. Even his interest in the hyper-traditional food at St. JOHN emphasizes its construction, not only in the mise-en-scène just discussed, but in the way Bourdain and food critic Jay Rayner assert no one would have thought to elevate, or even eat, traditional British food if not for Henderson, and in the way their conversation culminates in Rayner claiming, "what's 'great' about Britain" is, partially, its "*weirdly* cosmopolitan welcoming environment in which the history of immigration into the country has defined a much more open culture."

In fact, almost every food discussion comes back to either its construction, such as chef Marco Pierre White instructing Bourdain to add vinegar to their mushy peas and teaching him to make a "chip butty" out of chips, butter, and bread, or its diversity, such as his discussions of Jamaican cuisine with musician Jamie Hince and the history of Scottish egg exportation with cookbook author Nigella Lawson. Similarly, when Bourdain visits White's hotel-restaurant outside of Bath, he invokes a Romantic, Emersonian vision of nature only to instead depict the environment (and nature) as constructed by White, assisted by the chef's assertion he is quite literally causing nature to "increase." Elsewhere, when the duo fishes on rough seas, Bourdain declares "nature overrated" and they retreat to a fish restaurant. Similarly, it is a quiet pub at a quiet time of day with good food and conversation that Bourdain declares "an argument for England," prompting Lawson to respond, "we can *pretend* all is right with the universe." What is great about England is not innate, but, rather, a constructed space where one can embrace an aesthetic to converse with people. Thus, Bourdain does not declare Henderson's meat pie "a traditional dish that exemplifies everything that I believe in" because it is innately British; rather because it is simple and constructed in a way that tells a story.

Bourdain concludes by tying these themes together in a most personal way. The last montage of media coverage bridges the transition between a scene in which Bourdain drinks at a pub with Hince, pessimistically discussing Britain's future, and a scene where he wakes up with a hangover and heads to Lawson's apartment. The media "noise" ceases as the camera places us in the perceived intimacy of Lawson's kitchen, with tight close-ups emphasizing familiarity. "When the world seems like it's spinning out of control and the inside of your skull feels like it's being gnawed on by angry wolverines," Bourdain transitions, "it's good to have a friend who, without judgment, gives you a shoulder to cry on and maybe a simple, good thing, like some eggs and sympathy." Telling Lawson, he feels "shame and regret," she universalizes his experience, invoking Brexit, saying "you're not the only one," and proceeds to make him a "hangover cure," all while explaining both the dish's history and construction, finally declaring it "*something* we [Britons] can be proud of." Bourdain leaves the apartment to uplifting non-diegetic music and asserts, in perhaps the most optimistic tone of the episode, "These are frightening times for many. The world is changing and there is no stopping those changes, but in such times, there are always two ways to go: run and hide, build walls, cower in fear and suspicion . . . or stand up and try, at least *try*, to build a better world. To look for, instead of a man on a horse to save us or a wall to keep us apart, to our better angels." In this case, as in many for Bourdain, those better angels are embodied by food, the simple construction of which allows people to connect and empathize.

Bourdain never shied away from politics; he simply approached politics from a distinctive viewpoint that is less overt than how we are trained to imagine political coverage, thereby offering an alternative way of imagining the world around us. As this chapter's second epigraph claims, Bourdain's viewpoint is "incredibly political without being didactic," consistently "humanistic and very anti-hierarchical." Few filmmakers follow this approach. After Bourdain's death, CNN journalist Christiane Amanpour memorialized,

> I think the world really misses Tony Bourdain whether it knows it or not. What he provided and the places he took us every week on CNN, and before that in his other incarnations, it's something that's really missing in our world, particularly if you look at the overwhelming focus in our media, on just the politics, on just the person of the president. For many people it's an exhausting and partisan and often toxic environment that we're forced to inhabit. What Tony Bourdain delivered was the exact antidote without being overtly political. But just being about humanity and community and people. It was what we needed, and we don't have that now.[22]

Journalists such as Amanpour strive to depict political subjects truthfully, working in a genre and in an aesthetic that tends to disguise bias. Some political documentarians, like Errol Morris, strive to expose bias by revealing political figures, like Robert McNamara in *The Fog of War*, as constructed by the media, thereby asking us to question what we thought we knew. Bourdain did the same for everyday people, exposing the ways in which our imaginations of them, and their daily lives, are equally constructed. In the end, that may be the most political (and radical) filmmaking of all.

7
FOOD FILMS

I, personally, think there is a real danger of taking food too seriously. Food should be part of the bigger picture.

—Anthony Bourdain, *HuffPost*[1]

Foodways makes a special contribution to studies of food in film because it prompts one to expand analysis beyond the moments of food consumption most commonly depicted in film to consider the whole vista surrounding food, its production, consumption, and disposal. Drawn from the fields of folklore and cultural anthropology, the foodways paradigm throws into relief the fact that the movies designed and promoted to reach wide audiences emphasize the ease, pleasure, and emotional reward of convenient food consumption.

—Cynthia Baron, Diane Carson, and Mark Bernard, *Appetites and Anxieties*[2]

While I have outlined how Bourdain consistently resisted efforts to pigeonhole his work within the confines of any genre, particularly food, choosing to make a "stealth food show . . . rarely"[3] *about* food, there is no other single genre that so completely dominated how the world imagined him. Not only did Bourdain get his start in the kitchen and achieve fame writing about restaurant culture, but food was central to almost every episode he made. Further, Bourdain's television career began in the wake of a decade (the 1990s) that saw the first, clear identification of a food genre in film, and in which cooking shows proliferated on television, embodied by the founding of Food Network in 1993. More so, the height of Bourdain's television career directly coincided with the apex of that food genre, in which it transcended its previous confines within independent cinema and how-to cooking shows, dominating the way media depicts food in forms as diverse as mainstream Hollywood production, documentary filmmaking, animated movies, and an ever-expanding number of food-TV shows, most no longer situated inside a kitchen.

Bourdain both anticipated and participated in this genre expansion, even as he repeatedly critiqued its intentions and defied its conventions. Bourdain did so by treating food not just as something to consume, but as a way of asking, and sometimes answering, larger questions; as he says in this chapter's first epigraph, food as part of a "bigger picture," or, as I argue in chapter 6, food as a lens for understanding a complex world. These intentions shape the relationship between food and his narration, subject matter, editing, and cinematography, and help him serve as a rare example of a filmmaker able to fuse a food-film spectrum divided between "utopian visions of food and society on one end and dystopian visions on the other."[4]

Defined by James Keller as a film "in which food production, preparation, service, and or consumption play an operative and memorable role in the development of character, structure, or theme,"[5] the basic approach to food that led to the identification of a genre was present from the birth of cinema, but came to more commonly serve as the backbone of entire films around the turn of the twenty-first century. As Laura Lindenfeld and Fabio Parasecoli point out, films as diverse as *Big Night* (Stanley Tucci and Campbell Scott, 1996), *Ratatouille* (Brad Bird, 2007), and *Julie & Julia* (Nora Ephron, 2009) share a key commonality: they "are all about food, prepared in the kitchen, served at the table, and offered to global audiences for visual and emotional consumption. Above all, cooking and eating shape the character's lives and adventures, while dishes and ingredients, luscious and appealing, often steal the scene."[6] Food films manipulate the spectator into imagining a complete, full-sense response to a medium that is strictly visual and auditory, a medium that can simulate neither smell nor taste.[7]

As such, food is attractive as filmic material precisely because it is popular, consumable, and an easy way to use a visual image to advance narrative because (similar to what I argue in chapter 6) it serves as a marker of politics, culture, economic class, race, ethnicity, geography, gender, sexuality, history, and much more. Essentially, "The marketability of food . . . suggest[s] that narratives about eating constitute a highly contested arena in which cultural, social, economic, and political tensions converge."[8] The stakes only increase with the genre's shift from its roots in independent and foreign cinemas, e.g., *Big Night* and *Babette's Feast* (Gabriel Axel, 1987), to the mainstream, e.g., *Julie & Julia*, *Ratatouille*, and *Chef* (Jon Favreau, 2014).

That duality of a genre that represents a subject that both literally exists to be consumed, *and* is intrinsically a marker of a wide variety of consequential things, opens it to criticism. For instance, many argue the genre depicts food identities in a homogenizing way that treats identity as shallow, existing for the filmmaker's profit and the spectator's consumption, the very thing Bourdain repeatedly criticized in food TV. Again, returning to Lindenfeld and Parasecoli,

> Participating in the reproduction of the existing cultural and social order, food films play an important role in defining our sense of what is normal, natural, and appropriate, while keeping their mechanisms and strategies invisible. The virtual experience of eating while exploring different lifestyles and unfamiliar cultures provides audiences with seemingly safe and ordinary spaces to play out anxieties about racial differences, alternative sexualities, class distinctions, and all sorts of power issues. Food films, however, often end up highlighting consumption behaviors and lifestyles that privilege mainstream value systems while offering a virtual, vicarious touristic experience of various kinds of otherness.[9]

While these tensions are clearly not limited to food films, in fact they are present within all filmmaking, they are intensified and exacerbated by a genre centered on a subject that, on its surface, directly evokes emotion and nostalgia (for flavor and smell), while often ignoring, or at least underemphasizing, broader implications. As a specific example particularly pertinent to Bourdain, food films and food TV often participate in "celebratory images of ethnic food traditions" that "promote an agenda that ignores issues of power, advancing the idea that assimilation and appropriation are the proper strategy," romanticizing minor differences in flavor, taste, and thereby culture, "but only to a minor degree that does not fundamentally disrupt the status quo" but, instead, "reiterate[s] the legacy of colonialism."[10]

While these tendencies present themselves within the narratives of food films, they are most dominant within the genre's form, creating an approach to editing, cinematography, and mise-en-scène Bourdain dubbed "food porn." Typically, the form emphasizes pleasure in the consumption of food and inspiration in its preparation, while situating artistic genius in the person who prepares it. In so doing, food films establish a highly identifiable visual language catalogued by Lindenfeld and Parasecoli as a progression "from the ingredient detail to highlight its material qualities to the handheld shots that glorify dexterity and skills, moving to larger shots that include table, instruments, and dishes, as well as the face of the cooking character, all the way to wide shots that reveal the cooking environment and the interactions with other characters."[11]

The shot sequence is foundational throughout both narrative food films and food TV. Midway through an episode titled "Food Porn" (NR S5E6), Bourdain restages a cooking show with an attractive female cook and breaks down this standard shot sequence, emphasizing its relationship with porn in its manipulation and exploitation of the audience. Bourdain's overlapped narration describes how both genres begin with an establishing shot of the home/kitchen, followed by a medium shot as man meets woman/cook meets food, and eventually transition to a back-and-forth between close-ups of the action and point-of-view shots providing identification of the person doing the action; Bourdain concludes by equating porn's "money shot" with catchphrases like "bam!" and "off the hook!," trademark terms for food-TV celebrities Emeril Lagassé and Guy Fieri.

In fact, though largely played for laughs, "Food Porn" is a cohesive, thorough expression of Bourdain's problems with food genre conceits. The episode adheres to a 1970s porn aesthetic, made to appear as if it is shot on low-quality '70s film stock; Bourdain shamefully covers his face with his hands in an allusion to Paul Schrader's *Hardcore* (1979) as he watches his own episode from a seat in a mostly empty theater, further breaking the fourth wall by commenting upon the footage before, after, and while it plays. His guest line-up of celebrity chefs is given porn-star intros, which serve as clear commentary upon the genre's obsession with the chef as genius/artist. Bourdain describes how early food films directly borrowed from contemporary porn aesthetics, before beginning his dissection of how film form treats the consumption of food.

While Bourdain admits similarities between the body's response to food and sexual intercourse, he critiques food films for capitalizing on shallow images that remove food from broader cultural contexts. Sitting in a porn house, watching chefs cook, Bourdain turns to the camera and tells the spectator, "Millions of people are watching but by no means doing. Like the peep shows of old, food has become an almost entirely voyeuristic activity, a popular kink. . . . so many close-ups of moaning, eye rolling, lip-smacking, and oohing and aahing on basic cable *right* now, that if you listened from another room, you'd think it was a dirty shag carpet."

Bourdain's open invocation of the genre, viewed through the lens of porn, to deconstruct the fetishistic effect that permeates food films, is simply an intensified version of his overall approach. As I have argued, Bourdain draws attention to the artifice of filmmaking to expose bias, undermining genre. Think, for instance, of my discussion in chapter 1 of Bourdain denying an image of food simmering in "Hanoi" (PU S8E1), forcing the spectator to visualize from memory in a way that reveals how television typically constructs incomplete images for them. Or my discussion in chapter 2 about the time when, eating schnitzel in "Budapest" (PU S5E6), Bourdain (a) breaks the fourth wall and explains why he does not describe food as much anymore, providing reasons similar to "Food Porn," and (b) subsequently turns to a food-TV aesthetic and mockingly oohs, aahs, and snaps a selfie of his plate, the previous commentary still fresh in the spectator's ears. Further, think of my discussion in chapter 6 about Bourdain drawing attention to the fact the family meal in "Laos" (NR S4E11) is made for television, as well as the scarcity of meat in the region. In fact, Bourdain *regularly* talks about and depicts food at its source, draws awareness to its availability (or lack thereof), and discusses how all that shapes the dish we see on television; rather than a consumable delight created in a moment of spontaneous inspiration by a genius chef, cuisine is part of a larger narrative, tied to its geography, with both positive and negative connotations.

As such, Bourdain employs a foodways approach to de-exoticize and de-glamorize food. For instance, consider "Peru" (PU S1E7), in which Bourdain travels with Éric Ripert to find rare, white cocoa beans to produce fair-trade chocolate. Rather than a romanticized pilgrimage further and further into remote Peru, Bourdain emphasizes their status as outsiders within an ancient civilization. He interjects an extended montage laying out the history of cocoa production and exportation, its links to colonialism, the degree to which it was fetishized precisely because Europeans imagined it as exotic, and the ways mass-market chocolate extraction has hurt both the quality of the product and the people who live in the region. Bourdain is even careful to discuss how fair-trade *also* utilizes a shallow image that often does not lead to fairness for Peruvians. Typical for Bourdain, the approach is complex, multifaceted, and avoids glamorizing, denigrating, or, above all, exoticizing his subject. Relevantly, at the end of "Food Porn," Bourdain compares *Bizarre Foods with Andrew Zimmern* (Travel Channel, 2006–18), a show in which Zimmern travels to sample foods not typically eaten in the West, to kink porn and asks pointed questions about the effect of exoticizing cultures: "Bizarre? Kinky? What does that *mean* if *most* of the world gets off on it? . . . I've learned that just about anything goes *somewhere* in the world." Thus, consistent with his own filmography, Bourdain emphasizes how food films "play an important role in defining our sense of what is normal, natural, and appropriate."

Bourdain thereby creates a space for himself between two extremes within the genre. Specifically, critics draw a contrast between the overwhelming breadth of food films and food TV partaking in the "utopian visions"[12] already discussed, and a wave of documentaries, beginning with *Super Size Me* (Morgan Spurlock, 2004), *King Corn* (Aaron Woolf, 2007), and *Food, Inc.* (Robert Kenner, 2008), that takes a broader foodways approach. By showing activities that lie outside the frame of consumption, such as processing and disposal, foodways documentaries provide commentary on larger social values and "tacitly highlight the food and film industries' power to control representations in consumer society,"[13] but they typically struggle to reach broad audiences through mainstream media platforms precisely because of their approach, limiting their potential impact.

To be clear, the distinction is not a simple line between narrative and documentary. While foodways approaches most commonly are found in documentaries, other documentaries reinforce food-film norms. As Lindenfeld and Parasecoli are careful to point out, documentaries that glamorize chefs, *El Bulli: Cooking in Progress* (Gereon Wetzel, 2010) and *Jiro Dreams of Sushi* (David Gelb, 2011) for instance, "contribute to the formation of a cosmopolitan canon of practices, norms, and values that naturalize the concept of the knowledgeable chef trained in a prestigious culinary tradition as the professional ideal" and rely on "a repository of images, ideas, and values that are perceived as based on reality rather than fiction."[14]

I believe the same can be said of a lot of the post-Bourdain food-TV shows influenced by his documentary aesthetic. Shows like *Chef's Table* (Netflix, 2015–present), *Taste the Nation with Padma Lakshmi* (Hulu, 2020–23), *Stanley Tucci: Searching for Italy* (CNN, 2021–22), and *Somebody Feed Phil* (Netflix, 2018–present), are heavily influenced by Bourdain, but they *also* adhere to "utopian visions." For instance, *Somebody Feed Phil* emphasizes its host's lack of prior knowledge, as well as the importance of learning local nuance, such as the host carefully repeating pronunciations back for local approval in Lisbon (S1E4); yet each episode still concludes by offering a sense it has given the spectator a complete, authentic view of a national cuisine the spectator may one day consume. Similarly, consider the way Tucci is not shy about exposing Italian cuisine's peasant roots, or in the case of episodes in Rome (S1E2) and Sicily (S1E6), the current plight of immigrants; yet, Tucci ends each segment on a yum or a joyful moan, coaxed by ingesting food prepared by a genius chef who has manifested that impoverished context into something beautiful and delicious. Or, in Milan (S1E4), when Tucci boldly pushes back against his anti-immigration host William Cavadini with tough questions, tells us in narration he thinks food and politics are interconnected, but allows his host to smooth things over in real time so as to not hinder the enjoyment of the meal. In short, despite a heavy Bourdain influence, these shows remain within "a larger media and cultural framework that commercializes the desire for authenticity" even if "definitions of what counts as authentic are subjective."[15]

It is not just that Bourdain partakes in a documentary aesthetic; it is that he partakes in a specific *type* of documentary that embraces a holistic approach to completely (not partially) upend the paradigm. Hence, while Bourdain shares a foodways-based approach with alternative documentaries, it is the intersection of his anthropological approach with the wide audience available to him as a television host that distinguishes him from much of the genre.

That is not to suggest that some early, foundational food documentaries do not in fact walk a line between glorification and dystopian political messaging. Les Blank's *Garlic Is as Good as Ten Mothers* (1980), for instance, is a love letter to garlic and the dishes for which it is an ingredient, yet still highlights sustainable agriculture, depicts workers harvesting, and pointedly utilizes a freeze-frame to superimpose a picket sign reading "Support the people who grow the food we eat" over a produce box bearing the emblem of the United Farm Workers. Such documentaries had limited audiences, however, and while documentaries became more marketable and readily available in the wake of *Roger & Me*'s (Michael Moore, 1989) financial success, the availability of streaming platforms, and television's subsequent attraction to a documentary aesthetic, the aforementioned split actually widened between documentaries that reinforce the conceits of narrative food films or those which deconstruct them in support of a specific political critique, typically with a niche audience in mind.

Bourdain cast his net wider, but what I find even more compelling is how comprehensively dedicated he was to his approach, even within subject matter that would seem to *most* glorify food, that would seem to *most* squarely fit within the genre's normative conceits. For example, two *No Reservations* episodes dedicated to Ferran Adrià's El Bulli (S2 Special Episode and S7E12) and a *Parts Unknown* episode dedicated to Rene Redzepi's Noma (S2E4), center themselves not, primarily, around genius chefs at exclusive restaurants, but, rather, the way those chefs (and restaurants) represent the end result of larger foodways conversations, conversations in which their work participates.

When Bourdain was first granted what was, at the time, unprecedented access to El Bulli, then widely considered the best restaurant in the world with a multiyear waitlist for a table, he famously expressed skepticism about molecular gastronomy, a technology-based food approach popularized by Adrià. It would have stood to reason that the 2006 special "Decoding Ferran Adrià," which documents Bourdain's conversion into an Adrià fan, as well as the 2011 follow-up episode documenting the restaurant's final days, would embody a chef-centered, romantic vision of cuisine—akin to Gereon Wetzel's documentary *El Bulli: Cooking in Progress*, released in the interim between the two episodes. Instead, the episodes collectively serve as a cohesive expression of Bourdain's culinary worldview, working against romanticism. Similarly, Bourdain's 2013 *Parts Unknown* episode at Copenhagen's Noma, the restaurant that supplanted El Bulli as the consensus best restaurant in the world, also defies food-film expectations, especially when compared to Pierre Deschamps's documentary *Noma: My Perfect Storm*, which appeared two years later (2015). In both cases, Bourdain utilizes his typical foodways approach to argue the best restaurants are not simply the result of individual genius, to be consumed by patron and spectator alike. Rather, Bourdain depicts their food as both a product of—and participant in—cultural conversations rooted in geography, the understanding of which shapes every aspect of identity.

Bourdain begins his introduction to each restaurant making it clear he is visiting despite predispositions, in the case of El Bulli, reluctance to eat the "foam dude's . . . weird science approach to cooking," and in the case of Noma, disdain for fairytale locations, accompanying establishing shots with the warning, "Once upon a time in a land far, far away there was a place. A very special place. A clean, orderly, and nice place. Usually I hate clean, orderly, and nice." In each instance, Bourdain is swift to admit he was wrong and structures the rest of the episode around providing necessary context for understanding how these restaurants, and their chefs, are part of those larger conversations.

Much like the food-film documentaries about these very restaurants, all three episodes go to painstaking efforts to document and communicate Bourdain's experience working his way through tasting menus, each over thirty courses. Unlike those documentaries, however, Bourdain's meal is never the apex; rather, the dishes and their progression are dissected as a means of better understanding and expressing the larger context of the episodes, and the cinematography, editing, and mise-en-scène deny the basic tenants of food-film form. Sitting back in his chair at El Bulli's chef's table at one of the last meals ever served in that restaurant, Bourdain jokes with Adrià, "No human being in the world deserves this, I certainly don't. I feel guilty. I feel like I just fucked my best friend's wife. I feel guilty showing anyone pictures of that, I feel guilty telling anyone about it, I feel guilty *eating* it." There is much to learn from (and cherish about) these restaurants, Bourdain suggests, but abject glorification of consumption is clearly not his goal.

Both El Bulli episodes spend significant time outside the restaurant as Bourdain traces not just Adrià's biography, but, more important, the way that biography links his cuisine to Catalunya, home to Adrià and his restaurant, and Andalucía, from where many in his hometown migrated. The first episode opens at a *jamonería* Adrià chose the first time he met Bourdain, and ends at Rafa's, a straightforward fish restaurant that became the inspiration for a key course on El Bulli's tasting menu. The second episode opens with Bourdain walking around Adrià's hometown with chef José Andrés, sampling tapas, talking to locals, and playing miniature golf at the tourist camp Adrià once worked at. While the attention to simple cuisine could seem incongruous to a three-star restaurant, Bourdain makes those connections apparent. For instance, Bourdain uses *jamon*, Spain's *most* traditional product, to repeat a point Adrià made at their first meeting: "what's *wrong* with transforming food? The making of ham is a *process*. Iberico ham is *better* than fresh ham, no? Just like good sherry is better than the grapes it is made with." Bourdain's instinctive disdain for processed foods effectively deconstructed, Bourdain comes to understand what Adrià does at El Bulli is an extension of tradition rather than a rejection of it. By the time he eats at Rafa's with Adrià, Bourdain declares he no longer sees incongruity, claiming, "It is here, I think, that the true nature of Ferran Adrià revealed itself." The two restaurants are, Bourdain claims, "all of a part" because Adrià wants his food to remind you of your first taste of fish, a claim that echoes Adrià's own words when he presents Bourdain with the El Bulli dish inspired by Rafa's: "there are *new* things [at El Bulli] but they're not strange. We have the memory of these tastes."

Bourdain reinforces these connections within his experience of El Bulli's progressive tasting menus across both episodes. Bourdain generally avoids stereotypical, local music, yet the first El Bulli episode utilizes Spanish guitar music at almost every turn, de-emphasizing the international, homogenized vibe typical of Michelin-starred restaurants. Such a normalizing of the space is reinforced when his narration claims, "The first thing one notices when entering El Bulli is it is, indeed, a restaurant," the cinematography depicting typical tables and decor. Eating an oyster dish, Bourdain proclaims of the tasting menu, "When eaten in sequence it takes the tongue on a wild—yet strangely familiar—trip around the world and then right back to your first oyster"; Bourdain then looks straight at Adrià and declares, "I feel like I've eaten that dish my whole life." In the second episode, Bourdain and Andrés discuss how a gazpacho dish served with *ajo blanco* "brings" them "right back" to Adrià's hometown, Hospitalet, and Andalucía before that; Andrés going so far as to claim, "so this is an entire region with centuries of history [distilled] into one dish." As Bourdain summarizes his first tasting menu at El Bulli, "There is no *fusion* here, there's no blending of flavors into a muddy, sort of general crowd of flavors, all combining to make one flavor. There are individual, clean favors put together." Adrià is not inventing technique, he is building upon the tradition of flavors and techniques present within the culture in which he is rooted.

Such an innate connection to geography, culture, and tradition is the central point Bourdain seeks to convey. As Adrià tells Bourdain in the first episode, "If I make you a Spanish omelet, I'm doing something I already know how to do. Here, we try to do things we don't know how to do. Whoever created the first omelet created a technique and a concept." Such a connection lays at the heart of the return episode as well, in which Bourdain's early narration confidently proclaims, "the roots . . . of Adrià's cooking are traditional Catalan," one in which the *only* true food-porn cinematography Bourdain utilizes is reserved for a traditional Catalan stew Adrià makes at a campsite after consulting with a fisherman. Bourdain carefully points out, "What's interesting and instructive to notice about this process is this: watch one of the best chefs in the world here taking advice from a local fisherman. It is *assumed* that they both know in their bones how to make this most traditional of dishes." This act leads to a conversation between Bourdain and Andrés in which Bourdain declares, "There's a direct relationship between something you cook on a beach, that this gentleman has been cooking, and fisherman and farmers have been doing for centuries." Andrés interjects, "I agree, maybe some people that do avant-garde cooking, unfortunately they don't have the tradition behind them." Bourdain corrects him, "the *majority* of the time, they are cooking to show you how smart they are . . . and they forget about *this*." Andrés ends the conversation, "If you don't have connections to the traditions and the past, it's *impossible* you can have connections to the present and the future." It would seem reasonable to therefore question if one could reasonably appreciate food at such a restaurant, either as diner or food-TV spectator, if one lacks an understanding of that very connection, if one imagines a restaurant or food TV as pure expressions of artistic genius meant to be consumed.

Bourdain approaches Noma through a similar lens, reimagining Redzepi's influential interest in foraging not as nouveau, but rooted in tradition and place. Bourdain makes a point of taking Redzepi to a simple restaurant to discuss Danish food traditions, and he chooses this location to quiz Redzepi about his Macedonian youth. Here, Redzepi shares the story of his first food memory, his father roasting chestnuts collected on a family trip to the mountains, served with fresh milk. Redzepi connects the two topics, proclaiming, "Now you have a generation of young cooks like myself—and they are all over town—looking for the flavor of a region, what is the flavor, what are the ingredients we have, and how do we combine them in a way that tells something of where you are in the world." Suddenly, the fact Noma's product comes almost exclusively from within sixty miles seems less a high-end gimmick and more about rooting haute cuisine in familiar flavors and local traditions. As Bourdain claims when he first sits at Noma, "the technique, you don't notice it, you notice the flavor," or after eating Redzepi's butter, "you can pretty much taste what the cow ate. You know, anybody who's milked a cow, this is a flavor of childhood." Toward the end of the tasting menu, the soundtrack shifts to traditional Scandinavian music, reminiscent of the effect of the guitar at El Bulli, and one of Bourdain's guests, Alessandro Porcelli, discusses visiting the Yucatán and finding chefs who "say I want to be number one in the world" but "don't even know how to make a tortilla, they don't even know what a tortilla is made of. They kind of lose touch with what the tradition is." Almost immediately, Bourdain cuts to Redzepi introducing his next dish, violin music still in the background, "It's good for you to try this, the herring, the rye bread, the smoked fish, the traditional stuff. Because when you grow up as a cook here you think this is old-fashioned, you don't see it as inspiration for your future endeavors as a cook." Bourdain's camera suddenly cuts to Redzepi serving traditional Danish flatbread, laying bare the difference between avant-garde for the sake of fame versus what he believes Noma (and El Bulli) to be.

Bourdain's insistence upon linking food with culture is not an alternative romanticism via *terroir* strategy, which imagines (and markets) a connection between land and food,[16] but a refusal to romanticize lone, genius chefs. Such a distinction is evidenced by the lengths these episodes go to emphasize the collaborative nature in both restaurants. In the case of Noma, Bourdain shows the kitchen staff presenting their own creative, innovative dishes. Redzepi praises these dishes, but refuses to steal them, emphasizing the talents of all involved. Meanwhile, rather than only including foraging scenes about the individual agency of a chef, Bourdain spends a lengthy sequence interacting with a farmer who grows product for Noma, Søren Wiuff. Bourdain explains Wiuff's approach to farming, how it influences (and enables) Redzepi, and Wiuff's bravery working against market demands when he began. To quote Redzepi, "the future is cutting out the middle-man, the farmer," and that is a worry because "a chef can't know shit about this land." Similarly, the first El Bulli episode starts at Adrià's lab, where Bourdain declares, "There's one concept at the heart of *every*thing . . . while the world writes and speaks of Ferran Adrià, within the *taller* there is an environment of *team*work." Bourdain then cuts to Adrià insisting, "One of the very important things is the *team*. Normally the chef is the center of the universe in the kitchen. I might be the media star, but they are part of the history of El Bulli. They participate in the creativity at the same level I do . . . They never say 'I,' 'I did,' 'I make,' it's 'we.'" Further, Bourdain shows El Bulli's family meal as more complex than is typical at other restaurants, reintroduces by name the chefs Bourdain met at the *taller*, and depicts a sous chef teaching Bourdain how to make the entire tasting menu. Bourdain thereby wholeheartedly denies the heroic individualism embodied by most food-film chefs.

Bourdain's denial of genre conceits within his narrative is supported by his denial via form. Despite choosing the world's most sought-after food as subject, and meticulously documenting his tasting menu experiences, Bourdain almost entirely avoids the approaches to cinematography and editing he helped dub "food porn." With some isolated exceptions, such as the depiction of the rustic Catalan stew contrasted against haute cuisine, by and large Bourdain keeps the spectator at a distance from the food and its consumption, utilizing blocking within his cinematography, cutting away to shots of other people preparing the dishes while Adrià sits with Bourdain, keeping the camera far from food on the plate, and emphasizing distracting conversation that often has little to do with the dish. Even depictions of food preparation are typically over the shoulder, part of the body blocking, to not clearly establish the face of the cook. In particular, the second El Bulli episode's visit to Adrià's other restaurant, Tickets, uses an even *more* distant camera that remains even *lower* to the table, awkwardly preventing the perfect framing typical of food documentaries. Near the end of the first episode, Bourdain does provide framed overhead stills, which I believe are influential to Wetzel's documentary four years later, but the narrative layover continues the discussion typical throughout the episode. Taken in tandem with the stylistic approach in the remainder of the episode, it makes clear Bourdain is decoding the dishes rather than mystifying them like Wetzel (and most food documentarians). As Bourdain asserts, Adrià "goes at the dining experience like a film director. It's about timing, and pace, and thrills, and surprise"; rather than an artistic image of a plate as the expression of individual genius, Bourdain emphasizes it is a construction; it tells a story.

Bourdain mostly utilizes the same distancing approach depicting food and its creation at Noma, but he augments its effect by stylizing the entire episode after Terrence Malick's *The Tree of Life* (2011). Malick, one of the most experimental and avant-garde filmmakers working within the margins of Hollywood, is known for unique approaches to cinematography and editing. In the case of *The Tree of Life*, Malick relies on handheld camerawork to capture mundane moments and frame them to emphasize their beauty and meaning, often via metaphor. The film, itself, is ostensibly a coming-of-age story, interspersing, with little context or chronology, faded memories of the protagonist's early family life with imagery of the origins of the known universe and the inception of life. The themes of humanity's relationship with nature, as well as the importance and relevance of memory upon identity, are clearly evocative of the themes of "Copenhagen," but more important, it is an example of Bourdain using filmic illusions to move the purpose and intent of food shots to issues beyond the glamorization of consumption. Wanting to mimic *The Tree of Life*, Bourdain intentionally denied the editors establishing shots because he wanted his subjects, including Redzepi, to "fall and wander out of frame."[17]

Bourdain's focus is not the genius chef, or even the consumption of his food, but, the relationship between Noma and larger contexts that led to it. Hence, while the episode is structured around the tasting menu, the menu is not its apex. Instead, Bourdain ends with a picnic with humble but tasty versions of the restaurant food, riding a boat with Redzepi and his children as they observe Danish Midsummer celebrations, the visual style heavily leaning on Malick; family memories, cultural traditions, and cuisine thus intersect.

It is dangerous to entirely dismiss the idea of imagining food as a form of art. First, it is, in fact, a form of expression. Second, it is, historically speaking, one of the few forms of expression available to minority voices, the underprivileged, racial and cultural Others, women, everyday working people. Too often, however, society's desire to romanticize all modes of expression places so much emphasis on individual genius that it ignores the cultural context from which it comes and, inevitably, reinforces a status quo that imagines food *only* as art, thereby elevating privileged chefs at high-end restaurants. In so doing, such an approach returns us to Lindenfeld and Parasecoli's claim that "culinary tourism is embedded in a larger media and cultural framework that commercializes the desire for [subjective] authenticity."[18]

Throughout his filmography Bourdain continually questioned the very notion of authenticity, routinely forcing his spectator to consider larger contexts that emphasize nuance and uncertainty. Time and again he uses film form, style, and content to deconstruct the touristic, consumerist aims of food TV in locations around the world, even in episodes dedicated to the most exclusive of cuisines. Concluding his final episode at El Bulli, Bourdain declares, "What I'll remember: the gin tonics on the patio as the dining room emptied for one of the last times ever; I'll remember what Ferran [Adrià] has talked about all along, the emotion; I'll remember José [Andrés], struggling to control his voice as he talked about what El Bulli and this man meant to him, and to the world." For Bourdain it is not about food or its consumption. It is about the people who consume it, and how it connects them to each other, as well as to a history (both real and imagined) that brought those people—and ingredients on the plate—together.

III
DÉGUSTATION

8
HONG KONG

I begin the Dégustation with "Hong Kong" (PU S11E5) because there is no spot in Bourdain's filmography where the disparate themes I have explored thus far converge more completely or seamlessly. Speaking of one of his own films, *In the Mood for Love* (Wong Kar Wai, 2000), episode guest Christopher Doyle proclaims, "everything we did before was preparation." I argue the same could in many ways be said of Bourdain before "Hong Kong," a *Parts Unknown* episode that so clearly expresses so much of what he wanted to say about cinema, the world, and how cinema depicts and shapes that world. Opening with "Hong Kong" allows it to serve as a lens for understanding all of Bourdain's work that came before (and after).

"Hong Kong" draws its visual style from one of Bourdain's cinematic heroes, Wong Kar Wai, but contrasts that style with that of Wong's longtime cinematographer Christopher Doyle—who takes over as Bourdain's director of photography midway through the episode—as well as Simon Go, whose photography features prominently. Both Doyle and Go's voices also feature prominently, as does the presence of Asia Argento, who guest-directs. The episode works to break verisimilitude, to draw one's attention to competing visual perspectives and biases, and to emphasize discussion of the ethics of filmmaking. The episode is framed around a conversation about gentrification and definitions of progress, what is lost within such processes, and what is at stake regarding those issues when one documents a city in transition. Bourdain is interested both in depicting what is unique about Hong Kong and making the spectator aware of how Bourdain's interest in those qualities is preconstructed by his love of Wong. More than anything, the episode draws the spectator's attention to the fact it is doing all of this: offering both a sense of realism and a deconstruction of it, a sense of Bourdain's perspective as well as how the episode is shaped by other voices, and an attempt to document rather than preserve while making the spectator think about the space between those two approaches. To quote Bourdain, "We threw out our Pelican cases full of gels. Avoided, wherever necessary, the fascistic concept of continuity. Messed (often mid-scene) with the equally tyrannical and artificial notion of blocking. We filled the frame with living, breathing people—moving through the busy streets, markets, houses, and teahouses of Hong Kong as they do."[1] In my opinion, it is the culmination of where Bourdain's filmmaking had been heading for at least a decade and an embodiment of his greatest qualities as filmmaker.

Airing June 3, 2018, only five days before his death, and arriving with additional fanfare because Bourdain aggressively advertised the episode via press interviews, social media, and an editorial published in *Hollywood Reporter*, where he called the episode "the most intensely satisfying experience of my professional life and a show that I am giddily, ecstatically proud of,"[2] the episode has come to serve as a touchpoint for debates about Bourdain's legacy. In particular, Morgan Neville's 2021 Bourdain bio-doc, *Roadrunner*, isolates the episode as the moment that "broke"[3] *Parts Unknown*, as, to quote *Film Cred*'s Cory Stillman, "The episode is characterized as a gross betrayal of all that preceded it, an egregious departure from the formula that came to define both *Parts Unknown* and *No Reservations* before it."[4] Specifically, Neville's documentary emphasizes an interview with one of Bourdain's producers, Helen Cho, who expresses dismay about Bourdain's "obsession" with Argento, whom Bourdain brought in to direct the episode when the planned director had to undergo gallbladder surgery; the purported onset firing of longtime cameraman Zach Zamboni, which Cho calls "a huge red flag"; and Argento's decision to allow Doyle, acting as cameraman, to interrupt a very personal interview with two asylum seekers in order to "re-set" the table and the shot, something Cho claims Bourdain "would have never, ever done." It is worth noting Neville disingenuously includes footage of this interruption without contextualizing the fact the interruption is actively included and emphasized in Bourdain's episode.

Asserting "Hong Kong" marks a clear departure from Bourdain's established approach ignores multiple levels of evidence to the contrary, not the least of which is Bourdain's claim, penned days before his death, that it was the professional achievement of which he took the most pride. Pointing to the firing of Zamboni as a "red flag" ignores the high expectations (and claims about willingness to cut ties) present throughout the quotations from Bourdain I use in chapter 1, as well as Zamboni's discussion about the tenuous nature of working for Bourdain for so many years in a 2017 interview.[5] Talking about this episode as a departure also ignores the fact that Bourdain and his crew worked for over six years to secure Doyle to fulfill their long-held plan of shooting Hong Kong in relation to the filmic depictions of Wong[6] and had already twice experimented with Wong visual references in "Shanghai" (PU S4E1) and "Buenos Aires" (PU S8E7). Further, such assertions isolate Bourdain's approach to a static formula across episodes and programs, rather than the constantly evolving, persistently self-aware (and self-reflexive) approach I argue defines his development as a filmmaker. As such, returning to Stillman, such critiques ignore "the fact that the strongest throughline in Bourdain's career was his refusal to abide by traditional storytelling conventions."[7] Even more precisely, I believe they ignore that the common threads across Bourdain's disparate storytelling approaches are all embodied in the themes of "Hong Kong." Reviewing the episode at the time of its release, *IndieWire*'s Eric Kohn felt the same, "The 42-minute episode celebrates Wong and Doyle's work, but in a broader sense, it feels like a natural extension of Bourdain's homegrown oeuvre—it's a lush, riveting overview of Hong Kong's history, its struggles with gentrification, and multicultural inhabitants."[8] Again, the episode represents a culmination, emphasizing the disparate perspectives that influence and shape Bourdain.

Descriptions of how the disparate voices that constructed the show—namely Bourdain, Argento, and Doyle—worked together sound not only symbiotic, but reminiscent of the collaborative, experimental approach Bourdain utilized across his career. Bourdain claimed the group "hit it off" immediately because of a "shared affection for a 'dirtier,' more natural, more reactive shooting style" in which "the oppressive notion of 'continuity' was largely discarded in favor of emotional impact."[9] Argento echoed this claim, "Chris, like me, isn't looking for the perfect shot. Through what other people may see as mistakes, there is a search for beauty and immediacy."[10] Argento points to the influence of Doyle's *Ruined Heart* (2014), which she is attracted to more than his more acclaimed films because of its "immediacy, an urgency, and many 'mistakes' which make it very alive for me . . . The movie was shot for very little, but it had an unprecedented depth in its search for what may resemble truth—something that always moves me in cinema and documentaries."[11] I find shades of Werner Herzog in a low-budget "search" for something that "resembles truth," and thus a shared commonality with the interest Bourdain explored across at least the second half of his career. Meanwhile, the embrace of and emphasis placed on "mistakes" is quintessential Bourdain. To return to Kohn's review, "Argento's own work on both sides of the camera tends toward rough, visceral narrative experiences, and her sensibilities prove a natural union with Bourdain, whose baritone voiceover and John Wayne swagger sits at the cross-section of Hong Kong's evolving identity."[12]

"Hong Kong" is bookended by sequences that exist outside the episode's timeline, seemingly outside its diegesis altogether. This is a tone-setting device Bourdain uses somewhat regularly in the later seasons of *Parts Unknown*, but the mood here is far more personal and the repetition of using different *versions* of the same scene as bookends is unique within Bourdain's filmography.

The opening sequence begins with a slightly off-putting counterpoint sound that turns hopeful and complete as the camera slowly finds its focus and Bourdain begins to speak. Bourdain sits alone on the bow of a ferry writing in his journal, the lights of Hong Kong behind him. Bourdain reads as he writes, "Chapter One: to fall in love with Asia is one thing, to fall in love in Asia is another. Both have happened to me. The Star Ferry to Kowloon at night. Lights of Hong Kong behind me. It's a gift, a dream, a curse. The best thing, the happiest thing, yet also the loneliest thing in the world." As Bourdain says "loneliest," the nondiegetic sound goes silent and the camera cuts to an angle taken from inside the ferry, emphasizing Bourdain's solitary status.

At episode's end, we return to the same shot, but the sequence continues; suddenly, the camera cuts to a different angle, exposing Argento and Doyle filming the angles previously shown. Next, Bourdain walks off the boat and onto a viewing deck, surrounded by a cacophony of tourists with cell-phone cameras. All the while, we hear the soundtrack that has dominated the body of the episode, highly reminiscent of Wong's *In the Mood for Love*. The message is clear: every image we see of Hong Kong

The arms of director Asia Argento guide cinematographer Christopher Doyle as he shoots Bourdain "alone" on the bow of Hong Kong's Star Ferry. This reveal comes at episode's end, after their presence was hidden at its beginning.

is Bourdain's, but Bourdain's imagination has been indelibly shaped by that of others. Meanwhile, every image and imagination, from his supposedly private journal to Hong Kong itself, is constructed by and for cinema, and every act he participates in is itself a construct, which simultaneously renders Bourdain never alone and always lonely.

The opening of the actual episode, after the credits, serves as the thesis for both "Hong Kong" and Bourdain's worldview, and, even as it points to the global, it is evocative of the highly personal bookend sequences I just discussed. The camera roves crowded streets, set to the original score evocative of *In the Mood for Love*. Every single shot of this extended sequence is, at very least, reminiscent of the style of cinematography found throughout Doyle and Wong's collaborations, and some of the shots are precise re-creations of shots from their films. Bourdain opens, "All of us when we travel look at the places we go, the things we see, through *different* eyes. And how we see them is shaped by our previous lives. The books we've read, the films we've seen, the baggage we carry." As Bourdain finishes that line, the camera moves to one of the direct Wong references, but this time it cuts straight from that copy to the original clip from *Chungking Express* (Wong, 1994). Bourdain proceeds to scroll through a series of Wong shots and his copies of them, exposing the references he has been using throughout the sequence, his voice-over declaring:

> Years ago, when I first watched the stunningly beautiful films of director Wong Kar Wai, it shaped forever the way I'd see Hong Kong. From that point on, my hopes, my expectations for this city would be seen through that lens, a lens that was—in nearly every case—pointed by, focused by, this man. Christopher Doyle. Longtime resident of Hong Kong, known by his Mandarin name Dù Kěfēng. His earlier works with Wong Kar Wai were distinguished by unspeakably gorgeous images of beautiful people moving through spaces both unfamiliar and yet painfully intimate. Ultimately jagged, frenzied, innovative, languid, composed, chaotic. I *obsessed* over his work. Fetishized it. Longed to see Hong Kong like the characters in so many of his films longed for each other, and I feared, like those characters, I would be denied. I was wrong.

Again, personal experience shaping cinema and cinema shaping personal experience, and an awareness the entire episode will be an exploration of the space therein.

Wong rose to international fame first as a member, and eventually as the leader, of a group of filmmakers Ackbar Abbas identifies as "a new Hong Kong cinema,"[13] a generation of filmmakers who learned technical competence working on television crews while simultaneously being exposed to international cinema. This generation emerged partially in response to a changing Hong Kong, which, after Margaret Thatcher's 1984 visit, was bound to be united with China in 1997, with assurances of only fifty years of retaining their own system of government. To quote Abbas, "The Joint Declaration caused a certain amount of anxiety . . . it made Hong Kong people look at their country with new eyes. It is as if the possibility of the disappearance of this social and cultural space led to seeing it in all its complexity and contradiction for the first time: an instance, as [Walter] Benjamin would have said, of love at last sight."[14] Wong, eventually teaming with Doyle as cinematographer for six of his most important films, became internationally known and respected for his lush visual style, which captures a sense of movement on Hong Kong streets. Many of his films, particularly *Chungking Express* and *In the Mood for Love*, exert a nostalgia for the ebb and flow of architecture in specific neighborhoods and in specific moments in time, but a nostalgia that is always situated in a state of continual change (as in *Chungking Express*) or set in the past (as in *In the Mood for Love*), thereby denying any imagination the filmic representation is anything but temporal. To return to Abbas, "Hong Kong people have little memory and no sentiment for the past . . . But history exists, if not in surviving monuments or written records, then in the jostling anachronisms and spatial juxtapositions that are seen on every street; that is, history is inscribed in spatial relations."[15] As such, Hong Kong's ever-changing history is best embodied in Wong and Doyle's cinematography, and it is that cinematography Bourdain draws upon as he tries to understand his visit to his own version of a disappearing Hong Kong.

While Bourdain's visual style references the Wong-Doyle films, as do many of the conversations and locations, even more of the locations are determined by the work of the photographer Simon Go who, like Doyle, appears in the episode. Go's black-and-white photography primarily documents small, family-run businesses that are disappearing across the city, partially because of global economics but also because of trades dying out within modernity. Bourdain shows us these photographs, commenting, "All this is disappearing. All this could be gone. It's vanishing before our eyes." Bourdain visits and interviews several such proprietors, such as Sun Nga Shing, who owns Hong Kong's last umbrella repair shop, Ho Sau-Mei, the last female maker of handmade mahjong tiles, and Lau Fat-cheong noodle shop, where Bourdain first tastes and explains the painstaking process of making bamboo noodles the "old school way," and then, in the episode's final moments, shows Lau Sum Kee, one of three remaining noodle makers, silently going about his craft. Bourdain shows Go's images of these places, but Bourdain shoots them in the style and color palette of Wong-Doyle and sets the interview to the music reminiscent of *In the Mood for Love*. His interview with Go inside China Café is also shot in that film's green palette, as Go talks about nostalgia for showing locals and foreigners "the old Hong Kong" as he seeks to "preserve some memories." Talking about the loss of establishments to urban development, Go claims he has a "mission to preserve that." When Bourdain asks if it is "realistic" to "protect" these businesses in a city that has always been defined by change, Go answers he hopes it can happen through his work, that "when the government and the Hong Kong people see more about our own unique culture so many people try their best to fight for that." Go says all of this sitting in an old school diner, China Café, which permanently closed just one year after Bourdain's episode aired.[16]

While Bourdain returns to Go's locations throughout the episode, never letting his perspective disappear, he continually contrasts it to Doyle's and eventually his own. We last see Go, sitting at China Café, reminiscing about how the smell of traditional food brings back powerful, nostalgic memories of his grandparents, and asserting his hope that his photography can spark change. Bourdain immediately cuts to a scene with Doyle on Lantau Island, one of Hong Kong's last remaining fishing villages, and the location of his most recent film, *The White Girl* (Christopher Doyle and Jenny Suen, 2017). Doyle ends up sitting at an open-air fish café next to the docks, a location that could just as easily be a source of nostalgia as Go's diner. Instead, Doyle asserts no documentarian can ever achieve Go's desires. Doyle and his co-director Jenny Suen readily admit they chose the location as a "metaphor" for a "disappearing" Hong Kong. Unlike Go, however, Doyle asserts, "The only function of what we do, of art, or of anything, is to give voice to the unspoken. To give it a form that it's never been perceived in before. We can't change the evolution of history or the gentrification. You can't stop that, but at least you can say, look what you're losing. That's all. All we can do is give an image to an idea." Bourdain places special emphasis on this quotation as the camera pulls back and switches to increasingly cinematic shots of Lantau, all set to a slowly building soundtrack of a Cantonese remix of "House of the Rising Sun" created by *Parts Unknown* composer Mike Ruffino.

This perspective, which obviously has much to say not only about Hong Kong but also the very nature of documentary film, is preceded by a complex interchange between Bourdain, Doyle, and Suen, which has much to say about Bourdain's perspective on cinema. Bourdain asks Doyle what he describes as a "tricky, moral question": "We are changing the world by looking at it through cameras as happens every time you look at real people, the real world, real places, where does that fall in your comfort zone, as the character of the place changes?" Doyle instantly responds, "That's true, we're part of the problem." Suen interjects, "The only way is just not to be cynical about it. We want the audience to feel a certain way, but if the process is open, then I think it has integrity."

Doyle continues her thought, "If we've done it with love and integrity. If we've tried to be as true as possible to how we see things, perhaps, *perhaps* it transfers."

Almost everything I have discussed about Bourdain's view of cinema is embodied in this single exchange: an emphasis on conflicting perspectives and the nuances between them, a belief that film can never represent reality, doubt that film can spark positive change, and a tentative belief that if film can achieve any type of truth at all, it is an abstract truth that draws attention to the presence and perspective of the filmmaker. It is for these reasons that Bourdain's belief that the purpose of art—to return to Doyle's words immediately after this exchange—is to give a "voice" to the unspoken, a "form that it's never been perceived in before," and "an image to an idea." In short, an embrace of cinema.

What comes next is Bourdain's own demonstration of this approach, in a powerful, cinematic transition between scenes. Precisely as Doyle says the words "give it a form that it's never been perceived in before," Bourdain visually demonstrates Doyle's achievement of this goal by cutting to shots of Lantau and Hong Kong that directly borrow first from *The White Girl* and then *Chungking Express*. The instrumental lead-in to the Cantonese "House of the Rising Sun" remix builds throughout Doyle's quotation but it comes to a crescendo as Doyle finishes, the lyrics begin, and the sound completely fills the soundtrack. The camera instantly cuts to Bourdain, alone, walking out of Lantau through back alleys. These images are exact copies of Wong's first film, *As Tears Go By* (1988), which was partially shot on Lantau, and which represents Wong's filmmaking before his collaboration with Doyle. Much as Ngor, Wong's protagonist in that film, leaves his girlfriend's fish restaurant to return to the city, the episode immediately cuts to Bourdain back in central Hong Kong, only, now, the images are exact copies from *Chungking Express*, one of Wong's most influential films, a film Bourdain has already spoken about in the episode, and one of the films that most embodies the Wong-Doyle collaborative visual style. We see Bourdain enter Chungking Mansions, a sprawling urban mall that features prominently in *Chungking Express*. Bourdain tells us, "The *infamous* Chungking Mansions sit right smack in the center of high-end Tsim Sha Tsu, right around the corner from swank hotels and surrounded by shops selling luxury goods and designer brands. Five housing blocks and seventeen stories containing, well, everything and everybody who the rest of Hong Kong would like to ignore." As Bourdain finishes, the remix stops, and we suddenly hear the loud noises of a shopping mall filled with African and Middle Eastern refugees, as well as their diegetic music, all of which remind the spectator that Bourdain is, by interviewing these refugees, giving voice to people ignored not only by mainstream culture but by Wong-Doyle films.

What Bourdain thus achieves, almost entirely through filmic choices rather than voice-over, is a transition between scenes that is the pure embodiment of his approach to documentary filmmaking. What happens once we get inside Chungking Mansions becomes the culmination of Bourdain's approach rather than a "betrayal" of it. When Bourdain situates us inside and moves to naturalistic sound, he interviews African immigrants who run a restaurant for refugees, and then interviews an Iranian and a Somali refugee over lunch. For most of the sequence Bourdain asks short questions and lets the refugees speak for themselves. We see them in close-ups, we see the space and layout of Chungking Mansions, we hear natural sound, we hear the refugee's voices and stories. Then, suddenly, Bourdain interrupts mid-sentence and says, "Hold on one second, let me re-set." We see Doyle enter the frame and interact with Bourdain and the guests. We see Doyle direct the crew to move the table and rearrange food. We see Doyle, now back behind the camera, making decisions with Argento. Finally, after twenty-five-seconds of behind-the-scenes reality, Bourdain says, "all right, let me know when everybody's up." He pauses, nods, and the episode returns to its previous style as the refugees talk about lack of hope. The sequence gives "voice to the unspoken," lets refugees speak when society typically does not care about their story, but Bourdain has just argued the depiction can only have "integrity" if the spectator is aware it is, in fact, a depiction, that none of this is real, that all of this is being done in front of a camera, a camera Bourdain has just told us always "changes the world." Lest the spectator forget Bourdain's presence, he reasserts not only his presence but also that of countless crew. Similarly, Doyle's presence as cinematographer reminds us Bourdain was not actually alone, was not actually 'leaving' Doyle when we saw him walking out of Lantau; Doyle was filming him the entire time. The filmmaker is always present; he is always the one providing an "image to an idea."

Bourdain's image of a city and culture desperately trying to adapt to global and political realities while retaining a core sense of what makes it unique is a quintessential and omnipresent obsession of Bourdain's (one which I will continue to diagnose and investigate throughout the remainder of this book) but is also heavily influenced by Wong's films. The degree to which "Hong Kong" draws the spectator's attention to the influence Wong has over not just this episode, but Bourdain's worldview, also seems quintessential Bourdain.

Returning to Abbas's identification of the "new Hong Kong cinema," of which Wong was at the forefront, Abbas defines what he calls a "new localism," an approach to preservation of culture in a globalized, late-stage capitalist world. Abbas claims that prior to Wong's generation, the use of Cantonese in Hong Kong cinema represented "the local [as] an ethos of exclusions: it defined a narrow homogenous space where foreigners and foreign elements had no place."[17] With Wong and his generation, however, "New localism . . . investigates the dislocations of the local, where the local is something unstable that mutates right in front of our eyes, like the language itself."[18] As such, a new type of cultural resistance is possible, one that seems to closely match Bourdain's approach across at least *Parts Unknown*. Allen Cameron explains: "Old-fashioned localism fails because of the difficulty of locating authenticity, marginalism because it cedes power to the colonial centre, and cosmopolitanism because it fails to account for difference. Relying upon dislocation, impurity, and hybridity, new localism succeeds where others have failed by exploring the disjunctive zones where the local and global intersect."[19] Therefore, "the skewed perspectives, blurred images, and fractured continuity in Wong's films" become "strategies for critiquing the colonial gaze, which depends upon stability, order and clarity in order to function."[20] Seen in such a light, Bourdain's films, particularly "Hong Kong," are best seen as critiques and subversions of the homogenizing, outside gaze of global capitalism, colonialism, and Western mass media. By interrogating traditional film form and complicating (rather than objectifying) ideas about localness and difference, Bourdain partakes in strategies of new localism.

It is for these reasons Bourdain's camera at once romanticizes what is lost and alters and destabilizes interpretations of those spaces. Bourdain shows us Go's black-and-white, nostalgic images, but then shoots those locations using Wong-Doyle's green filters and digitally pushed red hues, which he shows to be a different type of nostalgia, removed yet again from Bourdain's own perspective. Bourdain employs these strategies because, at heart, his films are about the space between documentation and preservation, and the degree to which the act of filmmaking actively participates in both even as it changes the world it depicts. To quote Emily VanDerWerff, reviewing "Hong Kong" after his death,

> Bourdain was never interested in progress for the sake of progress because he was always curious about what might be lost. A city could become a gleaming edifice, but it might bury what had been truly valuable beneath those buildings. To Bourdain, the city builds from the ground up—the food nourishes the people, who build the city. When the reverse happens, when a powerful few eradicate the spaces those people lived and ate in, in order to build ever-taller, ever more valuable real estate, there's a tragedy inherent to that, in the eyes of Bourdain . . . Bourdain was one of the few people who believed that television could make the world not sleeker and more modern but more human, less cold. Television doesn't have to be a window into other lives. It can be a door, too, held open and inviting.[21]

Thus, I would posit an embrace of new localism invites the outsider to partake and respect what is unique and distinctive about a culture while remaining wholly aware they are not a part of it and that the outside world can pose a threat to it. It is not just that the physical spaces foster and forge the culture. It is, to return to Abbas, about how the relation between the two are depicted; a "history" that "exists" in "jostling anachronisms and spatial juxtapositions that are seen on every street . . . history inscribed in spatial relations."[22] The culture can thus best be expressed through cinema, which captures movement across space, creates visual (and narrative) juxtapositions, documents a moment and space in time that is otherwise already history at the moment of its completion.

Abbas's notion that ever-changing spatial relations define Hong Kong's culture much as cinematic representations of those spatial relations determine the city's cultural memory, is a dominant, recurring theme in Bourdain's episode. Bourdain and Doyle discuss it explicitly in a conversation on the Central-Mid-Levels Escalators, a conversation to which I will return shortly, but we also see this interest within Bourdain's mediation between Doyle's and Go's conflicting ambitions for what they think can be achieved when they film disappearing spaces. Elsewhere, at Happy Paradise Restaurant, Thierry Chow explains feng shui and shows Bourdain how she designed the restaurant around its concepts, explaining "when you're in a restaurant, when you're eating the food, *the space matters*. It changes the way you taste the food." Earlier, Janice Lau and Jason Chung, frontpeople for the punk rock band David Boring, tell Bourdain the way China silences dissent is not by stopping them from saying what they want to say, but, rather, by removing a space in which to say it. "You're actually allowed to play music," they explain, "you're allowed to do whatever you want, but there's no venue, there's no space for you to practice. I think this is how the society is limiting the possibility of young people." Echoing Abbas, Douglas Young tells Bourdain over noodles, "Hong Kong is always going through change, and nothing is precious. If something is old, it's torn down, thrown away, destroyed. That's Hong Kong." What's left, at least for Doyle, Abbas, and Bourdain, is an emphasis on *how* one depicts the culture interacting with those disappearing spaces.

This interest in spatial relations dominates Zero Point Zero cinematography across Bourdain's career, especially "Hong Kong." We see it in Bourdain's assertion that the episode's intent was to "fill the frame with living, breathing people—moving through the busy streets." We see it in the multitude of shots of the people of Hong Kong walking and interacting with the urban environment surrounding them, almost always shot in ways that create physical juxtapositions. We see it in the manner the episode depicts Bourdain riding the ferry, observing the skyline from a perspective only distance provides. We especially see it in his first meeting with Doyle on the hectic and crowded Central-Mid-Levels Escalators.

The camera finds the pair riding the moving walkway just as Bourdain finishes declaring he was "wrong" to "fear" he would never really "see" Hong Kong, implying this chaotic ride through the city center is of special importance. With Bourdain's very first question for Doyle, "What do you look at in Hong Kong?," the camera pulls back to frame the two inside the diagonal beams of the escalator's wall, with buildings behind them. Doyle's response is about both the ever-changing location around them and the films he made in that neighborhood: "We have people coming and going, we have the city passing us by. To me, the energy is the noise. It's the people. The films that we've made are only this way because we made them here . . . It doesn't exist anymore because the energy changes, *but* to tune into the energy. Aha. Hello? Then we have a movie. Then we have this conversation. Then we have something that the cameraman is going to fall over backwards trying to film." As Doyle proclaims that the energy changes, the soundtrack doubles in speed, changing the energy for Bourdain's spectator, and throughout the sequence Doyle and Bourdain are framed and juxtaposed against their physical surroundings. As Doyle references the cameraman, the shot pulls back and reveals a cameraman scrambling to stay ahead of them as they ride the walkway. Thus, the act of filmmaking is foregrounded, as is the way in which cinema makes its meaning by capturing finite moments and spaces in time, and which finds its value by how it connects to the energy created by the people of the city—an energy (and a culture) that is also in a perpetual state of flux.

Much as the episode's depiction of a disappearing Hong Kong relies on juxtapositions between subject and environment, the narrative structure relies on juxtapositions between the disparate viewpoints around which the episode is structured. As VanDerWerff asserts in her review, "What was key to Bourdain's approach was how rarely he inserted his own explanation of what was happening. He, instead, let those he interviewed speak about what they thought."[23] I posit Bourdain's perspective comes via cinematic choices, as well as his use of narrative juxtaposition between the conflicting voices, and the way that editing works to highlight what those voices have to say to, and about, each other. Toward the conclusion of the elevator sequence, Doyle makes a statement that uncannily mirrors—even as it pointedly differs from—the perspective Bourdain expressed in his thesis statement moments prior. Doyle claims, "I think we are just preparing all the time. For example, you've watched some of my movies. Or we read a book. Or we go out drinking with friends. And then Bam. We are doing something which all of those energies focus in a way that somehow connects with other people." Both men feel we are the sum of all we have experienced before, and their goal is to find a way to focus that experience into art, which connects across difference and expresses one's own unique perspective. Turning specifically to his own work and experience, Doyle asserts, "I think everything we did before [*In the Mood for Love*] was preparation. If you find this in your life, you actually say one sentence, or you make one dish, or you make one image that is true. That's pretty good. Because not many people get there." As I said at the onset of this chapter, the same might be said about Bourdain and "Hong Kong."

In the interview on Lantau, Suen asserts, "There is something that I think binds us all together, which is we are trying to reinterpret Hong Kong culture in a way that makes sense to us." Suen is speaking specifically about Doyle and herself, as the duo had recently co-directed *The White Girl*. In a sense, however, Suen highlights the point of the entire episode. Like all cinema, "Hong Kong" comprises a multitude of perspectives, in this case, Bourdain's, Doyle's, Argento's, Go's, Wong's, Suen's, and many more. What binds these perspectives is that each is trying to "reinterpret" Hong Kong in a way that makes sense to their own experience, their own perspective, their own "preparation." They are further bound because Bourdain exposes and juxtaposes these perspectives; what they share, what they differ on, and what is at stake within those differences. Bourdain asserts we can never know Hong Kong, past or present, and, even if we could, what we knew or understood would already have disappeared. The best one can do is try to express, through art, one's own personal truth in a way that connects with the spectator, and which makes clear it is just that, the artist's perspective, not objective truth.

After Bourdain hands Doyle the camera in a boat on Lantau, a camera he would ultimately retain for the remainder of the shoot, Doyle slowly adjusts the aperture and adjusts the lighting, bringing Bourdain's face into focus. Doyle is in no hurry, however. He takes his time. The construction of the ultimate image is part of the art. When Doyle finally achieves what he calls "one of the most beautiful images in all of your films," he asks Bourdain, "Do we have a movie?" Bourdain answers confidently: "We have a movie." Both men laugh happily, and Doyle leans forward and kisses Bourdain right next to the mouth. It serves, I argue, as a metaphor for the entire episode: disparate voices working in tandem to make a movie about the making of movies.

9
MONTANA

In the months preceding the death of Jim Harrison, Bourdain returned to Montana to shoot a *Parts Unknown* episode (S7E4) with the poet, novelist, and gourmand who had previously appeared on *No Reservations* (S5E17) seven years prior. By the time "Montana" aired May 15, 2016, Harrison had been dead for almost two months, sparking a reedit of the conclusion to frame it as a tribute to Bourdain's friend and literary hero. Despite the episode's focus on writing—it opens and ends with Harrison poems—its argument, as well as the larger discourse it enters, is almost entirely visual, and largely filmic. Even when the central influence is ostensibly a literary figure, Bourdain's work has more to say about cinema.

Specifically, the visuals of "Montana" place it in direct conversation with the romantic way the US West has been imagined (and reimagined) from the beginning of US history; a discourse that has always been dominated by visual culture, first paintings, then photography, and thereafter motion pictures. Bourdain's voice-over directly, if briefly, invokes the filmmaker Sam Peckinpah, and the visual representations of a landscape Bourdain calls "one of the most beautiful places on earth," are wholly evocative of how filmmakers like John Ford and Howard Hawks framed similar spaces. Even Harrison's poems become poignant for the way Bourdain juxtaposes physical spaces they evoke against landscapes that could only be created by cinema. Thus, "Montana" becomes about how *visual* images shaped the myths of the US West—myths of rugged individualism, loner-heroes, and limitless possibilities—in ways that impact the people who live in the harsh environment that is the actual West. Most notably, Bourdain invokes the Western genre so he can deconstruct its romantic constructions and reposition the West (both historic and filmic) as inherently social rather than primal, communal rather than rugged individualist, an evolving civilization rather than an empty frontier.

The romantic mythologization of the US West began almost as soon as Europeans began to explore it. By 1893, the year Frederick Jackson Turner declared that the US Census Bureau's 1890 admission that the "frontier" was no longer delineable "marked a closing of a great historic moment,"[1] the reimagination of the West was unfettered by any concrete notion of time and place. As historical interpretation, Turner's thesis, "The existence of an area of free land, its continuous recession, and the advance of American settlement westward, explain American development,"[2] has always been controversial for justifiable reasons. But Turner's influential assertion, right or wrong, that US history has largely been defined by the colonization of the West,[3] almost undeniably serves as a near-perfect means of articulating why US artistic production, particularly visual art, is obsessed with reimagining the frontier.

Painters like Frederick Remington and later Georgia O'Keefe depicted a landscape of unlimited possibility and shaped the way filmic Westerns, *the* dominant genre of the first sixty years of US cinema, approached the same spaces. For instance, John Ford explicitly attributes his approach to framing horizons to nineteenth-century painted art.[4] To quote Bourdain's voice-over from early in "New Mexico" (PU S2E3), "The Western myth has pretty much captured the American imagination. None of us can escape it. For ages, we identified ourselves with the images of the lone cowboy, the perception of frontier values: self-sufficiency, rugged individualism, the freedom of wide-open spaces."

A significant reason that this individualistic version of the Western myth so strongly shaped US identity lies in the combination of this version of the myth having almost a century as the dominant representation and that representation being predominantly visual, and hence widely accessible and pervasive, as "the history of the West has always been closely bound up with the forms of its representation—and misrepresentation,"[5] since its nineteenth-century "invention."[6]

The subsequent, pervasive perspective, which treats every landscape as a metaphor, every person as a loner-hero, lies at the heart of classic iterations of the filmic Western, a genre exemplified by Ford and Hawks, and a genre particularly noted for its visual representations and masterful use of mise-en-scène. Specifically, critics have largely attributed

Ford's greatness as a director to his "gift for visual composition, his ability to use film as an eloquent, often wordless means of expression."[7]

These images are so pervasive as to be inescapable, largely forcing all filmic depictions of the West to invoke similar metaphors even when their purpose is to deconstruct them—such as Sergio Leone's violent spaghetti Westerns, Robert Altman's feminist *McCabe & Mrs. Miller* (1971), Dennis Hopper's anti-establishment *Easy Rider* (1969), or Paul Thomas Anderson's anti-monopoly capitalist *There Will Be Blood* (2007). It is into this metaphor-laden landscape that any filmmaker inevitably steps when they choose to shoot the US West; the images, framing, and mise-en-scène are all too ubiquitous, too ingrained in the American consciousness to be ignored.

Earlier Bourdain episodes partially embrace romantic versions of this cinematic history, but the aforementioned "New Mexico" exemplifies a turn of thought and approach that eventually manifests itself in "Montana." Bourdain's plans for "New Mexico" seem to have been to invoke a romantic view. For example, it opens and ends with overt allusions to the iconic opening and closing scenes of two classic Westerns, George Stevens's *Shane* (1953) and John Ford's *The Searchers* (1956), respectively. Bourdain drives Route 66, replete with its own history of romantic television depictions, and the opening monologue asserts, "Since I was 14 years old, I always wore cowboy boots. Maybe because my little boy role models were always . . . Men with pasts. Men from somewhere else who found themselves in the great American West. A place where reinvention, a new life, was always possible, as long as you were ready to kill for it." After exploring New Mexico, however, Bourdain's tone markedly shifts. Late in the episode, he asserts, "I didn't know this show was about this, but I've been thinking about it a lot: this sort of cowboys, Mexicans, Indian, romantic ideal. A lot of Easterners came out here and fell in love with this romantic notion of the West. Was that a good thing?" Elsewhere, he posits these landscapes as "where the myth of the American West took root, where so much romantic lore began, history was being re-written almost as soon as it happened. This was never the Big Empty. As Dan Flores writes, 'the idea of a wilderness is itself a cultural construct.'" Much as Werner Herzog sees nature as a human construct that reveals more about the culture(s) that imagine it, Bourdain thus draws attention to how the concept of the US West is a construct with roots which predate cinema, even as cinema has come, in turn, to dominate that culture's articulation of that construction.

Having drawn his spectator's attention to the way film constructs how we see and imagine landscape as metaphor, Bourdain ends "New Mexico" by embracing metaphor to revise it. Bourdain claims, "the expression of American power and identity has always been the lone cowboy with a gun," but he contrasts that construction of identity with an alternative reading: "If you are an Easterner and you come out to New Mexico you start to see metaphors in everything. But actually, if you were to stretch a little bit you could say New Mexico is a *perfect* metaphor for America. It is a total mutation. It's got Spanish, Mexican, original American, and add a tinge of radioactivity." A metaphor of a diverse society, not a loner-hero. Where the (primarily Eastern) US construction of the US West emphasizes a loner-hero, removed from capitalist ambitions or connection to society, finding meaning for his own life via rugged, individualistic existence, Bourdain depicts a diverse collective working together to become the complex culture that embodies the values often imagined as existing only in the East. Such a shifting of the story the Western genre wants to tell, that of rugged individualism and idealism justifying Manifest Destiny over an untamed frontier, to a story about community, colonization, and the merging of diverse cultures, is the driving, unifying lens behind *Parts Unknown* "Montana."

"Montana" opens and ends not just with Harrison's Western poetry, but also images of Bourdain driving the author in a pickup truck as they explore the wide-open spaces near Livingston and Yellowstone. In both sequences, as well as many moments between, the camera romantically frames natural beauty and wide-open spaces in a manner evocative of Ford and Hawks. Bourdain and Harrison's conversations similarly emphasize the vast landscape. At episode's end, as a coyote runs away from the pair, Harrison claims, "You never feel hemmed in, in any direction you could go for miles and miles," the camera cutting to a longshot emphasizing such possibility. The episode's opening similarly emphasizes space and possibility as Bourdain proclaims, "Some people must live in great spaces. Where the sky goes on forever. Where *every*one must bend to the land." Upon close examination, however, this is a deviation from traditional descriptions; Bourdain's emphasis on "*every*one" frames this space as a great equalizer where people are connected to each other and the earth via shared experience, not an individualistic space outside of society's bounds.

This point is further emphasized when Harrison's diegetic comments interrupt Bourdain's narration. Harrison points to the horizon and indicates where the Cheyenne and Crow fought a great battle, reminding us there were civilizations on this landscape long before Europeans, as well as telling Bourdain the landscape has not changed much in the past two centuries. Such a repositioning of the West as social and communal informs Bourdain's subsequent visit with members of the Absaroka (Crow) nation, his depictions of cordial disagreements between landowners and hunters about land use, and the ecological destruction and political unionization embodied by Butte.

Bourdain's Montana has existed much longer than historic renderings of it, and it has always been a place filled by diverse people with conflicting perspectives representing a multitude of cultures. The present culture is no different from past iterations; it is influenced by, and comprises, influences from all people. When Bourdain concludes his introduction to Harrison by declaring the vast landscape on-screen "his home," he subtly articulates his view of the West: a shared space for diverse people to establish roots, not a space to wander and conquer.

The poems Harrison reads similarly deconstruct traditional depictions of the physical West. The common theme across the poems Bourdain chooses, and the ordering he gives them, is the way they use landscapes or other physical bodies as metaphor for the finite nature of life. This theme renders the individual similarly finite against time and vast landscapes, rather than empowered by an imagination of a limitless future and infinite possibilities. As Harrison reads in the opening sequence, "Am I as old as they am?,"[8] the camera connects Harrison's questions to a filmic image of the ancient mountains. Harrison continues: "Maybe not. Time is a mystery / that could tip us upside down. / Yesterday I was seven in the woods . . . sixty-eight / years later I could still inhabit that boy's / body without thinking of the time in between. / It is the burden of life to be many ages / without seeing the end of time."[9] In another poem, time "sinks" away "to the deepest part / of the Ocean, the Mariana trench,"[10] and, upon finishing that reading, Harrison looks at Bourdain and says "I get a little tentative when I hear" there are "90 billion galaxies in the universe." In his final reading, lightning illuminates the valley below the speaker and reminds him "of a battle from two / hundred years ago when the Cheyenne / from the east attacked the Absaroka / in this valley."[11] Harrison's poem explains the Cheyenne warriors were painted as "the wolves of heaven." As the credits begin to roll, the camera shuffles through intense close-ups of beautiful nature, Harrison claiming he, too, "want[s] to be a yellow wolf of heaven" and "disappear into the lightning."[12] Harrison's speaker is inextricably connected to cultures across centuries and is limited by the nature in which he wants to disappear. Similarly, Bourdain's camera concludes on intense close-ups of Yellowstone rather than John Ford's infinite vistas; both are beautiful, but Bourdain's (and Harrison's) landscape is one that puts humans in their place rather than emboldening them.

Framed at both ends by this inverted depiction of the West, what lies between is an exploration of the community of Montana—a community that serves as metaphor for an alternative imagination of US identity precisely because it is diverse, interconnected, and defined by a history driven by capitalism rather than idealism—or, if it *is* defined by idealism, a real-world idealism that cannot be magically divorced from real-world realities like capitalism.

As Bourdain leaves Harrison in the opening, the images continue to mirror classic Westerns, but Bourdain's voice-over begins a subtle repositioning. Appearing in the year of the 2016 US presidential election and Donald Trump's "Make America Great Again" campaign, Bourdain's answer to political division and imaginations of national failure is to invert US national identity as inherently social, using the same landscapes where Trump's individualistic egocentrism finds its intellectual roots to embody his counterargument. In Bourdain's words:

> Next time you turn off a news cycle filled with shouting bobbleheads, convinced that America is devolving into a moronic inferno, questioning the greatness of your nation, maybe you should come here. Here are your purple mountains majesty. *This* is the landscape that generations of dreamers, despots, adventurers, explorers, crackpots, and heroes, fought and died for. It's one of the most beautiful places on earth. There is *no* place like it. Montana. Many have come to claim their piece over the years, but before the prospectors and explorers, there were the Plains Indians.

Bourdain immediately delves into a lengthy, detailed, and sympathetic history of the Absaroka, emphasizing the length of their history with the land long before Europeans arrived, as well as the complex interplay between their culture and other Indigenous societies. Bourdain thus posits Montana's greatness is defined by a beautiful landscape that has been the home to interconnected cultures and conflicting aims for centuries. The landscape is indeed a metaphor for US identity, but a very different metaphor (and identity) from traditional depictions.

Transitioning from eating Indigenous dishes with an Absaroka family on their own land to arriving by helicopter at Bill Gault's 100,000-acre ranch to fish for trout cannot help but shape how one is supposed to react to Bourdain's rhetorical questions, "Who *owns* this land? Can *any*one really own it? Who gets to use it? These are *big* questions that cut across traditional ideological lines out here." Bourdain frames an argument between Gault and a friend about the 1984 Stream Access Law, which declares riverbeds public access even if located on private property, as the inverse of 2016 political divisions, asking, "They disagree on land use, a major issue, remember when you could do that and still be friends?" Part of a community that must remain amicable even as they debate, Bourdain also uses these men to demonstrate the tensions between individualism and collectivism present from Montana's earliest incarnations.

Later, when Bourdain goes hunting with Joe Rogan and *Field and Stream*'s Hal Herring, he returns to this theme, informing us "one-third of Montana is public land." Bourdain's defense of what he calls a "socialist idea" is yet again linked to national identity defined by Western landscapes, claiming, "Have you ever been out on an open body of water where you're just surrounded by the ocean, or the desert, or here actually for that matter? You do begin to understand your place in the universe, meaning, at the end of the day, I'm not that different from that pheasant I shot today." Shortly thereafter, Herring adds, "We're all in it together. The elk, and me, and the wolves. What we do to the world we do to ourselves." In other words, a social connection defined by nature, the land, and innate responsibility to the people, animals, and environment that surround one's home.

This is a perspective more closely linked to the visual allusions to Robert Redford's *A River Runs Through It* (1992), itself a film about timelessness and connectivity, which dominate the sequence on Gault's ranch, than to the allusions to Ford and Hawks that begin the episode. On Gault's ranch, as in Redford's film, the camera stays close and bright, romanticizing interaction with nature, as humans fly-fish in seeming harmony with their environment. When Bourdain returns to Ford-Hawks imagery while discussing social obligations with Herring, he thus repositions that imagery.

Bourdain's invocation of the strain between capitalist ambition and social obligation is not accidental, and it re-invokes themes present not only in the nineteenth-century West, but also in foundational Westerns, even if the cultural perception of the genre tends to overlook them. For instance, the protagonist of Hawks's *Red River* (1948), Tom Dunson (John Wayne), is a venture capitalist who heads West and takes a large spread of land by force to start a large-scale cattle operation. The justification he gives for grabbing all of Don Diego's land north of the Red River is that Diego "took it away from whoever was here before, Indians maybe" and four hundred miles is "too much land for one man. Why, it ain't decent. He has all this land aching to be used and never has been." The film's climax is a fistfight between Dunson and his adopted son, whom Dunson has threatened to kill, but instead of resolution by victory or defeat, the fight is resolved when a woman points out the love they have for each other, and the older man agrees to share his business. Similarly, Ford's *Stagecoach* (1939), depicts a group of disparate strangers working together to survive a journey. As Gaylyn Studlar and Matthew Bernstein claim, "Returning to the film now, one is struck less by its classism than by its disturbing darkness, visually and thematically, and its 'Popular Front' resonance with the class and social issues raised by the Great Depression. In this respect, Ford's *The Grapes of Wrath* and a Western such as *Stagecoach* are linked by their championing of the common citizen who is 'under attack.'"[13]

It is therefore not so much that classic 1950s and '60s Westerns are unaware of the West's colonial history, nor that they actively promote unrestrained capitalism, but as they struggled to project romantic imaginations of rugged, transcendent individualism among wide-open spaces, the genre had to create a false separation between communal spaces and individualistic ones and reposition capitalist ambitions within those spaces. As Peter Lehman claims of Ford:

> I contend that it is only by repressing the role of money, trading, and capitalism in the West that Ford can represent his ideal communities and families . . . Ford's ideal families figuratively wash their hands of money, leaving it to those who threaten the very cohesion of the family and the community. Ford's Westerns do not represent the evils of capitalism; instead, they represent evil capitalists living at the margins of families, military units, and communities that are tied to the land in ways that do not seem to be economic.[14]

This attempt to imagine landownership and enforcement of colonization as unrelated to economics required not only a denial of history, but a repudiation of US identity as communal; wherein the West is viewed wholly in juxtaposition to the very society and culture it is supposed to represent. In the words of John Baxter, writing about Ford's *Fort Apache* (1948) and *She Wore a Yellow Ribbon* (1949), "The shadows of encroaching urban values," are "suggested . . . by the corked 'sutlers' whose capitalism destroys the balance of power of which the cavalry depends."[15] Pointing to *Stagecoach*, Baxter continues, "The 'town' characters are associated throughout with self-seeking and a lack of community spirit, to Ford twin aspects of Capitalism."[16] It is to this forced separation between urban and rural, and the inherent shifting of capitalist aims away from the individualistic loners and onto American communities, that Bourdain responds.

While I have explored the way the entire episode argues Montana is defined as a social space, nowhere is this more readily apparent than in its depiction of Butte, a fourteen-minute sequence that takes up a full third of the run time and serves as the episode's philosophic heart. Bourdain depicts Butte as founded for wholly capitalist ambitions that have negatively impacted both the environment and culture. However, Bourdain also depicts Butte as a culture that has survived (and thrived) because the unrestrained capitalist aims of its founders have been tempered by the socialist tendencies of its inhabitants. He depicts Butte as ethnically and culturally diverse, an example of the other dominant US myth, that of the immigrant, and he depicts that diversity as the city's strength. Most importantly, he posits that all of this stands not in stark contrast against the rest of Montana, but, rather, in tandem with it, much as he thinks Montana embodies US identity at large.

The camera frames Butte's decaying cityscape and industrial wastelands the same way it frames the mountains and vistas; for Bourdain, they are just as beautiful and contain no less metaphor. Aaron Parrett, a literature professor and Bourdain's first Butte guest, proclaims the city "the essence of Montana" and that he thinks of it "the way Europeans Romanticize those ruins in Greece or Rome. Butte is America's Acropolis." Bourdain responds, "Like in Detroit or Buffalo or Cleveland, you can see the aspirations of the builders, or the people who they were building for." This town, Bourdain asserts, is what "built, well America. That helped power the country, defend it against Germany and Japan. Without this hill, well, no electricity." Essentially, Butte's relevance to national identity matches Ford's patriotic vision, but it is a relevance born of community not isolation. As such, the episode shares more in common with "Detroit" (PU S2E8) and "Pittsburgh" (PU S10E4) than with "US Southwest" (NR S4E15) or "Far West Texas" (PU S12E5).

Bourdain's depiction of Butte as representative of Montana, rather than juxtaposed against it, is reinforced by his cinematography and mise-en-scène. The sequence's first shot is an extreme close-up of nature, specifically a leaf, situating the spectator comfortably within the natural spaces they have already assimilated. Next comes a slow fade into a longshot of a portion of a Butte mine, and then to a series of industrial shots—all of which are also long shots that match the Ford-Hawks framing approach. Bourdain's voice-over assists with repositioning these images, "At first look you'd think this is the worst place on earth. A ravaged, toxic, God-forsaken hill threatened from above, riddled with darkness below. But you'd be wrong . . . It is, in fact, heartbreakingly, poignantly beautiful. The gallows frames seem eyesores for only a second before it becomes clear why they are points of fierce pride for locals for whom they signify and commemorate everything."

This invocation of metaphor out of urban decay is reinforced when Bourdain turns his attention to the Berkeley Pit, a mirror-black, toxic lake filled with thirty million gallons of water and toxic waste. The camera slowly pans across it in longshot, rendering it, without context, one of the most beautiful, classic Western shots of the entire episode; it quite literally looks like it comes straight from a foundational Western. Again,

Bourdain's voice-over asks the spectator to seek metaphor, as Bourdain describes, "a monument to greed and heedless exploitation of the earth and something eerily yet tragically beautiful." Asking Parrett if it sparks "a weird, perverse pride" for locals, the scholar responds, "you've nailed it. Obviously, The Pit is an enduring emblem of that rapacious, capitalist greed. But you also have people here that are proud of where they live." Thus, by the time Bourdain's audio turns to the only Harrison-read poem visually separated from the poet, and pairs that poem with nostalgic home videos of 1950s Butte shot in the same style as home videos of Harrison's childhood shown previously, the rural-urban opposition is diffused; the two share more similarities than differences.

Having emphasized the idea of an urban-rural divide as socially constructed, Bourdain deconstructs portrayals of the US West as culturally homogeneous. While classic Westerns depict predominantly Caucasian loner-hero cowboys and townspeople existing in stark contrast to Native Americans and Mexicans, the historic West was diverse, not only via the cultural impact of Indigenous and Hispanic cultures, but also in the makeup of its colonizers. Specifically, approximately one-quarter of the workers in the range cattle industry between 1860 and 1880 were Black,[17] Asian immigrants composed a significant percentage of the workforce,[18] and white populations largely consisted of immigrants

Butte's Berkeley Pit shot John Ford style. Rather than emphasizing urban decay, Bourdain leans on classic Westerns to reposition our perspective of the US West.

themselves originating from the colonized cultures of the British Isles and Central and Eastern Europe. Bourdain highlights Butte as "very ethnically diverse," asserting "people came from all over the World to make their fortunes here, or simply for steady work, a better life," as he and Parrett refer to Cornish, Welsh, Croatians, and Serbs. Butte is, in Parrett's words, "a micro-version of New York City." The duo eats at a supper club, a type of restaurant born in Meaderville, an Italian American neighborhood flooded and destroyed to make room for the Berkeley Pit. While eating, the duo discusses how the combination of food could only have originated via the specific types of diversity intersecting in Butte. Aside from cultural and ethnic diversity, Bourdain's final interview of the sequence, State Senator Jim Keane, asserts, "[mining is] intensive. I mean you need engineers; you need guys running ventilation, mechanic, or a carpenter, or a pipe fitter. It's just such a diverse asset to have all these different types of people, that's what was good about it . . . The community worked to support the people."

Bourdain's articulation of the West as a diverse community defined by tensions between capitalist aims and the needs of the community those aims claim to serve is invoked in Bourdain's conversation over beer with the owner of the Silver Dollar Saloon, Brian McGregor, and former State Representative Amanda Curtis, both Butte natives. Bourdain introduces the bar with close-ups of wall stickers advertising organized labor, which Bourdain's voice-over illuminates: "As you might have gathered by now this is a working-class town and unusual in that it is a union town. A proudly union town, in an otherwise *very* red state." Discussing labor history and working conditions in pre-union mines, Bourdain counters, "That was then, this is now. This is the era of 'I've got mine Jack,'" to which Curtis interjects, "That's what makes Butte different. It's *not* I've got mine . . . We've grown this community out of taking care of each other," echoing Keane's image of a community working to support people.

Despite the way this conversation draws contrasts against Montana's (and the US') contemporary political landscape, Bourdain continues to demonstrate the ways Butte, and the West in general, serve as a metaphor for US historical identity. First, McGregor asserts, "Butte is the most interesting, important town in America that nobody knows about." Then, Curtis adds, "We call ourselves Butte, America. When you got off the boat in Ellis Island it said 'Butte' pinned to your shirt. And it wasn't 'Butte, Montana,' it was 'Butte, America.' We were founded by European immigrants who came from socialist countries with all these crazy socialist ideas." In short, it is *because* of the ever-present tension between capitalist and social aims, as well as the melting pot of diverse cultures, that Montana serves as a metaphor for US identity.

Such tensions between the individual and their community have been present from the start of US history and were the driving force behind Western expansion. No matter how hard filmic Westerns work to alleviate said tensions by creating contrasts between those "who wash their hands of money" and "evil capitalists living at the margins," the reality is both aims were present, simultaneously, in almost every family, almost every community. To justify a romantic metaphor, filmic Westerns framed these disparate aims as oppositional, despite the history of the US West largely having been defined by the constant negotiation of—and resolution between—those aims. Further, no matter the ability of filmic Westerns to reinforce an imagination of loner-heroes freely riding across the prairie unrestrained by social obligation, the reality is that was always an image, no one can remain in perpetual motion, the loner-hero always had to return to one of the communities that enabled him. Further, time spent alone in nature, away from support of the community, was largely dangerous and difficult, not transcendent and redemptive. What is so bold about Bourdain's "Montana" is that it directly invokes those visual images—images so powerful that Bourdain claims "none of us can escape" them—to reposition the spectator's understanding of the US West through his own lens.

Sitting in a union bar he tells us is located where Butte's Chinatown once lay, Bourdain listens as Curtis asserts, "we serve as the example of what happens if you allow *unfettered* capitalism." Bourdain's response invokes patriotism to shift its meaning, yet again, in an alternative direction: "I feel I'm a patriot, but if you are taking jobs away from America to export them overseas, you're not." Unrestrained capitalism that does not serve the community that enables it does not, for Bourdain, represent US history or identity any more than the lone cowboy can serve as a metaphor for American aspirations.

The Butte sequence ends when a miner tells Bourdain what he loves about the profession is "you meet some of the most interesting people."

In an example of free indirect subjectivity, Bourdain rotates between highly stylized shots of diverse individuals staring directly at the camera: individuals we mostly have otherwise not seen, with different backgrounds, different modes of dress, different ambitions, but all part of the same collective, seeking the same result in the mines. Similarly, at episode's end, while Harrison reads his final poem, Bourdain's camera yet again invokes the landscapes of Ford and Hawks only to abandon them, as the final frames return first to Harrison's face and then to Harrison sitting on a bench amid the landscape. What matters to Bourdain, at every turn, are the diverse people who compose the community of Montana, and his depiction of that community employs a visual representation which alters the dominant discourse about the US West.

10
ROME

Late in his final "Rome" episode (PU S8E9), Bourdain sits in a hyper-local restaurant whose name he refuses to disclose and asks his lunch guest, the Roman filmmaker and actress Asia Argento, "Is it possible to look at Rome in a non-cinematic way? I mean, it's a city that kind of demands it." While I will return to Argento's answer later in this chapter, this question haunts the episode, framing Bourdain's depiction of the city at most every turn. Bourdain depicts an extraordinary Roman culture existing at the margins, filled with ordinary people with everyday concerns, surviving in counterpoint to (and in spite of) the imagined, filmic Rome and the tourist culture drawn to it. Moreover, Bourdain is aware his Rome is *also* an image, albeit an image that emphasizes how all depictions of Rome are constructions used for disparate aims, such as the relationship between fascism and film, architecture, and photography discussed throughout the episode.

Rome is the most Western of cities, the place that first comes to mind when one thinks of colonial empire. Meanwhile, because of the long and influential history of Italian cinema, it is also among the most filmed cities in the world. This duality renders it both the embodiment of the Western gaze and one of the most common subjects of it. It is therefore not without irony that Bourdain uses this city as the source for one of his most comprehensive and nuanced deconstructions of the filmic gaze, a deconstruction that provides a lens for understanding how Bourdain similarly deconstructs the Western gaze when depicting non-Western cultures. Notably, Bourdain uses cinematic approaches, particularly ones that draw upon the work of Pier Paolo Pasolini, as a means of achieving said deconstruction, much as Bourdain typically uses cinema to draw the spectator's attention to the space between subjective truth and objective fact.

The evolution of gaze theory toward an awareness of the spectator's participation in a Western gaze is pervasive within discourse about travel and food television, the primary genres Bourdain's filmmaking inverts. In prototypical travel TV the binaries of West and East are reinforced as Western adventurers travel to places in Asia and Africa, places the Western screen surrogate and the Western spectator both imagine "as more 'authentic' and 'exotic.'"[1] Whereas, as we have seen in "Jamaica" (PU S4E8), "Polynesia" (NR S3E10), and beyond, Bourdain deconstructs notions of authenticity and exoticism, in *normative* travel TV, "the 'Western' Self who travels to such places, puts into motion a colonizing mission to search for new and exotic places with which to enrich, or reinvigorate his/herself."[2]

Much as Bourdain argued that popular imaginations of paradise pose a threat to local cultures (and people), the result of a genre centered on the needs of the spectator rather than the needs of the subject results not only in the objectification of the culture but, eventually, its consummation. As Lori Kido Lopez argues, travel TV "inspires its viewers to be good consumers on many fronts—they desire the food, the locale, the culture, the adventure, to be theirs, and if they want it, they just have to pay for it. But as these shows move from the glitz and glamour of New York or Miami Beach into underdeveloped countries . . . ethical dilemmas begin to arise."[3]

Bourdain's "Rome" explores how such approaches are destructive at all levels, how "ethical dilemmas" are already present even in the most Western of cities. While the stakes may be even higher when one depicts an underdeveloped country, a similar ontological threat is posed to local cultures and local populations whenever they are objectified by a curious, controlling, filmic gaze.

The notion Rome might "demand" to be imagined cinematically should come as no surprise given the scale of its architecture, history, urban planning, and the weight of its diverse and iconic film history; even Bourdain used his first "Rome" episode (NR S6E20) six years earlier as a chance to shoot in black and white as homage to the visual images that shaped his imagination of the city, particularly Federico Fellini's *La Dolce Vita* (1960). What makes Bourdain's deconstruction of *that* Rome so compelling—and so quintessentially Bourdain—is that Bourdain's effort to "look at Rome in a non-cinematic" way is *also* formulated entirely through cinema.

Bourdain shot the *Parts Unknown* episode that aired December 4, 2016, on an Arri Alexa digital camera with anamorphic lens. As Bourdain wrote in an editorial for CNN, this was his first "episode [shot] entirely in widescreen, letterbox anamorphic format—like so many of the movies we admire," something he called "a mammoth undertaking" that "networks don't like" because of the added costs and distribution issues in markets where televisions are still square.[4] Bourdain's approach required additional equipment, including enhanced lighting for every scene, as well as a sizable Italian crew and an entire original score to provide, in Bourdain's words, "music adequate to the scale of the subject."[5] "Rome" also references films and filmmakers at most every turn, ranging from Bernardo Bertolucci's *The Conformist* (1970), which dictates the episode's color palette and some of its locations, to direct visual quotations from the films of Dario Argento, Asia Argento, and Abel Ferrara, the latter two of whom appear on-screen in person. Most notably, Bourdain uses Pasolini's *Mamma Roma* (1962) as a framing device, directly invoking it in his narration and borrowing key elements of its approach to cinematography and editing, as well as its philosophic approach to depicting the plight of Romans amid modernity.

Pasolini's early films, *Accattone* (1961), *Mamma Roma*, and *Uccellacci e uccellini* (1964) in particular, depict post–World War II, post-fascist Rome, and focus wholly on working-class citizens displaced by urban planning that left them on the city's periphery, struggling to survive. Pasolini's approach begins at the level of location and subject. Choosing to primarily shoot Rome's extensive urban wastelands, locally referred to as the "*disabitato*," Pasolini "draws viewers into increasingly liminal states, physically as well as psychologically bewildering. From vacant lots and half-built overpasses to shantytowns and collapsing farmhouses, commonly recognizable monuments almost never enter the screen. Confirmation of location by reference to the city center is consistently and carefully denied."[6] Instead, Pasolini shoots the architecture of the suburbs—architecture built to diminish the role of the individual much as his films argue Rome's embrace of an image of itself as a space of consumption fails to serve its inhabitants.

Bourdain limits himself to the same cityscapes, the same type of subjects. In Bourdain's words, "there was one important constraint: we would shoot NO classical Rome. The entire episode would feature ONLY the architecture of Mussolini and post-Mussolini era Rome: brutalist, futurist, and rationalist structures, mid-century housing blocks, suburbs, the decidedly downscale and not particularly romantic seaside community of Ostia."[7]

These self-imposed limitations are far from the most important connections between the two filmmakers, however. The more important similarities are *how* they depict these people—similarities that have far-reaching implications about the rise of the modern city, film, and the relationship between the two.

Pasolini's early films draw upon a history of Italian neorealism in a manner that inverts neorealist aims via a process similar to the "poetic realism" articulated by Vilmos Zsigmond, emphasized in "Budapest" (PU S5E6), and discussed in chapter 2. Specifically, Pasolini's shooting style in *Mamma Roma* "expresses a profound skepticism toward the project of architectural neorealism and this skepticism toward Rome's built environment attaches itself to and is consonant with the film's corrosive take on cinematic neorealism, whose legacy is everywhere alluded to in the film, from its title to its casting decisions."[8] Pasolini thus treats filmic neorealism, postwar architecture, and modernist urban planning as part and parcel, exposing all three as destructive to the individual. Even as Pasolini depicts a bleak environment, he uses it as a metaphor rather than as deterministically as a neorealist would.

Pasolini's use of another film movement's cinematic language to invert its intentions manifests itself in a type of painterly cinematography that, much like Bourdain's, uses framing to create metaphor via the positioning of the individual in relation to their environment in an expansive (rather than deterministic) manner. As Manuela Mariana and Patrick Barron argue, Pasolini thereby "create[s] 'a mannerist re-composition of reality.'"[9] As specific example, they point to Pasolini's framing of shots in *Uccellacci e uccellini*, which "almost always includes elements of the scattered city, from lone houses and medieval towers to cheap apartment buildings and worn-out roads—underlining, as many renaissance paintings do, the connections between landscape, its inhabitants, and their spiritual and moral beliefs (or lack thereof)."[10] As such, Pasolini's strength is not technical, defined by elaborate camera movements, but rather his "masterful, pictorial framing of characters combined with their environments" typically shot "at the level of the human eye."[11] Pasolini's films therefore do not represent the trauma of an individual at the hands of their environment, but, rather, a collective trauma of a community, even an entire city, represented by that individual. Put another way, Mamma Roma's grief is that of Rome's.[12]

The Rome Pasolini responds to (and which interests Bourdain) is a Rome built in two waves, the first under Mussolini's fascist regime, and the second in the postwar building boom that continued Mussolini's plans to reimagine Rome's center as it lured citizens to the periphery under the guise of affordable housing. Thus, the architecture and urban planning worked in tandem to relegate Rome's inhabitants to the margins to create a central *image* of a Rome that could be packaged and sold for business and tourist aims. Mussolini "was not merely isolating monuments so that they could gain visibility; he was displacing and, thus, isolating lower-class people as to render them invisible from inside the city center and controllable in their new homes outside it."[13] Instead of the environment shaping the individual as in neorealism, responsibility is thereby placed on the people who made the decisions to create that environment, an environment which was constructed as image and ripe for the filmic depictions that led to Rome becoming a "cinematic city."

Much as Pasolini places responsibility upon the people who chose to create the environment, one can evaluate the culpability of filmmakers who decide how to depict the city, as well as film critics who evaluate those depictions outside of their historical context. To quote John David Rhodes, in his book about Pasolini and Rome, *Stupendous Miserable City*,

> Much of [Henri] Lefebvre's writing on cities . . . is motivated out of his distress over the fact that cities have been almost wholly converted into arenas of consumption, theaters in which the serial tragedy of sheer exchange value is played out day after day. This state of affairs occurs as historic centers of many cities (particularly European) become exclusively the homes of the rich, open to other classes only as sites used for the consumption of commodities, whether these be cultural, comestible, or otherwise. The city center itself, once divested of any meaningful relationship to its actual inhabitants, comes to exist as nothing more than a product, ready and waiting to be consumed. Studies of the city 'in film' that

> are not responsible to the historical and material specificities of actual cities may run the risk of treating the city as nothing more than an evocative visual commodity.[14]

In my opinion, the last part of this quotation, which focuses on filmic depictions that assist in this consumption and critical studies of film that do the same by glossing over the specific, historical context of the respective cities the films represent, also applies to the genres of food and travel television that solely "inspire . . . viewers to be good consumers."

These imaginations of a city (Rome) and genres (travel and food TV) designed to propel a consuming spectator are those which Bourdain works against. While Bourdain called this episode "a very beautiful show. The most beautiful we've ever made, I think,"[15] the beauty he depicts, as with Pasolini, exists solely in Rome's periphery. More to the point, the *way* he depicts it, again drawing upon Pasolini, universalizes modern trauma through the metaphor of these specific people in this specific place.

Two different scenes, one the first of the episode and the other appearing near its middle, exist, without explanation, entirely outside the diegesis, and exemplify that approach. The scenes depict street performers at a local market. Bourdain's images are all "beautiful," emphasizing color and scope, particularly the singer's red hair and close-ups of artichokes—a vegetable that is in season and which Bourdain consumes throughout the episode. But the content of the songs works against any romantic, tourist image. Both songs are examples of *stornelli*, a musical genre specific to Rome that follows a sonnet-like structure but emphasizes insults and profanity and often makes light of death and murder.[16] Meanwhile, Bourdain's camera cuts between shots of the singer and shoppers. As with Pasolini, all these shots are "at the level of the human eye," as Bourdain depicts every day, local Romans at the market looking, at times, displaced, confused, bewildered. And then, in both scenes, the camera lingers several seconds too long, the performers staring back at the camera having already finished their performance—in one of the scenes the guitar player even strikes a match and lights a cigarette. We are left with a depiction of a hyper-local tradition performed at a market filled with local Romans, none of whom match any kind of filmic whole, other than the performers and the artichokes, both of which the episode draws attention to the construction and performativity therein, in the

Having finished their performance of a *stornello*, Roman street performers awkwardly freeze in place, breaking the fourth wall as the camera lingers "too long." The guitar player reaches into his pocket for a match to light his cigarette.

case of the singers with the lingering camera, and in the case of the produce Bourdain's perpetual eating artichokes in every set-dinner sequence in the episode. It is also worth noting that *Mamma Roma* opens with *stornelli* sung at a wedding and its title character sells produce for a living.

This destabilization of traditional narrative structure to highlight the construction of global, filmic Rome existing in opposition to an equally constructed, but marginalized, local culture is reminiscent of my discussion of Ackbar Abbas's "new localism" in chapter 8, an idea which presents itself throughout "Rome" and is best exemplified in the scene at L'angolo Amici, an off-the-beaten-path bar near Ostia's beachfront. On its surface it may seem a forgettable sequence precisely because of its lack of narrative structure, but this overlooks the ways it is emblematic of Bourdain's approach, and *Mamma Roma*'s as well.

The long sequence, which clocks in at over seven minutes, unapologetically depicts a Rome so local as to bewilder and confuse its host and spectator alike, augmented by a filmic approach that emphasizes rather than diminishes the untranslatable space between subject and depiction. One of the longest images of the beautiful, naturalistic beachfront is out of focus and partially blocked by caution tape in the foreground; the conversation in the bar is shot at eye level with such intentionality as to become awkward; the soundtrack for the establishing shots is Italian pop that is loud, off-putting, and indecipherable to the American viewer.

Bourdain introduces Ostia by reinforcing the spectator's awareness of urban planning's construction of an image, as well as its links to fascism. The sequence opens with what appear to be nature shots but, as the camera cuts closer, reveals flowers along a relatively ugly highway—a highway Bourdain declares "Italy's most dangerous road," built by Mussolini in a failed attempt to reimagine Ostia as Rome's "front door." Not only do Bourdain's camera and narrative emphasize this failure in the ugly, postwar, "decidedly working-class" beach town, but they point to a monument marking the site of Pasolini's murder, which Bourdain tells us may have been committed by fascists. In short, Ostia is a forgotten town with a marginalized population that represents just one of many attempts to reimagine Rome for alternative aims.

The dialogue throughout the sequence revolves around Bourdain trying to mediate an understanding of "local" Rome, but his attempts pointedly fail at every stage. Sitting on a patio with his friend and translator, Sara Pampaloni, whom we are told has also never been to L'angolo Amici, surrounded by a dozen bar regulars, Bourdain asks what a "typical" set of daily meals consists of. Realizing the question is too complicated for translation in this large group, he simplifies his question to what constitutes a typical Roman breakfast. One man confidently begins to explain it is an assortment of salami, a woman from another table talking over him to explain this is called "an Italian starter," all before a man at a third table yells over them both asserting the original man is from Sardinia, and that his suggestion is not a Roman breakfast at all. As the third man begins to explain what *he* thinks a Roman breakfast is, the woman who had just spoken begins to explain how she would like to have salami for breakfast, but cannot for health reasons, only to have a fourth man, unable to discern between her desires and intentions, start screaming at her, "What are you talking about? In your health condition? You have diabetes! So, you must not eat those things . . . You're talking bullshit!"

Through it all, Pampaloni struggles to keep up with translating the overlapping conversations to Bourdain, who sits with a clearly lost look on his face—a sense of confusion visible at multiple moments in the sequence as the regulars scream over one another and interrupt each other as they struggle to answer his questions. Meanwhile, the rapid written translation on the screen draws the spectator's attention to the fact (a) more is being said than could possibly be placed on the screen in type, (b) the type on the screen is far more than Pampaloni can understand in real time, and (c) what she understands is yet again far more than what she can translate to Bourdain. Rather than host as mediator, the sequence emphasizes Bourdain's inability to mediate, focusing, instead, on what is lost in translation. This communicative lack is further underscored when a fifth man, trying to simplify the discussion and end debate, simply jokes Ostia's culinary specialty is "grilled rats," deconstructing any romantic imagination of the "exotic" or "authentic," altogether.

The sequence at L'angolo Amici not only calls attention to the way the "local" is untranslatable to the outsider, in this case host and spectator, but also the way the very notion of "local" is, itself, a construction—even more so as the regulars are asked to perform that construction for television. One example is a moment when a local boxer invokes the cameras. The exchange begins as the boxer declares in Italian, "Ostia is a beautiful town." Pampaloni gestures at Bourdain and tells the boxer, in English, "Talk to *him*," before adding in Italian, "Who are you talking to?" The boxer points at a cameraman and replies in Italian "to him." Pampaloni gestures back at Bourdain and asserts, also in Italian, "Talk to him, forget about the cameras." Much as Bourdain's editing decision to include this exchange draws attention to performativity, the camera angle suddenly switches to a long shot taken from the very angle the boxer had pointed, thus further emphasizing the camera's presence. The boxer lightens the mood asking, "where are the cameras?" Everyone laughs and Pampaloni responds "that's right," but the boxer feels the need to add "I'm not used to this," again bringing performativity to the surface. Elsewhere, the same boxer recounts his athletic triumphs, only to be interrupted by a woman who undercuts his self-aggrandizations, asserting, "now he is a champion at changing tires."

All in all, every attempt to construct an imagination of self, be it individual or collective, is shown to be affected by the cameras, performed for an audience. The best Bourdain can do to mediate is to connect the tough-talking, jocular regulars to a completely disparate, filmic image his audience may be familiar with, saying Ostia "might be described, unflatteringly, as Rome's equivalent to the Jersey Shore."

The degree to which this local community of bar regulars is both untransmutable and untranslatable comes to a crescendo near the end of this sequence when the emphasis on translation moves, first, to *stornelli*, and just how bawdy they can be, and then, to the relationship between hand gestures and communication. Translating for an older lady, Pampaloni explains *stornelli* are "very romantic . . . like a serenade for a girl." Even as Pampaloni explains this idea in English, however, the subtitles continue to translate the older lady who is still talking in the background as she quotes a *stornello*, "Zucchini flowers are big, your girlfriend stinks like a pig." The sharp contrast between imagined romanticism and the way locals express romance sparks Bourdain to comment, "There are these wonderful expressions. Like, if you tell me, 'I'm having a baby,' I can say 'fuck your dead relatives.'" Pampaloni laughs but looks slightly confused until the boxer understands and tells her in Italian, "To your lousy dead." Pampaloni nods and points aggressively at him as if he has hit the nail on the head. The older woman further explains that she might say "to your bloody, dead relatives" in one tone to say, "hello," but in another to express "anger." Pampaloni continues to translate for the lady, interjecting her own perspectives, explaining the angle of the hand is the tell for how to take such a comment. In other words, this sequence shows a form of expression so hyper-local that it cannot be translated or understood from any single perspective, but, rather, with a collective (and contested) knowledge of multiple forms of communication.

This interest in new localism, specifically linked to language and cultural production, depicted as construction (rather than authentic) and as universal precisely because of its untranslatability (all localities struggling against hegemony) is further explored in the family dinner at the home of Asia Argento that follows L'angolo Amici. While the idea of a family meal, a chance to reflect on "local" cuisine in an "authentic" home, is a common trope in Bourdain's shows, and travel TV in general, this meal deconstructs the spectator's imaginations of "local" Rome and draws attention to the construction of those images.

Instead of the most famous dishes, which are also the ones most accessible to the outside palate, Bourdain is served tripe in ragù, oxtail, and ravioli with guanciale and fava beans. The table conversation focuses on how these preparations are uniquely *Roman* (rather than Italian) and how tripe is off-putting and unappetizing when prepared incorrectly—like a "human finger," Argento's teenage daughter asserts. Notions of "authenticity" are quickly questioned when one realizes Bourdain's hosts are one of Italy's most iconic film families—their room decorated with film memorabilia and Asian—not Italian—art. Argento's eight-year-old son, Nicola, answers "yes" when Bourdain asks if he likes living in Rome, but says it is because he "like[s] *this* neighborhood," a neighborhood which Bourdain has described as "*Roma Nord*, the burbs." Argento's sister tells Bourdain she does not know why she likes living in Rome and makes it clear she spent years abroad. The entire table talks about how they do not pay attention to the Colosseum, an eternal image Nicola deconstructs when he says it is "better this year" because "they" finished "cleaning" it—an idea echoed later in the episode when Argento and Bourdain question why anybody, particularly a New Yorker, would go inside the Empire State Building. In short, while the dinner scene might offer something closer to the imagined Italian soundtrack L'angolo Amici's soundtrack denies, the content undoes such imagination.

Bourdain's depiction thus answers Abbas's call to "evoke" culture's "indeterminacies" by drawing "attention to the problematics of perception, especially of visual perception."[17] To continue in Abbas's words (writing about Hong Kong):

> Images of the city [do not] show us very much about the city. This is the dilemma of every spectacularized society, where advertisements, cinema, television, monumental buildings and so on compete for visual attention. Images promote a certain kind of attention at the same time as they prevent another kind of attention. The trick then is to use the image in an unorthodox way, to invoke not the image's representational power, but what has been called 'the powers of the false.' That is to say, while images of the city do not show the city, they nevertheless fail to do so *in a determinate way*. This then is one method of discussing . . . urban culture: by attending to the kind of image used in writing, painting, photograph, cartoons, cinema, architecture, and so on, and asking whether these images can engage and transform the negative space of the city.[18]

Bourdain thus transforms Rome's spaces in similar ways, not just by depicting a *different* Rome, but by de-exoticizing imaginations of said difference.

Bourdain seems interested in suburban Rome precisely because it defies expectations via difference, but he also sees those differences as universal: markers of "the local" do not define them because what constitutes the local is a constantly changing construct. For instance, Bourdain and Argento shop for ingredients for the family meal at a supermarket; in and of itself revealing the "image" of the authentic, magically prepared-for-TV family meal. Moreover, the local chain supermarket they shop at is an obvious inversion of the farmers' market depicted in the street performer scenes—an inversion to which Bourdain draws attention by joking about "artisanal" canned goods. Meanwhile, Bourdain ensures that even this image of a "different" Rome cannot be mistaken for authentic, shooting it in a *highly* stylized and cinematic manner, culminating in Argento dancing with transvestites between shopping aisles.

Bourdain draws attention to the way images of Rome fail to show actual Romans in a "determinate" way by foregrounding this very conversation. For Bourdain, as with Pasolini, it is central Rome that exists in the margins, and it is exoticized precisely because it is constructed for universal consumption, rather than for the people who live and construct the culture.

The only shots Bourdain depicts of central Rome appear in the episode's introduction, and they are used in an "unorthodox" way, as called for by Abbas. Bourdain pairs the images of central Rome with narration explaining how his show is not going to be about "monuments, or statues, or the treasures of antiquity. This is about people, often extraordinary ones, living their lives in the Rome you don't see much of in the travel guides or TV shows."

The way Bourdain's camera shoots these images is equally unorthodox, showing portions of monuments and buildings and ruins in extreme close-ups that deny the spectator's desire to see the whole image. In fact, the only *complete* image of pre-Mussolini Rome to appear is the Altare della Patria, to which Bourdain shifts with a slow fade from a newsreel of a Mussolini speech shot at the same location from the same angle, thereby deconstructing the building's romantic nature even as tourist buses pass. By the sequence's end, the camera situates Bourdain, dining alone in a local eatery and pointing to a painting of Anna Magnani, the actress who played Mamma Roma. It is Pasolini's Rome that interests Bourdain, and it is Pasolini's influence as filmmaker Bourdain uses as a lens for his depiction of Rome.

Much as Magnani's portrait and the eyes of Mamma Roma loom over Bourdain as he eats his first meal, Pasolini's presence looms over the entire episode, Bourdain assuring it never falls far from the surface. Pasolini's influence on Bourdain's cinematography and editing is omnipresent, but typically subtle; Bourdain's narration, however, is more direct. Immediately after pointing to the painting, Bourdain calls Pasolini, "one of Italy's great filmmakers, a revolutionary figure in cinema who celebrated the working-class suburbs of Rome. He was a vocal opponent of fascism and of those that he felt allowed it to happen. His characters . . . were always, even at their worst, depicted as angelic in all their flawed and damaged glory. Rome's *true* heroes." Throughout this, Bourdain alters between images of contemporary Rome shot in Pasolini's style and clips borrowed from *Mamma Roma*. Later, Bourdain discusses Pasolini with Argento, points to the site of his murder in Ostia, and interviews Abel Ferrara about his Pasolini biopic. Elsewhere, without warning, Bourdain's narration returns to Pasolini, declaring, "To Pasolini it was the outskirts, the margins of Rome that were interesting and beautiful. The real Rome. Not the temples and monuments of a dead empire. A place where people struggled every day to live and to love . . . a city where you find the most extraordinary of pleasures in the most ordinary of things." Thus, even a spectator unfamiliar with Pasolini is made aware of the parallels between Pasolini's depictions of the *disabitato* in the 1960s and Bourdain's depictions of Roma Nord, Ostia, and other suburban neighborhoods in the 2010s.

Pasolini's presence also shows itself in the episode's structure. Rather than the tightly constructed argument that slowly builds upon itself to a crescendo, as we find in episodes like "Jamaica" and "Montana" (PU S7E4), "Rome" follows a structure more akin to Pasolini—cutting from one subject to another and back again, causing seemingly disparate images and conversations to comment upon one other through free indirect subjectivity and discourse. In this way, fascism, architecture, urban planning, filmic depictions of the city, and even Pasolini himself, can *all* be themes that are central to what Bourdain wants to say about contemporary Rome, much as Pasolini treated them as part and parcel in postwar Rome. Each of these topics fade away and come back, much as the camera often cuts away from whoever is speaking, not only to establishing shots of the suburbs, but also to non-diegetic images of everyday people staring back at the camera, not to mention the street performers previously discussed.

Similarly, Bourdain's exploration of the EUR district is separated by a nine-minute interregnum of restaurant scenes with Ferrara and Argento about everyday life, and newsreel footage of Mussolini giving speeches about making Italy and America "great" again come and go from the narrative, sometimes without explanation. Rather than becoming incoherent, the strategy uses repetition and juxtaposition to make complicated connections in ways, yet again, reminiscent of Pasolini. To return to Rhodes writing about *Mamma Roma*, "Pasolini's willful misreading of neorealist cinema and neorealist architecture reveals itself through its allusions, appropriations, and repetitions, as both an aesthetic practice and a political polemic intended to dislodge the viewers from any comfortable acceptance of modern urban—and therefore economic and social—reality. It is a reality too immense, too various, too complex to be represented accurately, or perhaps, at all."[19]

The way the nonlinear structure works in tandem with the beautiful, partial images of suburban Rome to emphasize the way no filmic representation could ever wholly capture the city, merges in a non-diegetic scene immediately after the opening credits. The brief but tone-setting scene depicts Bourdain and Argento walking up a narrow street, shot from behind. The images, themselves, are some of "Rome's" most naturalistic, yet the sequence is made cinematic by non-diegetic sounds of gunshots and graphic design lines exiting the screen reminiscent of Bertolucci and Fellini. As the duo walk, their conversation denied us, Argento looks left, and then up at a building. Bourdain looks at Argento, who then looks back at Bourdain before returning her gaze back to the left. At just this moment, the soundtrack shifts to the swelling, romantic score that accompanies most of the establishing shots throughout the episode. Immediately, a local man pops his head out of a doorway and looks each way as if to see what the commotion is all about, first looking at Bourdain and Argento, then directly back at the camera, and finally turning his body back up the street toward Bourdain and Argento again. Finally, a car and two couples enter the frame walking up the street. There is no narrative explanation for any of this nor its purpose. We are left uncertain which, if any, of these perspectives are intended to be ours, or even Bourdain's. Suddenly, Bourdain cuts to an image of a metro car in the *disabitato*. The soundtrack offers a sense of sublime wholeness that the camera and the (lack of) narrative deny, a mood eerily like Rhodes's description of a "mode of sublime" in *Mamma Roma*, in which "the Roman periphery resists not only its representation in film, but also its representation in the minds of its inhabitants. It is not, in Kevin Lynch's words, a place that 'can be organized into a coherent pattern.'"[20] Thus, Bourdain organizes his narrative and his images into a pattern meant to undo the weight of Roman film history.

I began this chapter asserting that Bourdain's question "Is it possible to look at Rome in a non-cinematic way?" serves as a revealing lens. Bourdain's framing of Argento's answer to that question, as well as the ensuing discussions as they tour the EUR, serves to clarify that lens. Argento's immediate answer, "To me, it's how to shoot it in a way it's never been shot," draws attention to the "determinate" way typical city cinematography depicts an unspoken ideology. The continuation of her answer, however, emphasizes the way alternative approaches to shooting the city are *also* ideological: "There are sides of Rome that Pasolini, for instance, who wasn't from Rome, but would shoot here, and he'd do the

A random man sticks his head out his door to watch Asia Argento and Anthony Bourdain walk a narrow Roman street. This shot is defined by an increasingly complex interplay of gazes.

suburbs, and you'd get this sense of the *real* Rome." With the very first word of this portion of Argento's answer Bourdain cuts to a clip from *Mamma Roma* and then fades into an image of the same suburban archway now shot by Bourdain's crew. Pasolini's approach is radical and new, but it is still a construction of what is "real" built upon filmic tradition.

Later, sitting inside an amphitheater in Mussolini's EUR neighborhood—a space Bourdain tells (and shows) us was used in both Elio Petri's *The 10th Victim* (1965) and Bertolucci's *The Conformist*—Argento and Bourdain discuss the relationship between film, photography, architecture, and fascism. A newsreel of Mussolini appears on the long, flat wall of the Rationalist amphitheater, as if it were a film screen. Silenced by the weighty discussion, the duo walks out of the amphitheater, Argento declaring, "Thank you for bringing me here. I don't think I've ever been or ever will come back. [pause] Maybe for *movies*." It is, she asserts, a space built for spectacle, built for cinema. These are the final spoken words of the episode, as Bourdain lets them quietly settle for the final ninety seconds as he walks the halls of the EUR's Palazzo della Civiltà Italiana.

It is no accident Bourdain places these moments in and around the EUR at the episode's end. They are the closest thing to a conclusion Bourdain can offer within a narrative structure intended to foreground complexity and the inability to resolve questions or images. These moments merge disparate discussions—architecture, urban planning, film, fascism—while positing the need of filmmakers like Pasolini and Bourdain to reposition said images.

When Bourdain first enters the EUR, before the Ferrara and Argento restaurant scenes, he narrates, "Built by Mussolini as the triumph of fascism, these buildings were not designed to thrill or elevate or warm with their beauty. They are designed to dwarf the individual. To intimidate, to remind constantly that the state is all powerful and supreme, that the individual is meaningless in the grand scheme of things, one person just like the other. Fungible, replaceable, ultimately worthless." The camera emphasizes these ideas as a staircase sometimes denies us Bourdain's face and we see the hands of an austere, uniformed guard, a clear view of whose face we are pointedly denied. The cinematography matches the architecture. Instantly, however, the soundtrack turns less austere and Bourdain's camera cuts to images of the *disabitato*, ugly on the surface but beautifully adorned with bright, cheerful graffiti, shot from inside a metro car filled with Romans shown at eye level, emphasizing their individuality. One of these women sits motionless in a carefully framed close-up, the metro playfully moving behind her as the train goes around a curve. It is a stunning sequence.

Once Bourdain returns from the restaurant scenes to the final images of the EUR, Bourdain's camera now emphasizes the Palazzo's high, expansive ceilings, and reveals the face of the (now smiling) security officer, all while intercutting images of smiling Romans in other suburbs. It is as if Bourdain's alternative city images have repositioned and reimagined the Palazzo just as Pasolini repositions images of the

Bourdain walks the Palazzo della Civiltà Italiana in Rome's EUR district. The cinematography and mise-en-scène emphasize how the architecture dwarfs the individual, obscuring their individualism.

An unidentified *romana* rides the Metropolina, a small smile beginning to appear on her face, the metro car playfully moving behind her.

disabitato. Finally, Bourdain leaves us with the quiet echo of his footsteps as he walks the empty building.

Unsurprisingly, *Mamma Roma*'s final shot sequence sheds much light not only upon Bourdain's final sequence, but his approach in general. Pasolini's final shot sequence intercuts between images of Mamma Roma and shots of Rome, thus "projecting the cause of her grief onto the image of the city"[21] since "the work of this shot sequence . . . is precisely to solicit our identification of the sequence *as* point of view. Further, an identification of the sequence as such solicits our identification *with* Mamma Roma. These solicitations, however, are lures, ideological snares. We are meant to understand that such a pursuit of identification (of shot with character's vision, of our emotions with those of Mamma Roma) is exactly what this film means to disrupt, to interrogate."[22]

Bourdain similarly disrupts and interrogates Mussolini's architecture and urban planning, as well as the weight of film and television history, which, intentionally or not, reinforces Mussolini's ambitions to reposition Rome's primary function for outsiders to consume it, rather than a space for locals to, as Bourdain says, "live and love."

Bourdain's images of the periphery, like Pasolini's, assist in this disruption. Lino Micciché claims Pasolini's cityscape in *Mamma Roma*'s final shot sequence "is never—*not even when it seems to be*—a *subjective image* but is instead always an *ideological image*, and it does not function within the film as a *diegetic surplus* (which would enrich the *story*) but rather an *ideological surplus* (which enriches the *meaning* of the film)."[23] Or, in Rhodes's words, "the image's logic and its message belong to the organizing intelligence of the film, to *Mamma Roma*, if you will, but not to Mamma Roma."[24] Similarly, Bourdain's use of non-diegetic Romans happily staring back at the camera, throughout the episode but particularly near its climax, are essential precisely because they express the episode's ideology, not because they help Bourdain tell the story of *his* experience in Rome. The non-diegetic scenes of the street performers work similarly. As such, we are asked to look at—not with—Bourdain as he walks the empty Palazzo, his body's relationship to architecture (as well as the echo of his footsteps) embodying the change of perspective his film has enacted.

Throughout the episode, Bourdain's images of suburban Rome repeatedly provide just such an "ideological surplus" as he reshapes not just how we see Rome, but how we imagine difference. After her answer about Rome vis-à-vis cinema, when asked about the "political health of the world," Argento asserts "I don't even care. I don't vote. I never voted. Never once. I don't go on the news. I don't want to bring that stuff with me. That shit is poison. . . . I care about my neighborhood, my children, my building. I care about that. That's a *lot* to care about already." At first glance it seems an entirely self-absorbed comment. At closer look, however, it is not *just* that; in a hegemonic, consumerist world, to care a "lot" on the microlevel is, in some ways, extraordinary.

Immediately after Argento finishes that quotation, Bourdain intercuts a shot of Rome almost identical to *Mamma Roma*'s final shot, emphasizing the space between her community and central Rome "out there." The shot is not Bourdain's perspective, nor Argento's, nor the spectator's; it is the ideological perspective of the episode. Global perspectives are shaped by visual culture, architecture, urban planning, and more; Argento implies as much herself, calling violent paintings of martyrs "the first horror movies" meant to scare people into a "buying mood." Rather than be assimilated into a global hegemony of consumerism, Argento champions her community. Jordi Maiso claims that "Pasolini wanted to reflect the language, the bodies, the culture of the people who lived on the margins in his work, the people who did not want to be assimilated into capitalist industrialized society."[25] The same can be said of Bourdain. And, like Pasolini, he most often depicts them through beautiful images exposed as subjective.

11
WEST VIRGINIA

The season premiere of what would come to be *Parts Unknown*'s final full season was an extended episode of fifty-seven minutes set in West Virginia (PU S11E1). Airing April 29, 2018, it came in the wake of the election of Donald J. Trump to the US presidency seventeen months prior, a topic to which Bourdain returns throughout the episode. It is an overt treatise on how the outside gaze has largely determined depictions of West Virginia since at least the nineteenth century, as well as how those imaginations have, in turn, shaped the state itself. Bourdain treats the thirty-fifth state like a foreign country to be studied and explored, opposed to most depictions that predetermine West Virginia for right or left-wing purposes. To quote Bourdain in an interview the day before it aired,

> I think the timing is right. I think because it's so different than the culture I grew up in and the place I grew up in, and the political landscape is very different than mine. I pride myself on trying to show up with an open mind and an open heart in places like Saudi Arabia, Liberia, Vietnam, Iran. Why not my own country? Why not show that same respect and empathy in the heart of God, guns, and Trump country?[1]

From the opening shots, Bourdain invokes his outsider status, as well as images of Appalachia shot by the outsiders who came before him. More than anything, Bourdain provides an effective and viable alternative not just to those imaginations of Appalachia, but to a contemporaneous example of such depictions, J. D. Vance's 2016 bestseller *Hillbilly Elegy*—a controversial and divisive memoir that dominated political discourse following Trump's election. Bourdain turns to his own filmic lens and, more surprisingly, influences ranging from the obscure, avant-garde California filmmaker Bruce Conner to a genre of mainstream, feel-good sports movies as means of asking his audience to completely reimagine what they think they know about West Virginia. It is quintessential Bourdain filmmaking.

One consistent trend in late-stage Bourdain was that his domestic episodes got more interesting when he began to treat them as wholly foreign subject matter akin to shows overseas; "Detroit" (PU S2E8), "Pittsburgh" (PU S10E4), "Mississippi" (PU S3E6), and "Houston" (PU S8E5), particularly come to mind. Much as I discuss in my chapter on "Rome" (PU S8E9), however, Bourdain's goal in emphasizing "difference" is not to exoticize, but, rather, to deconstruct how the filmic lens, and the Western gaze that lens creates, typically aids in such dangerous exoticization. Bourdain hints at this in his CNN field notes for "West Virginia:" "Like any other episode of *Parts Unknown*, whether in Vietnam or Nigeria, or any city in the United States, this West Virginia episode is a plea for understanding of the people whose personal histories, sense of pride, independence, and daunting challenges deserve respect. It's a walk in somebody else's shoes. The stereotypes about West Virginia, it turns out, are just as cruel, ignorant, misguided, patronizing, and evil as any other."[2] Early in the episode Bourdain declares, "this is *not* poverty porn," referring to a popular term for filmic representations of poverty, usually experienced by people of color, which affirm the stereotypes of a white, upper-class spectator.[3] Rather, Bourdain undoes such stereotypes by demonstrating how West Virginia should be admired, not pitied, precisely because of its diversity—a diversity of race, geography, politics, and culture.

Upon Bourdain's death, multiple critics pointed to these themes in this very episode as a signature moment. Erik Kohn, writing an obituary for *IndieWire* titled "Anthony Bourdain Was a Brilliant Filmmaker in Disguise," called the episode "an astonishing documentary investigation into the lives of working-class people."[4] Referring to a scene where Bourdain eats bear meat and talks politics while lunching with coal miners deep underground, Kohn continues, "Rather than constructing a bland plea for partisanship, Bourdain allows the men to simply exist within the specific parameters of their surroundings. It's thrilling to watch this kind of level-headed inquiry because so little of it exists in popular culture, which tends to regard others as either exotic objects or clueless products of less-enlightened circumstances. Bourdain worked to rewire those binary instincts and embrace the potential for experiencing new people and conditions. That's true movie magic."[5] Meredith McCarroll, in a retrospective for CNN titled "Anthony Bourdain Listened to the Voices *Hillbilly Elegy* Ignored," goes a step further, claiming, "Documentary has become another extractive industry with outsiders coming in to take what they need—in this case a narrow image of a complex place. A scapegoat for the rest of the country . . . Exploitation takes many forms and serves multiple purposes. Anthony Bourdain seemed to understand that he was in a position where he could judge, make assumptions, and dismiss. But he was also in a position to learn, to hear, and to have his mind changed through deep empathy and curiosity—which is what he chose to do."[6] The idea of documentary filmmaking as a form of "extraction" echoes John David Rhodes's discussion of filmic representations of the city for the spectator's consumption discussed in chapter 10, and Bourdain's alternative brand of filmmaking has similar goals for "West Virginia" that I have also discussed in "Rome," "Jamaica" (PU S4E8), and beyond.

The exploitation and oversimplification of West Virginia (and Appalachia as a whole) as representative subject dates at least as far back as nineteenth-century travel writing and has been reinforced by visual culture ever since.[7] Often serving as the abject, oppositional Other against normative, mainstream US culture, the imagination of Appalachia—as constructed by its representations—tends toward a whiter, less-educated, poorer, more homogenized population than has ever been reality. Think, for example, of John Boorman's *Deliverance* (1972), in which a group of brash city-slickers from Atlanta canoe through the Appalachian gorges of north Georgia. Toothless hillbillies and mountain rednecks subsequently rape, murder, and chase them downriver. It is not *just* that it is irresponsible of the film—and, to a certain degree, the novel it was based upon—to exert little effort exploring and examining its Appalachian characters, it is that the popular imagination of Appalachia is so ubiquitous (and so dominant) that shallow images serve effectively as stark, shallow archetypes that need no explanation. As Meredith McCarroll writes in "Hillbillies Need No Elegy,"

> Appalachia has been shaped by outsiders' images and strangers' descriptions. As a result, complexity gets simplified, the

> edges get rounded out, and what remains is an idea that Appalachia is somehow different than America. Appalachia has been written about and photographed in such a compelling (if fabricated) way that the descriptions of passersby took on more weight than the lived experiences of the people being described. What remains is a concept of a place that is both wildly romantic in its natural beauty and backward enough to justify the destruction of that very nature.[8]

In turn, real-world Appalachia is directly impacted as political discourse is shaped by the pervasive, depthless images across media, almost always serving the needs of the outsider.

Such short-sighted (mis)representations span political and cultural divides, and sometimes come from well-intentioned places. For instance, some of the most influential images of West Virginia come from photographers working for the Farm Security Administration (FSA), dating from the late 1930s to the early 1960s, particularly the work of Marion Post Wolcott, whose photographs feature prominently in Bourdain's episode. Founded by US President Franklin Delano Roosevelt in 1938 to engender sympathy for his New Deal and returned to by President Lyndon B. Johnson to promote his 1964 War on Poverty, the FSA sent photographers into the heart of Appalachia to document the impoverished.[9] These photographs, as Bourdain says, were meant to support "a good thing, yes?" And the photographers, particularly Wolcott, *did* capture a range of images: one of her photographs depicts a woman leaning forward over a porch rail with a smile on her face; another depicts a racially diverse group of men standing, nicely dressed, with dignity, in front of a Schlitz Beer advertisement. But, in the end, the most widely disseminated photographs were *not* images depicting any type of diversity. As Bourdain says, "the accompanying press tour portraying the people here as incapable and bewildered, helpless mass, missed the basic, essential character. The pride and the self-reliant core of the people here. That damage is lasting." In other words, the government's selection of images was determined for political aims and to reinforce stereotypes, "images meant to evoke sympathy, but which did not demand understanding."[10] The result of the FSA project(s) is representative of how Appalachia has always been depicted—as Bourdain told the *Bluefield Daily Telegraph*, "It doesn't seem to be in anybody's interest outside of the state to portray West Virginia as it is. The coverage has been ignorant, condescending, and hateful."[11]

The episode's opening minute, before the credits, draws from these themes as it emphasizes the divide between depiction and reality, providing alternative, redemptive images of West Virginia and West Virginians. Bourdain is entirely absent—we neither see his body nor hear his voice. Bourdain's camera cycles through images to which he later returns. Here, however, the images and sounds are all examples of locals telling their own story: a racially diverse football team plays a game and listens to a halftime speech; cheerleaders support a small-town parade; a coal miner talks about a "booming" past while black-and-white images show a thriving, urban downtown that the same voice declares "dead now"; leaves blow in an empty forest. At one point, a local voice asserts, "There's so much negativity surrounding this place that no one ever focuses on the positive. They see us as ignorant, or hillbillies. . . . There's really more here than just poverty, and illiteracy, and drugs. There's a *lot* of *good* people here." As he says "people," the miner on-screen turns his head back and makes eye contact with the camera following him, transforming from shallow image to real person. The music is slow and redemptive, a song to which Bourdain later returns, but, more than anything, it is unobtrusive. Bourdain, to the degree any filmmaker can, lets the locals speak for themselves. Simultaneously, by denying his presence, Bourdain leaves the spectator without a surrogate, uncertain of their place within the world he depicts. Further, even the images and quotations are edited in a jumbled manner that does not let the spectator get firm footing. All of this, meanwhile, is juxtaposed against what comes immediately after the opening credits.

While it is a trademark of Bourdain's approach to actively draw the spectator's attention to his presence, as well as how his biases impact his and their perspectives, it is rare to find an opening to any film, even within Bourdain's filmography, that goes to lengths as great as "West Virginia" to emphasize the contrast between the outsider/filmmaker and their subject(s). Reminiscent of "Congo" (PU S1E8), which ends with Bourdain back in his New York apartment, Bourdain returns from the opening credits to images of New York. While we still do not see Bourdain's face (or body), we finally hear his voice. The soundtrack shifts to an original composition by *Parts Unknown* composer Michael Ruffino, "Death-by-Canjo," which takes its name from a wholly Appalachian instrument born of poverty—a banjo made from a can. The song, however, is loud and jarring, and sounds more like Indian Panjabi music than Appalachian. The shots alternate between a roving camera shooting down upon Manhattan from the sky and New York's multicultural mass of people shot at street level. The quick, jumbled edits make the hustle and bustle seem all the more overwhelming when compared to the opening sequence. Bourdain's voice-over begins: "New York City. Where *I* live. And it's easy to think—having lived here nearly all my life—that *this* is what America looks like, thinks like. That the things that are important to me are important to everybody. That every place else is 'out there,' unthinkable. Maybe even unknowable." Bourdain thus exposes the divide between West Virginia and himself (as well as the spectator) and emphasizes the way the spectator can *never* get the sense of a "real" West Virginia as was implied (but denied) in the opening sequence. Every depiction is a filmmaker's construction.

Having foregrounded that divide, Bourdain creates another as his edit suddenly snaps back to West Virginia. "Death-by-Canjo" abruptly stops, the soundtrack filled only by water from a swiftly moving brook matching images of pristine natural beauty. The silence, and the nature, is almost jarring and empty compared to the abundance of sound and image we have just heard and seen in Manhattan, and Bourdain's narration highlights the juxtaposition between these worlds, asserting, "600 miles away from Midtown Manhattan is McDowell County, West Virginia. Another America. In the mind of many of my fellow New Yorkers . . . the existential enemy." A local man talks about how the mountains "protect" West Virginia from outside forces like "tornadoes and hurricanes," as Bourdain's camera shows the man in such a close-up that it cuts off a large portion of his face, much as the mountains cut the state off from the rest of the nation and emphasizing the construction of the man's image. The man seems anything but an "existential enemy," but the sequence reminds us just how different his world is from that of Bourdain's.

Bourdain does not try to bridge this divide; rather, he simply demands we understand it. To quote Bourdain's narration, "To think about, much less empathize, with somebody who comes from five generations of coal miners in a place that looks like *this* is, to our enduring shame, unthinkable. Why can't these coal miners get retrained? Maybe put up solar panels for a living? Why would these conservative, deeply religious people vote for a thrice married billionaire New Yorker? Well, I went to West Virginia. And you know what? [pause] Screw you." The pause and subsequent denial are reminiscent of Matt King's quip "Paradise? Paradise can go fuck itself" in Alexander Payne's *The Descendants* (2011), discussed in chapter 4. Unlike King, however, Bourdain is not speaking from the perspective of the insider as he rejects the outside construction. Bourdain has just bluntly shown us just how much of an outsider he is. It is his own perspective, as well as the spectator's, that is disavowed.

Bourdain thus uses the spectator's awareness of this dynamic—an awareness *he* creates—to push the spectator toward his repositioning of West Virginia. As the music turns to upbeat bluegrass, Bourdain continues, "Here in the heart of every belief system I've ever mocked or fought against I was welcomed with open arms by everyone. I found a place both heartbreaking and beautiful. A place that symbolizes and contains everything wrong and everything wonderful and hopeful about America." Almost every image from the episode matches this declaration—alternative images that deconstruct the dominant ones of the West Virginia the spectator thought they knew. We see a cosmopolitan Welch, described as "Little New York" and "The American Dream in miniature," and only abandoned after the rest of the country was done extracting "billions and billions of dollars." Bourdain repeatedly features people of color and tells us "mixed-race couples are common here." We hear "Little Liza Jane" played on a blues harp, subtly invoking the historical connections between blues and bluegrass via a song that shares both histories. That song then morphs into hip-hop at a high school pep rally before a game in which an entire community, across class and racial boundaries, comes together to root for a football team. We hear miners say they are aware the future is not coal, watch Bourdain interact with gun rights activists who look and act "nice," and see single mothers hunt food for their children as they worry about the impact of methamphetamines on their community. Bourdain eats dinner and prays with a seemingly prototypical family, only to be served spaghetti pizza attributed to their immigrant roots in Napoli—they even refer to peas as *piselli*. High school students say they want to be a mechanical engineer and a neuropsychologist, respectively. Instead of exotic, Bourdain's West Virginia is distinct—and in ways reminiscent of how America is distinct.

Bourdain's desire to take that which outside forces depict/determine as exotic (at best) or ignorant (at worst) and reimagine them as something distinctive, something to aspire to, is embodied in his approach to Appalachian cuisine. At various times, Bourdain is served squirrel, bear, venison, frog legs, turtle patties, rabbit, and desperation pie (vinegar and nutmeg used to replace costly lemon). Never, in any of these moments, does Bourdain depict the food as peculiar, nor joke about its humble origins. Instead, he declares, "Appalachia has a rich and deep culinary culture. Increasingly fetishized, riffed on, appropriated, for the genteel tastes of a hipster elite willing to pay big bucks for what used to be—and still is—the food of poverty." Chef Amy Dawson, declares ramp onions have become a new "extraction industry like coal and timber," and Bourdain calls the pawpaw "America's forgotten fruit," chiding mainstream culture for forgetting its culinary roots—something, he says, West Virginia "never forgot." Bourdain eats a feast served by local chefs at Lost Creek Farm while the camera nearly fetishizes the food with close-ups bathed in golden, natural light, the dishes plated like haute cuisine. "*This* is what heirloom looks like outside of Holy Foods," Bourdain asserts adoringly, pointing at bloody butcher corn, fat horse beans, and candy roaster squash—all more attractive (and distinctive) than anything at urban Whole Foods grocery stores. A chef proclaims, "We are often talked about as being this impoverished state, we are *rich* as can be in food and the things that we make as a culture and a community," to which chef Mike Costello quickly adds, "You look at something as simple as these pole beans. It took a community to save that seed." Bourdain concludes the sequence by agreeing with this sentiment, referring to the "friends" at the table as "interdependent, a community, an *economy*." Where the outsider sees lack and impoverishment, Bourdain sees abundance and plenty.

Such an inversion of lack and abundance mirrors Bourdain's framing of a conversation with Oscar nominated documentary filmmaker Elaine McMillion Sheldon and journalist Nick Mullins, both West Virginia natives. Bourdain begins by joking about lack of reliable cell service and suggesting the Trump and God signs in town might feel "threatening" to "many of my ilk." Bourdain then edits a quotation from Sheldon to put it in direct conversation with his outsider perspective, as Sheldon asserts, "*both* sides feel threatened by each other, and I would say a majority of people that live in this region want to be left alone. The traditions of this place—the things that we value, rather that be family or interpersonal communication, not having cell phone technology to distract us—those types of things sort of butt up against America's idea of progress. And it's why we've always been looked at as being backwards." As Mullins says the main thing people "need to know" about the state is "how much this area ha[s] been exploited," Bourdain's camera ushers the spectator through a powerful montage that treats the media (specifically a newspaper going to print), the FSA, national coal, lumber, and pharmaceutical companies, as well as politicians Lyndon Johnson, John F. Kennedy, Donald Trump, Bernie Sanders, and Hillary Clinton, as part and parcel—part of the same extraction economy reliant on misperceptions for profit, be it monetary or political. As the music returns to "Death-by-Canjo," previously heard in New York, Bourdain narrates, "it's always been too easy to come *gawk* at West Virginia. To make it a poster child for whatever the agenda of the moment was. Lazy depictions of stereotypical West Virginians, hillbillies, and hicks, tucked into isolated hollers to be pitied or made objects of laughter or derision."

One such depiction used for an agenda of the moment—the exact same political moment to which Bourdain's episode responds—is Vance's *Hillbilly Elegy: A Memoir of a Family and Culture in Crisis*. The highly influential book explores the relationship between Vance's parents' Appalachian values (they were raised in Kentucky) and the pervasive social problems of his hometown, Middletown, Ohio. Vance's narrative about pulling himself up by his bootstraps fit multiple, convenient narratives used to interpret Trump's surprise electoral victory, and the book became popular with pundits and readers on both sides of the political aisle, landing it atop *The New York Times* bestseller list, making it a common core-reading selection for freshman at many universities,[12] and eventually resulting in a major motion-picture adaptation (Ron Howard, 2020). A 2017 Brookings Institute report attributes its broad popularity to "its raw, emotional portrait of growing up in and eventually out of a poor rural community riddled by drug addiction and instability,"[13] but the pushback from journalists and scholars who live in or study Appalachia was swift. Eventually, West Virginia University Press published an entire volume titled *Appalachian Reckoning: A Region Responds to "Hillbilly Elegy"* (2019), in which forty essayists react to Vance's memoir, almost unanimously in critique. Explaining its popularity on elite college campuses, Elizabeth Catte explains the "appeal" of Vance's tale "relies on the gleeful curiosity of audiences who are happy to visually consume a version of Appalachia that, in many ways fits well-worn regional stereotypes."[14]

One of the collection's most compelling critiques, and the one most pertinent for understanding Bourdain's episode as an alternative, comes from Ivy Brashear, who accuses Vance of "display[ing] a willingness to sell out his family members by tapping into a long history of distorted, false, and intentionally made stereotypical images of central Appalachia that have been imposed on the region by outside media makers for nearly three hundred years, ever since the first white land prospectors were sent into the region by George Washington."[15] More broadly, she adds,

> *Elegy* has no class, no heart, and no warmth. It's a poorly written appropriation of Appalachian stereotypes about violent, ignorant, and slovenly hillbillies who refuse to help themselves despite having every opportunity to do so. Vance makes broad generalizations about class and wealth, insinuating that everyone living in the region lives in poverty, or among some mythical ruins of working-class life. He clings to that fictionalized past of working-class nostalgia and assumes that all our problems come from white men being out of work. He paints the region white, completely erasing the economic and cultural contributions and existence of Appalachian people of color. And perhaps most glaring of all, he blames the people of Appalachia for the economic and social problems they now face, which, in actuality, they had very little hand in creating.[16]

Vance's *Elegy* thus brings centuries-old discourses to the forefront as it appropriates Appalachia to explain US politics, and outside audiences accept the depictions precisely because they build upon said discourse, the very discourse Bourdain seeks to upend.

Where Vance shows lazy individuals who created their own circumstances and are now bitter about being ignored, Bourdain shows a squirrel hunting mom, Lola Kline, who asserts, "there's nothing I can't do, and if I don't know how to do it, I'll learn. We're not a bunch of pregnant women barefoot with no teeth, I've got all mine, you see?" For Bourdain, West Virginia is evidence that the narrative of self-reliance, central to the myth of the American dream and to Vance, is shallow precisely *because* the mainstream misrepresents Appalachians to exploit them. Where Vance sees "hollers" full of degeneration and resignation, Kline defines a holler as a place "where everybody is united, everybody speaks with one another, and takes up for one another"; as Bourdain said at Lost Creek Farm, "interdependent, a community, an *economy*."

In typical Bourdain fashion, the sequences that most clearly articulate what he wants to say about West Virginia as a misrepresented community and the extraction economy reliant upon that misrepresentation, come from the invocation of outside filmic lenses. What is surprising is that the lenses diverge between mainstream feature films and experimental shorts.

The first such lens is the Hollywood genre of high school sports movies, ranging from *Hoosiers* (David Anspaugh, 1986), *Friday Night Lights* (Peter Berg, 2004) and *The Blind Side* (John Hancock, 2009) to the documentary *Undefeated* (Daniel Lindsay and T. J. Martin, 2011). Time and again, small-town teams come together in the face of hardship to forge community, either resulting in surprise victory or defeat that binds them together. To a degree, Bourdain frames his entire episode around this construct: we see images of the Mount View Golden Knights practicing in the opening, early in the episode he talks about the importance of homecoming week and interviews players in a school lunchroom; and he closes with an eight-minute sequence depicting Mount View's improbable come-from-behind homecoming victory. The cinematography is stunning—of a quality far surpassing most examples of the genre, made more impressive because his cinematographers must work in real time, shooting a real game. More pertinent, however, Bourdain repositions the genre in the same way he wants to reposition depictions of West Virginia. Bourdain introduces his final sequence by stating, "For the citizens of Welch and McDowell County this is a *very* big deal indeed. Everybody knows everybody else's families. Asks after their kids by name. . . . There's an easy familiarity between people here." Later, addressing the team after the victory, the team's coach proclaims, "In anything you do in life, in school, in football, as long as you've got me, and these coaches, and this community, it's all you need." Namely, rather than community being forged by athletic endeavor as is typical in the genre, Bourdain depicts an athletic victory achieved because a thriving community is already in place. In so doing, a filmmaker who opened by claiming it "unthinkable" for US society to "think about, let alone empathize" with the citizens of West Virginia, ends with a feel-good victory rooted in the very type of community from which Vance idealizes escape.

Bourdain's other outside filmic influence, the visual artist and experimental filmmaker Bruce Conner's *Cosmic Ray* (1962), is likely far more obscure to Bourdain's audience, but no less essential to his argument. Conner's short films rely heavily on found footage, sometimes merged with depictions of models, and are almost always intended to provoke an open conversation about auteurship, the filmic gaze, and the juxtaposition of images and counterpoint sound. Conner is "enormously influential as well as completely inimitable. Formally meticulous and decidedly innovative . . . His visual lexicon ranges from the juxtaposition of disjunctive images to extremely concentrated abstractions."[17] In the case of *Cosmic Ray*, Conner pairs an upbeat soundtrack (Ray Charles's "What'd I Say?") with a frantic barrage of images edited together with a liberal use of jump cuts—images ranging from newsreels of cannon to Mickey Mouse dodging cartoon bullets to classic Hollywood depictions of masculinity to atomic explosions. The dominant subject, to which Conner perpetually returns, is a woman dancing nude, her body increasingly merged with or covered by weapons of war, as well as firework-like explosions that appear across her body. In essence, the four-minute film links patriotism to patrimony, the exploitation of war to the exploitation of the female body, all of which results in dangerous and destructive explosions.

Conner's films influenced a generation of American New Wave filmmakers, and I do not believe Bourdain's use of Conner is limited to "West Virginia"—the denial of image at the beginning of "Hanoi" (PU S8E1) is reminiscent of Conner's *Report* (1967) and the flittering of images in the introduction to "Charleston" (PU S6E8) almost definitely comes from Conner as well; Bourdain's use of *Cosmic Ray*, however, is more explicit, and is one of the most essential scenes in "West Virginia."

In a completely non-diegetic sequence, in which Bourdain neither introduces the poet nor offers any context, Bourdain uses *Cosmic Ray* as a lens for Crystal Good's poem "Boom Boom," merging images of strippers and strip-mining to draw attention to the extractive, exploitive economies that determine both West Virginia and how film constructs the (nearly) nude female body. The sequence begins when Bourdain returns from commercial to a close-up of honeybees working flowers, itself an extractive process. The camera then tracks a woman carrying a bag into a building; much like the episode's opening, the spectator remains on uncertain footing. Suddenly, the scene shifts to a locker room where women apply makeup, strip to normal shirts and panties, and then put on exotic outfits next to a sign reading "Mirror, Mirror on the Wall, You Are the Fairest of Them All," drawing attention to the construction of the female body for a sexualized gaze—much as *Cosmic Ray* draws similar attention by ending with the previously nude subject in a rapid succession of costumes waving a US flag. What had, for Bourdain, been an empty, naturalistic soundtrack, fills first with the opening lines of the poem, "Them boys say West Virginia girls are Golddiggers. / Them boys should know better cause in West Virginia there ain't no gold. / Just black, black coal." Suddenly, the soundtrack from the episodes' opening moments returns for the first time, the camera cuts to various images of the coal mining process, and Bourdain's narration sets the scene: "West Virginia was settled by people who were fleeing persecution, by homesteaders, people who just wanted to live their lives their own way. But the discovery of vast coal reserves and the big business that grew up around it changed everything." For the rest of the sequence, Bourdain's voice disappears; without explanation, we briefly see Good's face reading her poem twice, but otherwise Bourdain's camera, editing, soundtrack, and the poem stand alone as they reposition and reimagine *Cosmic Ray*.

The images in the "Boom Boom" sequence create a juxtaposition between poem and image, and between the disparate images of strip-mining and strippers dancing. These juxtapositions emphasize and expand upon the poem's argument, which closely mirrors Bourdain's throughout the episode; namely that West Virginia's identity has been determined by the outside gaze, exploited for the profit of others, all by people who imagine West Virginians as so uneducated as to deserve that exploitation. Further, Bourdain, Good, and Conner, all use the male, sexual gaze as a metaphor for the broader damage. We see this at work in the poem itself, as Good's voice continues:

Boom Boom
Them girls shake it.
Boom Boom
them girls dance.
Them boys know some of them West Virginia girls can't count
so they laugh
and call them names
like crazy
like whore
just after they take all their mineral rights.
Boom Boom
She was wrong.
Boom Boom
Forever gone.
Boom Boom
Them boys,
them girls,
them mountains,
explode.

But Bourdain, like Conner, makes most of his arguments visually. Essentially every single moment that is *not* "Boom Boom" juxtaposes close-ups of the strippers' nearly nude bodies and images of pristine nature, thereby drawing a visual connection between their bodyscape and the landscape, just as the poem merges exploitation of strippers and exploitation of the land. The lone exception is when Good reads, "all their mineral rights," in which Bourdain cuts to an image of a truck driving on company land with a sign attached, "We got rights too Mr. Stripper." Every single repetition of "Boom Boom," meanwhile, is matched with images of strip-mine explosions ravaging the land. The final word, "explode," is matched with fireworks, presumably taken from the football game, used to further invoke *Cosmic Ray*.

The sequence echoes an argument Bourdain makes later in the episode, asserting, "mining causes damage to the environment. Of this there is no doubt. But what cannot be grown must be mined. There are no cell phones, for instance, without a mine somewhere." In short, the spectator/outsider is complicit in the exploitation of the landscape just

Bruce Conner's *Cosmic Ray* (1962) intersperses images of hypermasculinity with partial images of a nude female body, repeatedly covered by explosions. Bourdain's "West Virginia" borrows from this approach as he pairs images of strip-mining and partial images of nearly nude female bodies ending in a slow fade to fireworks.

as gaze theory has long argued they are complicit in the exploitation and objectification of the female body.

His use of *Cosmic Ray* is one of the most glaring examples of a trademark of Bourdain's filmmaking: namely, using non-documentary film to destabilize notions of authenticity in documentary approaches. The "Boom Boom" sequence is thus emblematic of Bourdain's larger argument that distinctive cultures are exploited, objectified, and homogenized by an outside gaze in a deterministic way. Returning to Brashear, writing of one such narrative, *Hillbilly Elegy*, Vance's "narrative of the region also badly distorts its true demographic diversity. It ignores any person who is brown, black, queer, or progressive and, by default, assumes these groups of people simply do not exist in the region, and even if they do, aren't worth talking about or investing in."[18] It is for precisely these reasons Bourdain goes to great lengths to show the diversity that has typically been ignored as he tells the spectator that previous depictions have ignored that diversity and explores the damaging, real-world impact of those depictions and the spectator's complicity in them. He then pointedly tells the spectator he is doing all of this and employs influential filmic lenses to further expose and interrogate the gaze.

Rather than overkill, this layered approach is absolutely necessary when one considers Bourdain is up against the full weight of film form, cultural normalization processes, and centuries of ubiquitous stereotyping—all supporting agendas ranging widely from *Hillbilly Elegy*'s endeavor to legitimize Trump's victory to the FSA's desire to provoke sympathy and support for liberal causes. The weight of this history is the reason Bourdain (early in the episode) declares Appalachia "maybe . . . unknowable," and empathy for its inhabitants "unthinkable." By attempting to render difference as distinctive rather than exotic, and therefore universal because all cultures are distinct, Bourdain hopes to arrive at a spot where, at episode's end, he can ask his spectator to both empathize and understand. To quote Bourdain's final narration, "What are any of our hopes and dreams? A roof over our heads? Some security? Maybe even some happiness for our children? The opportunity to be proud of something? We *all* have that in common. *This* is America. And if you can't embrace it no matter how bitterly and fiercely we may disagree, there is *no* hope, for any of us."

The way in which Bourdain shifts how we see the Other is evident in a subtle, poignant, powerful montage sequence, which comes immediately after the scene where Bourdain eats lunch with miners. Having just had a conversation about politics, family, and the miners' aspirations—a conversation in which Bourdain simply asks questions and lets his subjects answer—the camera follows a trio of them out of the mines and then alternates between images of the men washing dirt off their bodies and the town's homecoming parade. As the miners' walk into the light, the soundtrack fills with the opening strains of Tyler Childers's neotraditional-country "Lady May." The song progressively builds in tempo and offers a redemptive quality to the montage, the cuts of which increase in tempo with the song, even as the images graphically match some of the song's imagery; for instance, a miner washes his face as Childers sings about baptism, a child smiles at the camera matching the lyrics "a smile across your face," children dance in the back of a pickup on parade as the song talks about letting "cares" go after the working day. Eventually, Bourdain's narration joins the soundtrack, positing, "It's so easy from afar to say that coal's time here has come and gone, that we should let the miners move, find some other work. *What* other work? The state's biggest employer is now Walmart. [pause] Whatever your views, *respect* these people. What they do, and what they've paid." Throughout the sequence, Bourdain's camera stays close to faces, usually at eye level, often letting his subjects break the fourth wall. For Bourdain, these *are* people "worth talking about" and "investing in," and his filmmaking demands such respect from his spectator as well.

12
SAN SEBASTIÁN

Bourdain made no secret that "Basque Country, San Sebastián in particular, is a place I make television as much as possible,"[1] but his final episode in Donostia–San Sebastián (PU S9E2) marks a shift in his approach to that city—a shift that is emblematic of late-stage Bourdain filmmaking, in general, and his increased interest both in micro-communities and in new-localist approaches, in particular. Airing May 7, 2017, the *Parts Unknown* episode is nuanced, sophisticated, focused filmmaking; it is one of his most complete episodes. In all aspects of his approach, Bourdain confidently calls into question everything his spectator thought they knew about European identity without offering a fixed, stable alternative. Bourdain visually references at least three films by the Basque filmmaker Julio Medem, yet uses these visual styles for his own purposes: to reposition how both his episode and his spectator imagine the Basque Country in ways that mirror, and sometimes even anticipate, the aims of the new Basque cinema movement that manifested itself largely *after* the peak of Medem's career. In so doing, Bourdain depicts a European culture that predates modern constructions of European identity to destabilize how we imagine cultural identity, hegemony, and nationalism, as well as highlight how the filmic gaze informs such constructions. Rather than a simple return to a favorite location—a chance, in Bourdain's words, to "take a deeper, more specific dive into who the Basques are"[2]—he articulates his increasingly complex conceptualization of how film shapes culture.

Bourdain's relationship with Donostia–San Sebastián spanned his career and evolved as his filmmaking matured. Bourdain first visited the Basque city in his first season of making television on *A Cook's Tour* (ACT S1E8), made life-long friends with chef Juan Mari Arzak, dedicated half of *No Reservations* "Spain" (NR S4E17) to the city, and brought chef David

Cheng there in season 1 of *The Mind of a Chef* (PBS 2012–17). Despite his clear affection for the region, however, his previous episodes rarely dealt with Basque identity head-on—focusing, instead, on the quality of Basque food for a tourist gaze, mostly avoiding topics like their ancient language, Euskara, the only language isolate in Europe, their cross-border culture, their history of terrorism, and the suppression of their language and culture under the fascist dictator Francisco Franco for much of the twentieth century. Instead, Bourdain's tone remained closer to one of his guests at the end of the *A Cook's Tour* episode, Visi Irizar, who turns toward the camera and declares, "This is a toast for all America, and we hope that you come here to our country and have a very good time," an articulation of a culture meant to be consumed by a spectator/tourist.

By his final trip to Donostia–San Sebastián, there is a marked shift in Bourdain's tone and interests. In the *Parts Unknown* field notes, Bourdain cites the retention of a distinct culture in the face of globalization and fascism as justification for returning: "Denied their own language, even the use of their given names under Franco, they refused to give up."[3] On speaking tours, Bourdain often talked of Donostia–San Sebastián, and sometimes told a story about being approached by two Spanish chefs after eating at their restaurant near Madrid. Speaking in what Bourdain calls "a very serious tone," one of the chefs asserts, "We read your book, and we like you very much in Spain. But people talk. They say things about you. . . . They say you are too close to the Basques."[4] Bourdain typically ended the story with a variation of, "I could hardly deny it. My love for the Basque, for Basque culture, for my Basque friends, is absolute. I hope I will be forgiven for this. But if not, I can live with it."[5]

Simultaneously, Bourdain's return to Donostia–San Sebastián serves as a culmination of his growing interest in subverting the Western gaze, manifested, in part, by shifts in choice of (and approach to) subject matter increasingly toward micro-communities, particularly those imagined as oppositional to national identity. Examples include "Kurdistan" (NR S7E15), "Sicily" (PU S2E5), and "Okinawa" (PU S6E3), and depictions of Appalachia, Glasgow, and Moloka'i within "West Virginia" (PU S11E1), "Scotland" (PU S5E3), and "Hawai'i" (PU S5E7), respectively. By emphasizing cultural nuance, hybridity, and difference in a way that turns the gaze back upon the dominant culture, Bourdain deconstructs the hegemonic manner dominant cultures imagine difference, showing, for instance, how even a location popularly defined by its imagination as "different," such as Hawai'i, will never conform to simplistic, single-toned imaginations.

This approach speaks to the way theorists like Homi Bhabha argue hybrid subjects offer a possible point of resistance to the totalizing repression of colonialism and neocolonialism.[6] For another example, think of the moment I have previously discussed in "Cajun Country" (NR S7E16), in which Bourdain begins in New Orleans so he can explore what Cajun and Creole, two distinct micro-communities, have in common, and why they "matter." Bourdain emphasizes Lolis Elies's answer to those queries: "If you think about what this represents, New Orleans still has a *regional* culture . . . We've got emblematic food, emblematic music, emblematic architecture, and we are an example for the rest of the country to rediscover those things about themselves because I don't *believe* that the people in Ohio didn't have anything to eat before they got McDonald's." As such, Cajun and Creole matter not only in their own right, but because they ask the homogenized, dominant culture that is gazing at them to reimagine themselves.

Such reimagination of a dominant culture by reflecting the gaze back upon them through a repositioned depiction of a micro-community is central to understanding *Parts Unknown*'s "San Sebastián." In *Imagined Communities*, the political scientist Benedict Anderson famously argues all communities are "imagined,"[7] not innate, and, once one accepts that, the only relevant question remaining is not *if* they are imagined, but, rather, "the style in which they are imagined."[8]

Bourdain does not portray Basque identity as authentic or primal, but rather, as no more (or less) constructed than dominant identities. If Bourdain offered a fixed, stable alternative, or outright accepted Basque historiography, the result would wholly legitimize Basque perspectives. Instead, Bourdain uses Basque perspectives to delegitimize dominant perspectives that he shows to be no less of a social construct. In other words, by questioning the narratives the spectator thinks they know, Bourdain uses micro-communities to draw attention to how all cultures are defined by false constructs and how those constructions are assisted by film form. By foregrounding perspectives of micro-communities and returning their gaze back upon the dominant culture, Bourdain lays the foundation for far-reaching implications that stretch beyond the Basque

Country, or even Europe. Think, for instance, of similarities to Bourdain's point-of-view shots of American Tourist running toward the spectator in "Jamaica" (PU S4E8). But nowhere is this approach more dominant and persistent throughout an entire episode than Donostia–San Sebastián.

Important context for Bourdain's approach lies in Joseba Gabilondo's reading of traditional Basque cinema, of which Bourdain's primary visual influence, Julio Medem, is a central figure. Gabilondo argues, "the gaze Basque cinema articulated during the 1968–2003 period is not Basque but Spanish; it articulated its gaze for the Spanish state and its cultural logic. Moreover, Basque cinema, in its Spanish otherness, is involved in the historical formation of the national Spanish imaginary."[9]

While Medem's two most influential films, *Vacas* (1991) and *Lucía y el sexo* (2001), both organize themselves around central themes of exposing and questioning the spectator's gaze—national in the former and masculine in the latter—both films are imagined for a Spanish audience and, in essential ways, affirm the spectator's imagination of that Other. In the case of *Lucía y el sexo*, by avoiding Basque identity altogether, and in the case of *Vacas*, by representing Basques "through their own violent self-cancelation or effacement, which, in turn, creates a structure of haunting, so that the Basque Other continues to haunt Spanish culture and its subject (the State) from its self-effacement."[10] In other words, even as *Vacas* deconstructs firm, authentic notions of identity at the level of the gaze, it still imagines Basque culture as a visual Other performing their difference for a Spanish audience informed by the weight of the history of Spanish cinema; accentuated by the fact Medem films in the Castilian (Spanish) language. As such, Medem's films share similarities to Bourdain's previous episodes, which, at times, expose the gaze, but rarely reimagine or return it. What may prove most interesting is that it is the visual style of these two films, particularly *Lucía y el sexo*, from which Bourdain borrows to reimagine the gaze-subject dichotomy, thus mirroring and anticipating new Basque cinema and repositioning Medem.

I am not implying that either of Medem's films affirm authenticity or a passive filmic gaze; in fact, the director's interest in disrupting both likely explains Bourdain's attraction to him. *Vacas*, for example, tells the story of two rural Basque families on opposite sides of the Third Carlist War—a war with particular significance to Basque historiography. Throughout the film, the Mendiluze family patriarch, Carmelo, obsessively photographs both the family and their cow; eventually the gazes of Medem's camera, Carmelo's camera, and the cow's eye merge in a manner that draws attention to both the construction of image and of history. While the film "on the one hand problematizes Basque identity, pointing to the holes so easily poked in nationalist myths, it is, on the other hand, a celebration of the Basque past, but a celebration outside the logic of a dominant, Western humanist (or Spanish) discourse."[11] Or, as Brittany Kennedy and I argue, the film's "primary purpose is to collapse any claims to an authentic identity . . . By foregrounding and exploiting the presence of a cinematic vision, Medem's purpose is to create images of Basque identity that show it to be unique, and hence worth preserving, but riddled with contradictions and claims to authenticity that he actively deconstructs as he denies the spectator easy answers."[12] *Lucía y el sexo*, similarly, uses disorienting camerawork that denies the spectator a firm awareness of where they are, and often tilts side to side, imitating both the on-screen legend of an island disconnected from the seabed and the ways the film metaphorically shakes the spectator out of a normative, objectifying gaze. Further, the cinematography matches the way the plot explores the arbitrary nature of narrative, as characters rewrite the plot at will.

While the two most common visual referents for Bourdain's episode come from these films, a third Medem film from which Bourdain also draws visual references, *La pelota vasca* (2003), can be seen as beginning the transition toward a new Basque cinema, a shift which Bourdain's episode philosophically embodies. Medem's documentary about the history of Basque nationalism, the highest grossing documentary in Spanish history,[13] is structured in a back-and-forth metaphorically mirrored by images of the Basque sport *pelota*, known as *jai alai* in the New World. Angering political observers on virtually every side of Spanish politics, the film lets interviewees speak in their own voice with little contextualization; Medem even insisted early festival screenings be without subtitles, rendering the spectator disoriented, almost regardless of nationality, listening to a mix of Euskara, Spanish, French, English, and other languages. Just as the film seems to foreground each individual narrative, however, Medem switches to opposing voices that deconstruct what has just been said. Medem offers an illusion of dialogue on the surface of his film coupled with editing that points out how each entity is speaking past each other, advancing an agenda—a perspective accentuated at the film's end when his camera sweeps past each interviewee, moving the conversation beyond what has been said. While the film angered both sides of the Basque-Spain dichotomy, Gabilondo argues it has particular importance for Basque cinema because it "presents the heterogeneity of Basque voices and people speaking for themselves, thus, renouncing the Spanish requirement of cancelling themselves as exotic or violent Others: they affirm themselves as rational subjects rather than as Others."[14] New Basque cinema therefore gives voice to a micro-community, captures a "global audience by transforming itself into what is considered 'art cinema,'" and forces "cinema [to] organize a different gaze, which no longer situates the Spanish state and its national culture at their center."[15]

Much as new Basque cinema disrupts a dominant (Spanish) gaze to forge a conversation between a hyper-local subject and a global spectator, Bourdain disrupts a dominant (Western, tourist) gaze that imagines a Basque *region* as exotic or exceptional in relation to Spain as a tourist destination to instead give voice to a distinct culture, the very acknowledgment of which calls into question basic, privileged assumptions about the cultural construction of national—and even Western—identity. Rather than depicting or performing difference for the audience's gaze, Bourdain's approach, much like that of new Basque cinema, forces the spectator to consciously partake in a Basque gaze, the purpose of which is to show the spectator how the dominant culture looks different to *them*. The result is not a reversal of the status quo; Bourdain does not attempt to cohesively argue, for instance, that Basque ideas of what constitute national identity are logical or correct. Instead, Bourdain forces the spectator to question why their ideas of what constitute national identity are any more (or less) arbitrary, and the degree to which their assumptions about nationalism and culture are based upon a history of a single, privileged perspective being the only one articulated. By making the spectator see the world from a new perspective that runs contrary to what they think they know, Bourdain fundamentally destabilizes the spectator, enabling deconstruction.

Bourdain's approach is unflinching. The episode opens with a nondiegetic sequence in which neither Bourdain, nor any Western surrogate, is present. Two (presumably) Basque musicians play a *txalaparta*, a percussive instrument that looks and sounds foreign to any non-Basque spectator, and an unattributed voice explains in Euskara (with subtitles), "We are because we were. What we were, who we were, we don't know. We don't know where our language came from. It's been mixed with several other languages. Twenty-five thousand years and all the people who crossed this sea. Our language is the one we have today. This language of ours is our nation, after all." The camera, reminiscent of *Lucía y el sexo*, swirls and rocks, never holding still; the speed of its swirl accelerates with the rhythm of the *txalaparta*; and when Bourdain cuts to shots in and around Donostia–San Sebastián, he utilizes an increasingly rapid rhythmic montage also dictated by the *txalaparta*. The effect is disorienting as Bourdain never allows his spectator a clear understanding of where they are or what they are seeing. The images contain close-ups of smiling, friendly Basques who break the fourth wall, as well as flashes of food, dancing, music, and surfing—the disparate elements Bourdain argues represent Basque identity. The montage culminates with the Basque flag, the *ikurrina*. All this occurs as the speaker defines nationality via language—much like the other images, an alternative imagination that is intentionally disruptive to normative definitions of such words, all made more nuanced by the speaker admitting the language has evolved, that it is neither "pure" nor "authentic." Additionally, it is the lack of contextualization that de-exoticizes the subject and challenges the Western gaze, precisely because the spectator can never find firm enough footing to objectify, or even fully understand, what they see. It is a jarring approach that upends the spectator's perspective without offering a stable alternative.

The opening of almost every sequence, particularly when Bourdain returns from commercial, serve as a similar assault on any notion of a fixed gaze as the editing and mise-en-scène disorient the spectator. When Bourdain returns from the opening credits and introduces his definition of what constitutes "the Basque Country," itself a destabilizing deconstruction of accepted historical narratives, the music is quiet, atonal, and contains an off-putting echo; the images are shot in a style evocative of *Lucía y el sexo*; and Bourdain's narration never explains exactly where one is nor what one is looking at. When the episode shifts to the first interviewees on a boat, Bourdain begins *not* by introducing them, but, rather, by letting them deconstruct assumptions a spectator would easily make about the visible landscape. It is almost two minutes before Bourdain introduces his guests (father and daughter novelists Edorta and Irati Jiménez), and he *still* never states where the boat is located. When the scene abruptly shifts to a more traditional introduction to the city of Donostia–San Sebastián, the camerawork, again like *Lucía y el sexo*, is handheld and jittery. As Bourdain moves about the old town with father and daughter chefs Juan Mari and Elena Arzak, the editing speeds up and becomes disorienting, even as Bourdain proclaims *he's* never "lost for long" in this city. In the meantime, the voice-over and dialogue assert the attractive architecture and food, which provide a visual surplus for Bourdain's camera, are all distinctly Basque. When Bourdain returns from the next commercial to the city of Pasaia, the soundtrack is even more aggressively off-putting, the introductory images shot in close-up to deny the spectator's ability to situate them, and Bourdain waits minutes to introduce the speaker, shipbuilder Xabier Agote. Bourdain never even mentions the fact the location shifts thirty kilometers mid-sequence to Jatetxea Elkano in Getaria, a restaurant he similarly does not introduce until the end of the sequence. This pattern continues throughout the episode as Bourdain makes his spectator constantly work to situate themselves.

While Bourdain's filmic choices affect the spectator's ability to situate themselves, Bourdain's definition of his subject matter, the Basque Country, is equally unsettling on a narrative level. Coming immediately after the opening credits, every word is carefully crafted to be as precise and uncontroversial as possible; yet, collectively they work to upend the imagined European map: "The Basque Country is an autonomous region, a place, a culture, where the Basque language is spoken." The choice of "autonomous" is evocative of the legal standing according to the Spanish government (one of Spain's seventeen "autonomous communities"), the other terms are carefully selected to stress the Basque Country as a distinctive place without stating anything technically inaccurate by normative definitions. Bourdain cuts to a map of Western Europe that redraws the lines to show a Basque Country on both sides of the French-Spanish border, as his narration continues, "Strictly speaking, it's an area straddling Spain and France at the Western end of the Pyrenees. They've been speaking Basque here long before the first Roman arrived in 65 BC. It is a very old language. How old, like the question of how far back their history goes, and where it begins, is not known. The best answer anyone can give you is long, long ago." Much like the opening sequence spoken in Euskara and edited to a *txalaparta*, Bourdain keeps his spectator on their heels, offering an alternative imagination of Europe that challenges accepted notions.

Bourdain remains focused on the powerful way historiography is constructed by things as diverse (and dominant) as cartography and filmmaking. Bourdain lets Basques speak for themselves, offering an alternative historiography he implies is no more, and no less, constructed than the dominant historiographies the spectator already knows; historiographies shaped, in part, by a fascist dictator, and, in part, by a Western, tourist, filmic gaze. Bourdain tells us Basque Country was the "center of the world for boat building," just as Agote tells us the Basques invented industrial whaling and hints they discovered North America but did not tell anybody because "they didn't want to attract the attention of other fishermen . . . You see the official maritime history has been written by kings that wanted to claim something, like this is mine, I want everyone to know that." Elsewhere, immediately after the opening introduction, the Jiménezes make even more jarring claims, that "25,000 years we are living here," that Basque DNA is wholly distinctive, that Euskara is "the only language in Europe that we know of that doesn't have anything to do with the rest of the languages." These assertions are, objectively, exaggerated—rooted in fact but romanticized—but they come immediately after Bourdain's narration informs us *no* one knows "how old" their language is "or how far back their history goes," that the "best answer anyone can give you is long, long ago." In other words, Bourdain actively *tells* his spectator Basque historiography is a construction, yet lets his subjects voice that historiography because it sheds light upon how the dominant historiography is *also* constructed. Agote "created Albaola twenty years ago because nobody knew about the Basques and the relationship with the sea," and says it is "important to us" that researchers are finding evidence of the Basque presence in Nova Scotia. In such a way, we see how all history, and thereby nationality, are constructions.

Like the opening sequence's cinematography, which shows *partial* images that shift and shape how we see a statue of Juan Sebastián Elkano—the man who finished Magellan's circumnavigation and a central figure in Basque historiography—Bourdain sees dialogue between historiographies as a nuanced debate between opposing constructions in which evidence must be examined closely, piece by piece, always aware of how it is being depicted, by whom, and for what agenda. One example is how Bourdain treats food, constantly asking a variation of the question "Why do the Basques, unique among their neighbors, obsessively insist on such high-quality ingredients for everything? Why here?" It becomes a framing device for the episode. For instance, much of the discussion about Basque exploration with Agote comes as the two eat Jatetxea Elkano's most iconic dish, grilled turbot, which Bourdain emphasizes is "portioned out expertly by owner Aitor Arregi to highlight each and every unique bit and its special characteristics," and which Agote describes as "finding every single secret of the fish." Rather than spectacle to be visually consumed, food becomes a means of investigating the secrets that make Basque culture distinct.

This use of food as a cultural text to be studied parallels Bourdain's approach to food across the later portion of his career; it stands at the forefront of "San Sebastián," however, because, in Bourdain words, "The love of food, the insistence on the very best ingredients is fundamental to the culture and to life here." In fact, Bourdain's episode, and his constant recurring question about their relationship to food quality, asserts it as a marker of nationality, much like language and *pelota*; another alternative way of understanding what constitutes collective identity.

The difference between Spanish *tapas* and Basque *pintxos* explored with the Arzaks thus becomes a way of understanding and interrogating difference, rather than a simple consumption of "incredible batteries of delicious, delicious things." At one point, before Bourdain even introduces Juan Mari Arzak, the internationally acclaimed three–Michelin star chef asserts, "Well, it's undoubtable I'm Basque, and here there's a kind of gastronomical atmosphere. We are prophets in our land and people talk to us about food wherever we go. We solve all our problems by cooking, because we have a kind of fanaticism towards food. I think it's one of the reasons it's so within me, in my heart, in my soul. But it's undoubtable that being Basque is a very important part." As Arzak speaks the last line, Bourdain's camera cuts to a sweeping aerial shot of Mutriku, a city Bourdain never visits or introduces, that is a direct steal from the end of *La pelota vasca*.

This assertion of one's relationship to food as part of a national, constructed identity, informs almost every answer Bourdain receives to his recurring question "Why *here*?" It is also emblematic of how Bourdain depicts Basque identity as simultaneously hyper-local and universal, related to Ackbar Abbas's "new localism,"[16] and an embodiment of the glocalization Gabilondo identifies in new Basque cinema.[17] For instance, Bourdain, eating international cuisine at Restaurant Arzak, declares, "The food is innovative, wildly creative, forward-thinking, but always, *always* Basque." Or, speaking of Viktor Arguinzoniz at Asador Etxebarri, "He is a master of what *looks* austere and simple but is, in fact, in an almost *Japanese* way, fetishistically *perfectionist* in his treatment of local ingredients. Viktor cooks everything *himself*, from his own charcoal, made from wood, he cuts *himself*." This food is thereby universalized by its expression of what is local and distinct and (in this case) simple.

As I have suggested, Bourdain's glocal articulation of Basque identity mirrors the shift in Basque cinema Gabilondo marks as beginning with *La pelota vasca*, and actively anticipates a film, Aitor Galdos and Jon Garaño's *Handia* (2017), which many see as the clearest articulation of new Basque cinema.[18] Gabilondo asserts "the new gaze that Basque film articulates is Basque, not Spanish"[19] as Basque filmmakers increasingly "frame" their films in the European art cinema tradition for global commercial appeal.[20] One clear marker of this shift is the choice of Euskara for the film's dialogue, rather than the Castilian favored by Medem's generation. On its surface, the use of Euskara could be seen as exoticizing, such as Garaño's citing a commercial advantage: audiences want to hear "that strange language."[21] The use of Euskara, however, is an essential part of a broad-based approach that forces the spectator to look back at dominant cultural constructions through the eyes of a Basque gaze, drawing attention to (and thereby thwarting) any easy allegiance to a Western gaze; filmmaking that is "eminently and globally Basque, in a way that only Euskara can channel and anchor."[22]

In the case of *Handia*, one of the film's overt plot themes is about such a gaze. The film is based on the historical figure of Joaquín Eleizegi, who suffered from gigantism and toured Europe much of his life, performing both his stature and his Basqueness to make ends meet, and his brother Martin, who learns Castilian to serve as Joaquín's business manager and wants to save money to move to the Americas to make a fortune. Gabilondo believes the film serves as the depiction of a Basque "tour throughout 19th-century Europe and America, in which the Spanish state can be represented as an ever-freakier perversion (the sexual gaze of the Queen) at the margins of a Basque condition that situates itself, beyond Spain, in a global geopolitical context. . . . The film gives the viewers a Basque-centered mapping of the world and its gaze."[23]

By offering a screen surrogate who suffers harm as the object of the gaze, *Handia*, and new Basque cinema collectively, turns a mirror on the Western spectator and exposes identity as a social construction with potentially dangerous side effects.

Bourdain thus uses his own filmic lens, as well as influences from Medem's repositioning of his Spanish audience's gaze, to turn a mirror on a global audience and achieve similar aims as the new Basque cinema movement that came of age after the peak of Medem's career and reached its fruition with a film, *Handia*, that premiered four months after Bourdain's episode. "San Sebastián" enters such an uncanny conversation because Bourdain similarly destabilizes his spectator and partakes in a "Basque-centered mapping of the world and its gaze."

As I have argued, this is a multifaceted approach that takes place (a) on a narrative level, as Bourdain repeatedly denies his spectator an introduction to where they are or what they are seeing, not letting them position it within the mapping they know; (b) on multiple filmic levels, particularly through editing, such as the rhythmic montage dictated by a Basque instrument, and cinematography, such as the jarring camerawork, which—similar to the lack of narrative introduction—prevents the spectator from wholly objectifying what they see and hear; (c) on the level of the mediation of historiography, as Bourdain depicts a Basque map, declares Basque Country the "center of the world" for maritime history, emphasizes Basque influences in the New World, and declares, "Basque language and culture exists on both sides of a border. Unsurprising as they predate *both* countries. This may be France, but it's *still Pays Basque*." Further, the approach also takes place (d) on the level of subject and representation, as Bourdain shows Basque instruments like the *txalaparta*, Basque sports such as *pelota*, Basque food like *pintxos*, and Basque people in the street happy and approachable, often, like the city worker cleaning the square in the first shots of the city center, breaking the fourth wall; and (e) on the level of language, as multiple guests speak Euskara without Bourdain drawing attention to or exoticizing it, and depicts Bourdain's own desire to partake in the language when

A sanitation worker drags a hose across the Plaza de la Constitución in Donostia-San Sebastián. Like countless Basques in this episode, he suddenly and pointedly makes eye contact with the camera.

he—seeing Elena Arzak about to make a toast—interjects, "*Osasuna*." Essentially, the only clear separation between Bourdain's episode and the aims and approach of new Basque cinema is Bourdain is not Basque, but, rather, a celebrity travel show host; a major feat that speaks to the degree Bourdain not only exposes, but actively subverts, the Western gaze.

It is not *just* that the episode employs the same strategies as new Basque cinema, but also that much of what it depicts or represents—ranging from language to sport to music to cuisine—are the very things most would agree constitute cultural identity, as well as nations, Anderson's "imagined" communities. Therefore, the emphasis on how one depicts or represents those subjects has far-reaching implications about how film form shapes and determines how we imagine the world. Much as "Rome" (PU S8E9) highlights the impact of film upon Rome's post–World War II reconstruction, both physical and imagined, as well as how films by Pier Paolo Pasolini (and Bourdain's episode) can reimagine the city, "San Sebastián" highlights the impact of film form upon the reconstruction of postwar Europe, and how new Basque cinema (and Bourdain's episode) can thereby reimagine it.

The implications are less about the specific micro-community than about the dominant culture, the construction of which is exposed when a film uses a hyper-local surrogate to gaze back upon the spectator. For example, Bourdain asks dinner guests to imagine a Spanish audience reacting to a Basque person "pissing" on Franco's grave. Not only do his Basque guests laugh heartily as they imagine the reaction, but the camera angles (which focus on Bourdain's own laughter) imply that he anticipates his audience will laugh as well. The spectator is now fully situated with a Basque gaze, laughing at the dominant, Spanish one.

This moment, much like this episode, serves as embodiment of Bourdain's increased interest in "glocal" exchanges between hyper-local and dominant cultures, with an attempt to universalize the local by demonstrating it as an ever-changing thing that should be embraced and preserved. Rather than the local as "authentic," it imagines the local as "different," in the way we are *all* different, and begs the spectator to respect and defend said differences rather than objectify and consume them. Much as Abbas's "new localism . . . investigates the dislocations of the local, where the local is something unstable that mutates right in front of our eyes, like the language itself,"[24] Bourdain's embrace of new Basque cinema is part of a broader, global resistance to hegemony. To return to Gabilondo, writing of new Basque cinema, "lines of flight, forms of resisting, persevering, and persisting, which, in its choice of Euskara and its haunted deconstruction of hegemony (masculine, Spanish, etc.) underscores its collective condition. Thus, Basque cinema might be a way out that highlights . . . a singular community defined by its language, its violence, and its negotiations with political hegemony. . . . This in/visibility appears to be universal these days."[25]

Thus, the very cultural markers that mark Basque "difference" represent a universal struggle to preserve and celebrate difference. For Bourdain, such an approach to a Western culture that predates modern conceptualizations of the West provides a unique opportunity to deconstruct firm notions of authenticity at the root of their philosophic home, Western Europe, thereby opening a wide swath of possibilities for deconstructing Western assumptions everywhere.

Bourdain concludes by pairing a response from Juan Mari Arzak with images of Donostia–San Sebastián in a way that concretizes Bourdain's use of micro-community to deconstruct firm, static notions of history, culture, and authenticity. The camera first depicts the old town's Plaza de la Constitución, followed by racially diverse Basque children on a playground, and, finally, people riding waves toward the shore, the water continuing, unstopping, even as the screen fades to black. The cinematography, particularly in the square, is heavily reminiscent of *Lucía y el sexo*, the camera rocking back and forth, mirroring Medem's island detached from the seabed. Arzak begins, "It's all been easy for me. And it's all been beautiful, which is the most *important* thing." Arzak's emphasis on "important" recalls *the* key moment in *Vacas* when Carmelo sets up a highly constructed shot on his camera of a seemingly random insect, and declares, "This is *important*. This is the *most* important thing." In the case of *Vacas*, Brittany Kennedy and I argue the moment emphasizes that, "Ultimately what is 'important' . . . are not answers or resolutions that resolve divisions between myth and history, but, instead, abandoning both."[26] Similarly, Arzak continues, "I always think that if you don't have creativity, you're kind of dead. You have to think like a child. You go to a square and see all the children there, and they're always making new things and they're always happy. And what I like is always being there, like the children. A child hasn't got boundaries. And we mustn't have boundaries. I don't know if this is difficult or not, but for me, it isn't." While Bourdain translates "*frontera*" as boundaries, a more direct translation is "frontiers," which allows dual inflections: philosophical "boundaries" and physical "borders," such as those between nations. The "happy" spot for Arzak, and presumably for Bourdain as it is the conclusion, is not in a fixed, firm location, but, rather, a liminal space connected to creativity and reliant upon the shedding of the fixed and firm ideas we have been taught in school and in film, and which determine, and thereby limit, how we see the world around us.

The implications of such an embrace of liminality, especially in relation to constructed cultural identity, is manifested in the way Bourdain uses a Basque song to bridge between two scenes of "happy" spots. The sequence comes immediately after a scene at a *txoko*, a Basque dining society in which a young man speaks in Euskara about the joy his ninety-year-old grandfather found in a final visit, and Bourdain eating at Asador Etxebarri, a restaurant he adamantly proclaims is where he would want to eat his "last" meal. Unlike most of the episode, both sequences are portrayed as idyllic, bathed in soft light. Between the scenes, Bourdain's camera cuts to an unidentified worker from Agote's ship-building company, Albaola, who stands in front of a perfectly framed view of Pasaia's port, the type of tourist backdrop Bourdain typically avoids. The man asks the cameraman, "Here?" We hear a muffled response, the man moves slightly to his left, and clears his throat. He then begins to sing in Euskara, "The first foundations of North America, / Were laid by Basque fishermen, / Where does our language have its origins? / Perhaps it was sent up from the bottom of the sea, / The Basque Country is like the sea, / It's always old, and always new." The matching images are the most romantic of the episode: a series of shots from a fixed camera depicting the harbor, mountains, a surfer, rural nature, the ocean, and finally ending on a string of Basque flags hanging across the courtyard in front of Etxebarri. As the song points to questions left unanswered by historiography, it offers an answer based upon myth, all while the camera, yet again, points toward the elements that make up an alternative definition of nationalism. Much like Bourdain's interruption of refugees in "Hong Kong" (PU S11E5), or the singer who lights a cigarette as the camera lingers in "Rome," the emphasis remains on the construction of what we see and how we see it. If all identity is a construction, all that matters is "the style" in which Bourdain asks his spectator to reimagine it, in this case, an alternative imagination that draws into question the dominant narratives they have accepted, a reversal rendered universal by a culture that is constantly changing, liminal even as it is rooted; "always old and always new."

13
BHUTAN

Airing June 24, 2018, the final episode of Bourdain's final full season of *Parts Unknown* was set in Bhutan (S11E8), a landlocked nation situated in the eastern Himalayas between China and India. "Bhutan" marks a reunion with the filmmaker Darren Aronofsky, a guest Bourdain first met when the two traveled to Madagascar (PU S5E4) three years prior. Both episodes share an interest in remote locations, the impact of industrialization upon the environment, the effects of environmental crises upon less industrialized cultures, and the role film plays in representing those issues. The episodes also collectively draw visual influences from Aronofsky's films, particularly *Black Swan* (2010), *Noah* (2014), and *Mother!* (2017). "Bhutan," however, is of particular interest for understanding Bourdain not just because it is one of his last episodes, but because it is perhaps the clearest embodiment of his search for "parts unknown." As Bourdain's narration asserts, Bhutan is "a kingdom that has existed contently in a state of self-imposed isolation for centuries," forbade tourism until the 1970s, and is where "the amount of foreign visitors each year is strictly limited to protect Bhutan's culture and environment." Further, as Aronofsky and Bourdain point out, few, if any, films have been set in Bhutan, let alone shot there, rendering it nearly unimaginable to the Western eye.

If, as Bourdain claims in "Hong Kong" (PU S11E5), "how we see" the world is "shaped by . . . the books we've read, the films we've seen, the baggage we carry," then Bhutan poses fundamental questions about a filmmaker depicting a culture with virtually no preexisting visual references. On the surface, one might anticipate the subject would be rendered more exotic; yet, Bourdain again largely subverts Western spectatorship, de-exoticizing difference and foregrounding himself and Aronofsky who serve as screen surrogates for Western tourists, rendering themselves, and the spectator, far more exotic than Bhutan.

This universalization of difference is a repeated theme in reactions to the episode. For example, Aronofsky, in an open letter addressed to Bourdain the week of its release, wrote, "Your shows bring the world closer together—not by making easy similarities but by revealing how unique we all are. You turned a light on what it means to be a human right now, right here on planet Earth. Thank you for letting me tag along and witness a master storyteller shape the unexpected into the relatable and unforgettable."[1] Eric Kohn, reviewing for *IndieWire*, claimed it "feels like a farewell—wistful, sensitive, and rich with existential yearning, it encapsulates Bourdain's underlying ethos. . . . Set to gentle acoustic rhythms and a constant montage of village lives, the episode flows with a meditative quality on par with its setting, while positioning these two white guys as the ultimate contrast to a culture defined by tranquility."[2]

As I have argued, Bourdain's approach of exposing spectatorship, and the problems therein, while foregrounding conversations about the efficacy of tourism, and the complicity of the spectator in it, are precisely the avenue from which Bourdain repositions how we see his subjects. To quote Bourdain, writing about "Madagascar," filmmaking is a "manipulative process. And not, inherently anyway, a bad one. I want you, the viewer, to feel the way about a place the way I want you to feel. I want you to look at it and see it from my point of view, if at all possible. Or at least consider other points of view. But it is, almost always, one point of view—or one lens through which you see: mine."[3] Time and again, Bourdain uses the awareness of the space between his perspective and that of his subjects to deconstruct the Western gaze and inspire the spectator to seek out differences in their own culture. In short, "Bhutan" is a microcosm of Bourdain's achievements, a universalization of difference made more emphatic because it is set in one of the most remote, unknown places on earth.

Bourdain's approach to depicting difference, and the way that depiction defies expectations of medium and genre, is central to Shelby E. Ward's "Anthony Bourdain's Cosmopolitan Table: Mapping the Ethni(c)ity Through Street Food and Television." Much as I describe him mediating content in his role as documentary filmmaker, Ward calls Bourdain, as host, "a translation machine" whose worldview "we read and see the world through."[4] Ward situates Bourdain within Jacques Derrida's idea of the "cosmopolitan,"[5] defined by Ward as someone who is mobile, open to others, willing to take risks, and retains "an ability to reflect upon and judge aesthetically between different natures, places, and societies."[6] As Ward discusses how such figures problematically "oscillate between hospitality and hostility,"[7] she points to Bourdain's "self-reflexive and accountable view of the city and Other,"[8] which complicates the normative dynamics of his genre. For instance, unlike most travel TV that "makes the host appear at 'home' or 'not out of place' in the city of the Other," Ward points to "Colombia" (PU S1E3) as an example when Bourdain uses his struggles with altitude to render himself "very much out of place," his "body untranslatable, and his position as 'guest' made explicit."[9] Ward's understanding of Bourdain as host thus augments my discussion of his equally self-reflexive approach to film form, as he repositions inherent assumptions present in film form, genre, and thereby the spectator. To quote Ward, while Bourdain's "authorial voice might produce an omnipresent and disembodied presence, it does so to complicate Bourdain's own image in relation to Otherness . . . It invites the viewer to consume . . . but in doing so, the viewer is also made aware of their own desires to consume. As such, the possibility to both confront and address the desire of the cosmopolitan becomes just as much a possibility as the consumption itself."[10]

This use of self-reflexive film form and a self-reflexive host working in tandem to subvert the dominant spectator-subject dynamic by exposing both that dynamic and the spectator's desire for it, is central to both Bourdain-Aronofsky collaborations, and underscores how "Madagascar" serves as prelude to "Bhutan." The former opens with an unidentified Malagasy asserting, "when I was a kid, my grandparents teach that there are some people who live in Madagascar *before* . . . they respect the environment. But then comes many people from other countries. From Africa, from Asia, Spain, from France." The two directors take a train trip and discuss the arduous nature of their journey as they sip champagne cocktails in an apparent reference to Bernardo Bertolucci's *The Sheltering Sky* (1990). The duo buy food from local vendors at a station, only to have children beg for it; the camera cuts away to iPhone footage Aronofsky shot of his own feet, emphasizing playful artistry, and later in the episode, returns to the train station scene, now edited by Aronofsky, emphasizing multiple, differing perspectives. Elsewhere children covet a village meal prepared for the filmmakers, leading Bourdain to declare, "it's one of those days when the artifice of television threatens to move dangerously into cruelty. Who gets to eat, and when, becomes a pressing concern." Bourdain subsequently implies Aronofsky's vegetarianism, though well intentioned, comes from a place of privilege, and, elsewhere, equates ecotourism with colonialism, asserting, "A lot of people feel that the future should be ecotourism. That they should essentially be working in restaurants and hotels for tourists. That's kind of a return to colonialism, isn't it?" Later, Bourdain repeats the idea, "local people cleaning rooms, cooking, performing traditional ethnic dances. To me, this is not an ideal option," but Aronofsky interrupts and asks, "What's an ideal option, though?" Bourdain stares back silently, a dissonant soundtrack intervenes, and the scene cuts away.

Thus, as two filmmakers visit an impoverished food culture, Bourdain repeatedly highlights the artifice of his medium, the status of both filmmakers as white, privileged outsiders, the degree to which there are no easy answers for the crises that have been brought to Madagascar from the outside, and the degree to which film is always the filmmaker's perspective. Bourdain asserts, "Over the years I've let a lot of extraordinary landscapes recede into a blur outside my windows. I've looked, maybe seen, maybe noticed, then gone. . . . We see things differently, don't we?"

Aronofsky's on-screen explanation for choosing Madagascar, "I guess it's one of the more extreme places that you hear about but know you'll never go to unless something weirdly summons you, and you are sort of that weird force," is a particularly telling admission as one considers their next destination, Bhutan, is even more remote. Further, Bourdain's introduction to "Madagascar," "Exotic, unspoiled, paradise? Or microcosm for the end of times?," and his subsequent episode-long deconstruction of those dichotomous, Western-centric questions, serves as a telling way of understanding his depiction of Bhutan, a nation that leaves Bourdain with more questions than answers as he shows how it cannot possibly embody what a Western spectator demands of it, nor is it Bhutan's responsibility to do so.

This denial of Western-based expectations is built upon a history of films, such as the aforementioned *The Sheltering Sky*, Jean-Jacques Annaud's *Seven Years in Tibet* (1997), Michael Apted's *Gorillas in the Mist* (1988), Sydney Pollack's *Out of Africa* (1985), Edward Zwick's

The Last Samurai (2003), or, even, to a certain degree, Bertolucci's *The Last Emperor* (1987), which collectively codify locations imagined in the West as "exotic," as either virginal, leading to epiphany, or formerly virginal, now actively in the process of being destroyed by encroaching industrialization. Both imaginations serve Western purposes and Western conceptualizations (e.g., Eden before the Fall versus after), a fact further driven home when Bourdain structures the first half of "Bhutan" around the most American of all genres, road-buddy films—a trope that pointedly disintegrates as Bourdain depicts Bhutan in defiance of Western expectations. Put another way, without a history of filmic depictions to draw upon, Bourdain chooses not to refer to films about "exotic" locations, but to instead use their dichotomous depictions as a framing device while invoking an even *more* Western genre that then fails, thereby emphasizing how *both* genres have little at all to do with their own subjects, nor Bourdain's.

These dichotomies are embodied in the episode's opening sequence and in the juxtaposition of that sequence with the lead-in to the more formal introduction that comes after the credits. Bourdain opens with up-tempo, Eastern-inspired instrumental music as the filmmakers' car traverses a dirt highway, which looks at once beautiful and unpassable. The camera repeatedly lingers on roadside animals, who sometimes stare right back at the camera, as the two men engage in a conversation inspired by a surface-level understanding of Eastern theology. Aronofsky asks Bourdain if he thinks "animals are sentient," to which Bourdain responds, "I think pain is, you know, pain. If you don't respond to that you might have something seriously wrong with you," to which Aronofsky comments, "That's very Buddhist of you, I think." Aronofsky's serious response sparks Bourdain to tell a story about steaming lobsters at a Cape Cod restaurant and how he now has dreams of anthropomorphized crustaceans locking him in a sauna. The perspectives manage to simultaneously be sophisticated, nuanced, thoughtful, comic, *and* stereotypical; the perspectives are inspired by the location, yet they are also Western-centric and linked to a desire to consume the culture they are road-tripping through via comedy related to their own lives. Returning from the opening credits, the soundtrack is mostly silent, dominated by the occasional ringing of a Bhutanese bell; the camerawork remains still and unobtrusive, colors slightly pushed; Bourdain's narration is serious and, primarily, about Bhutan's unknowability. Just as the opening emphasizes the duo's privileged position as cosmopolitan travelers, the self-reflexive depiction and the juxtaposition draw one's awareness to that very dynamic.

The (typical for Bourdain) nuanced positioning of his personal perspective between polarized oppositions also exhibits itself in the way his introduction walks a line between rendering Bhutan relatable to his Western audience and drawing their attention to its unrelatability, a line that also denies the duality created in most filmic depictions of "exotic" locations between virginal place of epiphany and Westernized wasteland. Throughout the introduction, and continuing throughout the episode, Bourdain draws parallels to Western surrogates his audience feels they know, such as comparing Bhutan's size to Switzerland. Time and again, however, these parallels are brief and incomplete, situated among a larger context that renders them mostly ineffective. In the case of the introduction, this is embodied by an emphasis on how few Western tourists have ever seen Bhutan linked to the difficulty getting there, a difficulty we see displayed through Bourdain's on-screen body as he is scared and ultimately relieved as his plane completes the harrowing approach between two mountains to land at Bhutan's only international airport. Rather than Bourdain's corpus offering a mediation rendering it easier for the spectator to visually consume Bhutan, the spectator is offered a surrogate whose body (and voice-over) emphasize how impossible it is to quantifiably experience Bhutan on their terms.

Instead of existing on either side of a Western epiphany–wasteland dichotomy, Bourdain describes Bhutan as "caught between the Old World and the New," and links the growth of its capital, Thimphu, a city of a relatively modest 100,000 inhabitants, as Bhutan having "begun the inevitable move away from a rural, agrarian lifestyle." This articulation destroys purist imaginations of the possibility of remaining in a kind of pre-industrial utopia by calling that move "inevitable," yet it laments what is lost with globalization and industrialization. Such an embrace of uncertainty is simply another embodiment of the embrace of nuance I have discussed across his filmography; as Bourdain told *Variety*, "Life is complicated. It's filled with nuance. It's unsatisfying [pointing to a tattoo on his arm]. It's from the Greek skeptics. The translation is 'I am certain of nothing. I'm not even sure I'm certain of that.' If I believe in anything, it is doubt. The root cause of all life's problems is looking for a simple fucking answer."[11]

In the end, Bourdain's "Bhutan" is defined by what the country does *not* share with the West, namely, "no Starbucks, no KFC's, no King, or Clown," and the fact "it's not on the tourist trail," directly telling his spectator, "They don't want you to come here, at least, *en masse*," thereby renouncing his own road-trip sequence from moments before. This perspective is an extension of Bourdain's ambivalence about the impact of tourist culture I have explored in "French Polynesia" (NR S3E10), "Jamaica" (PU S4E8), and "Rome" (PU S8E9) but taken to an even more extreme level by investigating its impact upon a country only beginning to face mass tourism.

Despite opening with Bourdain's declaration that tourists are not wanted, he goes to great lengths to highlight their presence. Most of the establishing cinematography consists of prototypical late-stage Bourdain images of locals in their own environment that, in terms of framing and color palette, are shot in a highly stylized approach reminiscent of Aronofsky's *Noah* and *Mother!*, which (sometimes utilizing CGI) render nature both more beautiful *and* threatening, and create contrasts between the nature depicted in the focus/foreground versus the distance/background. Bourdain, however, intermittently inserts pointed shots of Caucasian tourists gawking at and photographing local culture in a way that disturbs what would otherwise be a consistent visual style, as the shots of tourists almost always take a more classic, travel-TV, *cinéma vérité* approach. At several moments, such as while Bourdain is interviewing local journalist Kunga Tenzin Dorji, we see tourists moving past the frame with the sides of Bourdain's and Aronofsky's faces in the foreground, borrowing from the dominant approach of *Black Swan*, an approach which makes the person's "presence known within the mise-en-scène on the edge of the frame"[12] in order to achieve "eye-line as a proxy for eye contact."[13] In other words, we do not just see the tourists, we see them through the eyes of Bourdain and Aronofsky, rendering the tourists all the more out of place and disruptive.

The shots of tourists reach an apex in the conclusion, a scene to which I will return, but Bourdain never lets their presence—and potential impact—disappear. Introducing Punakha, the home of a monastery built in honor of Bhutan's "Divine Madman," Drukpa Kunley, Bourdain proclaims, "this is a *must*-see destination," using a verbal affectation to emphasize the cliché typical of travel TV. Elsewhere, Bourdain and Aronofsky purchase wooden phalluses, which Bourdain discusses as representing something important, something he as a Western tourist cannot adequately comprehend or articulate, yet he simultaneously mocks the way tourists "flock" to purchase them as souvenirs. In short, the spectator sees themself on-screen depicted derisively, imagined as posing a threat to local culture, and, with intended irony, linked to Bourdain's presence as filmmaker.

The connection between tourism and filmic depictions of locations perceived by Westerners as "exotic"—a central concern for Bourdain—is directly invoked in the first scene when Bourdain formally introduces his travel partner. Shot at Menzu Shiri, a restaurant situated on a backstreet in Thimphu, the camerawork emphasizes the ways the two filmmakers stand out like sore thumbs, juxtaposing close-ups of the locals' food choices and modes of dress in contrast to Bourdain's and Aronofsky's. The camerawork is assisted by the first bits of conversation we hear, in which Aronofsky tells Bourdain to "watch your head" as the tall men duck-under a low door to enter, and then sit at a table discussing their struggles with altitude. Again, as Ward argued about Bourdain's similar use of altitude in "Colombia," the discussion renders them even more "out of place," made all the clearer by a juxtaposition created between a local shown confidently swigging beer and Bourdain stating to Aronofsky that he will be "slowly dying" because of the altitude. Bourdain's narration introduces Aronofsky, "Fresh off the unjustifiably horrified reaction to what I think is his masterpiece, *Mother!* . . . an angry and thinly veiled warning that we are destroying our planet," a topic Bourdain relates to Bhutan, adding, "policy wise, Bhutan is something of an environmental wonderland." Sitting in the restaurant, the duo clearly depicted as outsiders, Bourdain asserts, "We want to protect the country from being overly influenced by foreign values, culture, you know all the bad stuff that happens with tourism. Has anyone made a film here?" Aronofsky answers earnestly, "I don't know, it's got to be hard to work here," causing Bourdain to laugh and add, "Yeah, plus talk about contaminating the values of the local culture." Aronofsky laughs and jokes, "Hollywood doesn't do that!" Thus, the threat to culture and environment posed by globalization is directly linked to the filmmakers' presence, as are the questions that are central to so many Bourdain episodes: What are the responsibilities of a filmmaker? Do filmic representations help or hurt? How does the style in which a subject is represented matter? How does one represent without essentializing?

While such questions trouble Bourdain, his allegiance to nuance, ambivalence, and asking questions rather than offering answers seem particularly well suited to Bhutan. Pressing the environmentalist Dasho Benji Dorji to explain the local manifestation of Buddhism, which follows what Bourdain calls "the middle path," Dorji explains, "It's all about an attitude, pick up and move on. His Holiness the Dalai Lama once told me, 'Every day when you get up you try to be as good a human being as possible.' That's more important than being religious." In other words, it is about a search, not clear answers, nor a stable destination. As I have discussed, Bourdain refrains from offering clear parallels that would make things he depicts relatable to his spectator because such comparisons mediate things into something they are not, and render too easy, Western-centric answers. For instance, he claims *momos* are his favorite Bhutanese food yet refrains from making easy comparisons to Asian or Italian dumplings.

In a remarkable moment, Bourdain talks about Bhutan's Gross National Happiness index as something important to which to aspire; yet, when Dorji attempts to explain it via comparison to foundational US ideology, saying, "you have in your constitution the pursuit of happiness, the right of every individual," Bourdain interrupts with a laugh, "Yeah, but we don't actually *believe* that." Eric Kohn, in his review of the episode, calls it "a definitive moment for the television host, whose acerbic personality was always a fascinating blend of cynicism and the sincere desire to find a better path forward."[14]

I, however, argue that the better path for Bourdain always lay in the realization of what cannot be related, what cannot be known, what cannot be mediated—essentially, a middle path. Dorji shows a slight misunderstanding of US history, attributing the quotation to the Constitution rather than the Declaration of Independence, while Bourdain's understanding of Gross National Happiness remains similarly vague as he listens to explanations he clearly does not fully comprehend. Even as Bourdain de-exoticizes his subject, Dorji uses the term to describe an edible orchid flower central to Bhutanese cuisine, saying "I always find it very exotic." Elsewhere, Bourdain quotes a local way of understanding the penis statues, the phallus as a "flaming thunderbolt of wisdom," then rapidly adds, "a term you or I are unlikely to get away with." The space between filmmaker and subject cannot be breached, the best a filmmaker can do is move forward.

Bourdain's invocation of the road genre is thus all the more nuanced because that genre's tropes have always been defined by oppositional imaginations of linear and cyclical journeys, imaginations themselves built upon Western perceptions of different ways of conceptualizing time in the West versus the East, and Bourdain shows that genre is an insufficient metaphor for understanding Bhutan's complex reality precisely because the genre does not foster a middle path.

The road story is the most pervasive of American genres; it permeates New World fiction, film, and musical production at almost every turn, ranging widely from Jack Kerouac's novels to the entirety of the Western film genre to the very core of blues and country music to art-house films like Alfonso Cuarón's *Y tu mamá también* (2001). The vast majority of examples can be divided into two oppositional categories, those which seek a specific destination, often marked by epiphany, and those which seek autonomy via a life of perpetual motion.[15] "Bhutan" denies both.

When Bourdain and Aronofsky talk road songs, invoking the type of music road films typically use to imbue a sense of meaning to the journey, the best Aronofsky can offer is John Denver's "Country Roads," which Bourdain openly mocks, the scene ending with the question otherwise unfulfilled. Bourdain notes the "road conditions get sketchier" as the duo move east on Bhutan's East–West highway, which was the nation's only road until fifteen years prior, but their journey is not significantly affected; we are neither asked to feel empathy for their inability to achieve autonomy via movement nor to feel the trip is somehow more meaningful because of difficulties. In fact, when the road is blocked by an avalanche, the camera shows the impact it has on locals while the two filmmakers crack jokes; later, on the roadside of a desolate stretch, Aronofsky invents Western-style cocktails with local ingredients for their pleasure.

Time and again we are reminded their journey has little to do with Bhutan and that the country's realities are too complicated to be pigeonholed into easy dichotomies. The modernization projects to which both Bourdain and the camera repeatedly draw attention are neither worrisome signs of industrialization encroaching on an isolated culture nor signs of progress; rather, they are both at the same time. Similarly, the forest they pass that, because of tradition, no one enters, and nothing is built within, is neither exalted as virginal nor depicted as myth to be mocked; rather, it simply is.

Most of the duo's roadside stops represent an attempt to understand and mediate difference in a culture shaping its own path by embracing a middle ground. Bourdain uses Bhutan's index of Gross National Happiness as a means of exposing and deconstructing Western assumptions of gross national product (GDP) leading to happiness; similarly, Kunga Tenzin Dorji claims Drukpa Kunley, the "Divine Madman" and source of the phallus glorification, is important to Bhutan precisely because he is "difficult" to "understand . . . because he breaks our own, our notions about what is right and what's proper." Interviewing an engineer, Nawang Norbu, about the massive hydroelectric dams that constitute about half of Bhutan's GDP, Norbu explains it is better to dam the same river multiple times, something that would be a tough sell in the West because of environmental concerns, because it is preferable to damaging multiple rivers, a justification based upon the environment. Elsewhere, Aronofsky asks a guest if Bhutan, being a Buddhist nation, has always eaten meat, only to have him explain not only have they always eaten meat, but at one time even human meat because, "culturally, because of terrain [and limited vegetables], we had no choice." In short, pragmatic, nuanced answers to difficult questions. In most every case, Bourdain and Aronofsky listen, seemingly open-minded, in a manner that legitimizes Bhutanese perspectives and does not essentialize them to fit Western preconceptions.

Nowhere is Bourdain's desire to depict difference without essentializing more apparent than in his approach to Bhutanese archery, which Bourdain calls "the national sport, an important community event that binds remote villages together in fierce competition and a rollicking good time." Bourdain again passes up easy opportunities to mediate similarities, such as the fact archery exists in most cultures or the degree to which the sport seems central to community pride much like European soccer or US college football, even as he actually shows cheerleaders.

If anything, he emphasizes difference, such as the fact that the archers shoot arrows five hundred feet, the arrows crossing over the highway, aiming for targets merely feet away from spectators, including children. The competitors are distracted by taunts from what Aronofsky terms "anti-cheerleaders."

Bourdain uses his own body to mediate these differences, as he and Aronofsky sit in the middle of the course, physically part of the action, yet verbally remind us of their intellectual separation from it. By placing themselves, as our screen and narrative surrogates, in the middle of the fray, and by neither mocking nor exoticizing from a distance, they, instead, depict difference as something from which to glean knowledge, something no less arbitrary or difficult to explain to an outsider than Western traditions such as college football tailgating or European soccer hooliganism. Like food, sport becomes another cultural artifact, and the degree to which it manifests itself differently in Bhutan only highlights and normalizes differences present in all cultures.

The final sequence is primarily located by a stream where Aronofsky and Bourdain leave Buddhist death offerings, called *sasas*, and discuss the state of the world through the lens of their trip, yet again emphasizing questions rather than answers. The sequence opens with a silent soundtrack and images taken out a car window that re-invoke the road genre, especially one shot with light appearing through trees evocative of Dennis Hopper's *Easy Rider* (1969). As the camera cuts to the duo descending into a gorge, a light, percussive instrumentation partially fills the soundtrack, which is still mostly dominated by natural sound. The location, itself, embodies dichotomies—known as the "Burning Lake," an oxymoron to a Western ear; Bourdain and Aronofsky claim it is actually a river.

The conversation is equally oppositional. Aronofsky asks Bourdain where he "think[s] this country is headed," sparking Bourdain to respond, "Honestly, I don't know what I believe. I don't know if it's good or bad. It seems like Shangri-La, but for the place that invented Gross National Happiness, they're content at under two dollars a day. I don't want *my* child herding yak, and I don't know a lot of parents that do, even here." The discussion of yak herding is a subtle invocation of a woman the two met in Pele La Pass who had just gifted her herd to her sisters so she could open a roadside shop to "go up the ladder" with "better opportunities."

As soon as Bourdain finishes speaking, the camera returns to images that have been present throughout the episode of workers paving the East–West Highway, as Aronofsky complicates matters further, “Having a fully paved road across this entire country, this country’s going to be a very, very different place in five years. The question is do they stay committed to happiness and not to consumption? Getting off the plane when we got here there were *many* flat screen TV’s.” The reference to TV’s is a subtle reinvocation of Bourdain’s earlier suggestion that it is difficult to say the Bhutanese should not have the same technology as the West, even as he fears the environmental realities that access presents. Bourdain’s answer is simultaneously cynical and hopeful, as well as self-aware and self-reflexive: “First comes electricity, then comes a television, then come pop stars and materialism. But maybe that’s arrogant, maybe that’s just easy for *me* to say. . . . I know it’s beautiful, I’m glad it hasn’t been fucked up yet by the world.” Unable to mediate contrasting opinions and desires into a simple answer, the best Bourdain can do is tell us what *he* “knows,” namely what *he* is glad about based upon what *he* has experienced as a filmmaker.

As their conversation ends with Bourdain declaring Bhutan not yet “fucked up by the world” while simultaneously implying such an end is inevitable, the soundtrack fills with a traditional Bhutanese chant, and the camera cuts to laborers chopping wood with an axe in support of the “improvements” on the East–West Highway, including a steamroller spewing black smoke. The entire tone abruptly shifts yet again as the soundtrack switches to a Western-style rap song performed in Dzongkha, Bhutan’s national language, and the camera begins alternating between stereotypical tourist destinations, a close-up of the rapper, masked and costumed dancers performing a native ritual, and hordes of tourists taking photos of said performances as well as selfies in front of the tourist sites. Without narration, we are offered no context for either the dance or the rap, and both destabilize Western perspectives and expectations, the dance through its surreal use of color and props and the song by its glocal mix of a hyper-local language with a Western genre.

Instead, the shots that linger the longest, that allow the spectator to contextualize (and stabilize) their perspective the most, are those of the tourists and their ever-present cameras. As such, questions Bourdain poses throughout “Bhutan” about the efficacy of tourism and filmmaking, as well as his equation (in "Madagascar") of "performances" for ecotourism with "colonialism," are all brought back to the forefront. As the soundtrack goes abruptly silent, filled only with hollow wind, the camera returns to the creek where Aronofsky tells Bourdain, "You're supposed to put [the *sasas*] somewhere where they'll last for a while and make a prayer." The two filmmakers do so, but we are offered no further information, and the camera cuts to images of natural beauty—one depicted upside down to be even more destabilizing—and then finishes with a close-up of a young Bhutanese girl silently staring back at the camera. As Kohn claims in his review, the "episode end[ing] without providing the specifics" of their prayers achieves a "masterstroke of a climax" as "*Parts Unknown* leaves us wondering if it's even within our right to know."[16] Similarly, I argue the conclusion asks if it is our right to gaze upon a remote culture at all; or, rather, if it is better that such parts be left unknown.

As I have discussed in several chapters, much has been written about the way depictions of a subject imagined by the audience as an Other inevitably partake in an objectifying, Western gaze, regardless of intention. For instance, Aaron Oforlea, claims that music theorist Alan Lomax unintentionally exoticizes and primitivizes blues music because he "doesn't know that an authentic black experience doesn't exist, and he can't explain to his audience the extent to which the white unconscious is inscribed in racialized discourses about black people. Lomax's white privilege impedes his ability to theorize blues performances as simultaneously taking place within and without white culture."[17] Jacqui Kong, writing of Bourdain's work in *No Reservations*, leans on the literary scholar and social activist bell hooks[18] to articulate why she feels Bourdain's self-reflexive approach allows him to move beyond depicting the Other as "merely a cultural commodity to be 'discovered' or experienced for one's own enjoyment."[19] To quote Kong, "exchanges between Self and Other can be characterized by feelings of discomfort and a displacement of the Self's ideals and authority. Through what bell hooks calls the 'mutual recognition of racism,' the acknowledgment of shared histories, the realization of one's privilege, and a willingness to listen to and understand one another, the binary of Self/Other is transformed into mutual exchange."[20] While Bourdain's auteurship makes it clear he feels it impossible for any Western filmmaker to completely achieve a "mutual exchange," I argue Bourdain's work, particularly in the final seasons of *Parts Unknown*, does more than just about any filmmaker to shift the Self/Other binary precisely *because* he does not believe in authenticity—of the filmic text nor its subject.

After seeing *Mother!*, of which "Bhutan" borrows Aronofsky's bright and contrasting depictions of nature to invoke the threat of global warming, Bourdain tweeted, "It is dark, dark, dark, brilliant and will upset the fuck out of people. A good poke in eye to convention."[21] Late-stage Bourdain similarly pokes filmmaking conventions in the eye—particularly those of documentary filmmaking—and destabilizes the spectator's relationship to an imagined Other by making television episodes an open discussion about how culture and film are both constructions. Thus, by embracing radical approaches, such as using Aronofsky's narrative films as a lens for mediating a remote, unknown location in a documentary, Bourdain calls the Other/Self binary to the forefront and asks all of us to re-think what "rights," if any, we possess as filmmaker or spectator.

For me, the episode's final shot may be the most enduring of Bourdain's career, as it ends with the eyes of a young girl staring back at the artifice of a camera, the entire point of the episode having been her unknowability and the unknowability of her culture. Because Bourdain imagines neither her culture nor his own as "authentic," this does not

A girl stares at (and past) the camera at the end of *Parts Unknown* "Bhutan" (PU S11E8), her unknowability largely having been Bourdain's entire point.

exoticize her. Instead, she is different because she has been constructed differently, in the same manner we have all been constructed differently. It is an embrace of difference rarely achieved in film. Because Bourdain's self-reflexivity is consistent across both his role as host and his filmic elements, film's role in shaping how unique individuals and unique cultures are constructed is all that we are left. That, in and of itself, is a remarkable legacy.

CONCLUSION

Modernist Filmmaker

> Maybe that's enlightenment enough: to know that there is no final resting place of the mind; no moment of smug clarity. Perhaps wisdom . . . is realizing how small I am, and unwise, and how far I have yet to go.
>
> —Anthony Bourdain, *No Reservations*, "Peru"[1]

> I tr[y] to open up a perspective that will reveal all sorts of cultural and political movements as part of one process: modern men and women asserting their dignity in the present—even a wretched and oppressive present—and their right to control their future; striving to make a place for themselves in the modern world, a place where they can feel at home. . . . To be modern is to live a life of paradox and contradiction.
>
> —Marshall Berman, *All That Is Solid Melts into Air*[2]

Completed after his death and lacking his voice narration, Anthony Bourdain's final "Indonesia" episode (PU S12E3) concludes with Bourdain's visit to a cremation ceremony. Bourdain's guide tells him Indonesian bodies are prepared for their next "journey" toward "mystery, the unknown," as a close-up unflinchingly depicts a human body being burned to a char. The episode eventually cuts to commercial and returns with more images of the ceremony as an unidentified narrator, used throughout the episode to describe shadow-puppet storytelling, proclaims, "time is circular, as is life. Death is but the beginning of another journey." As the narration concludes, we hear a non-diegetic motorcycle engine in the background, and the camera soon cuts first to establishing shots of Bourdain on a motorcycle, and then to point-of-view shots as he proceeds down increasingly rural, two-lane roads. The music, editing, and shot pattern are exact matches of the final sequence of Sofia Coppola's *Somewhere* (2010), a film that establishes both literal and metaphoric cyclical patterns until its final sequence when Johnny Marco completely abandons his life of privilege, taking to a life on the road. Its ending is evocative of one of the most dominant tropes in American literary and filmic modernism and utilizes *direct* visual references to Charlie Chaplin's *Modern Times* (1936), itself a modernist text. In both Bourdain's "Indonesia" and Coppola's *Somewhere*, an off-putting, atonal soundtrack slowly finds its tone and offers a redemptive quality as the protagonist abandons cyclical patterns for a linear path toward a frightening, uncertain future. Similarly, each protagonist emulates and alters a constructed, cinematic search for stable identity, imagined on spatial terms, and in a way that comments on the larger culture. In the case of Bourdain, it serves as a complex example of his nuanced, modernist filmmaking and its relationship to the relevance of his work, both in life and after death.

American literary modernism reached its apex in the 1920s, but more broadly defined, such as in Marshall Berman's *All That Is Solid Melts into Air* (first published in 1982), from which I draw this chapter's second epigraph, modernist philosophy dominated artistic discourse for at least a century. Such an approach "implies an open and an expansive way of understanding culture; very different from the curatorial approach that breaks up human activity into fragments and locks the fragments into separate cases, labeled, by time, place, language, genre, and academic discipline."[3] As such, core themes bind together modernist aims across diverse artforms: a desire for individuals to assert autonomy in the face of overwhelming social and economic obstacles, the idea that doing so is inextricably linked to the ability to identify and expose the forces and biases which construct us, a desire for the artist to give their work a unique thumbprint that draws attention to their bias and how it influences the work and the reader or spectator, and a belief in the necessity of perpetual change, both in terms of style and ontology, as all modes of thinking and expression eventually confine. If one looks carefully at Bourdain's filmmaking, one begins to see he largely embodies this definition in its totality.

As I have demonstrated, Bourdain takes a self-reflexive approach to documentary filmmaking that emphasizes nuance, contrasting biases, and uncertainty as he makes his spectator question the truths our media and our art offer us. He uses his own presence to embody this quest, even as he also makes us aware of his own biases, his own fallibilities. As I have argued in the final third of this book, he does so by deconstructing the dominant, Western gaze, giving a face, if not a voice, to filmic Others as he asks us to understand how they are as much a construction as are we.

As such, Bourdain promotes what Berman calls a "unity of disunity,"[4] in which the shared, common experience of humanity is that we are all defined by difference—difference that should be embraced, not objectified, as "modern men and women [attempt] to become subjects as well as objects of modernization, to get a grip on the modern world, and make themselves at home in it."[5] Bourdain's greatest gift lay not just in filmmaking that defied categorization and approached its subject matter in complex ways, but, rather, the result of that filmmaking: the ability to imagine and understand how different struggles, different lives are intertwined. So, when Bourdain concludes his depiction of an Eastern understanding of death as part of a cyclical journey by visually associating it with—and contrasting it to—a filmic history of Western, linear journeys often represented as suicidal, he emphasizes how both imaginations are a construction of the culture from which they stem.

That allusion to *Somewhere*'s ending, as well as the archetype it draws upon, is enriched when one realizes the most dominant, recurring manifestation of modernism in the US arguably lies in the road story, in which travel across space serves as a metaphor for perpetual ontological change, and a difficult life on the road allows for a darker, more nuanced depiction of individualism than available in Romanticism. As such, characters I term "hobo-heroes" are generally "portrayed as heroic" for "reject[ing] the society that entraps them, instead choosing a life of ceaseless wandering. In other words, if the human condition is one of uprootedness to begin with—as modernism claims—the hobo-hero at least retains a sense of agency unavailable to his static counterparts."[6]

Such figures take to the road and embark upon a perpetual, unachievable search for a more stable sense of self, what Berman calls a "home." This trope permeates a wide range of art, from novels, such as John Dos Passos's *Manhattan Transfer* (1925) and Jack Kerouac's *On the Road* (1957), to music, ranging from the blues to Bob Dylan to Gillian Welch, to an entire genre of films, from which the ending of *Somewhere* and "Indonesia" draw their meaning. In the case of *Somewhere*, I have argued that when Johnny abandons his privileged (but shallow) life in a transient home, Los Angeles's Chateau Marmont, ironically Bourdain's favorite hotel,[7] Coppola repositions a filmic image to "pose questions in response to many of postmodernism's assumptions" as she "defies postmodernism itself, even while expressing and exploring a postmodern landscape, a postmodern world."[8] Such a repositioning of an image—in a manner meant to draw attention to the fact it is both an image and a repositioning of an image—is quintessential Bourdain.

While it may well be an uncanny coincidence that the final visual reference of "Indonesia" is to a film largely *about* the embrace of a modernist trope to reject a postmodern world, Bourdain's use of visual references to invoke mood and meaning is central to his filmmaking. "Indonesia" is not even the first time Bourdain references Coppola; the introduction to *Parts Unknown*'s "Tokyo" (S2E7) reframes *Lost in Translation* (2003), including shooting inside Park Hyatt Tokyo's New York Bar. Further, the use of Bourdain's physical body in "Indonesia" to draw attention to competing perspectives, coupled with visual references to a modernist trope that inherently foregrounds questions about linear and cyclical journeys, while asking a Western audience to respectfully observe an Eastern cremation ceremony, renders this a keen example of how a modernist outlook informs Bourdain's filmmaking. Rather than simplifying a scene he knows will be difficult, even shocking, by either exoticizing or normalizing it, he instead contextualizes it in a manner that complicates it further. As Bourdain explained about "Jamaica" (PU S4E8), "It's easy to romanticize. But one shouldn't do that. Like a lot of our shows, we come to no neat conclusions, only more questions. Which is, I suppose, conclusion enough."[9]

Thus, juxtaposing a Western imagination of identity and journey, embodied by his own corpus and an overt awareness of archetypes, against an Eastern imagination of identity and journey, again reveals their nature as social, not innate, and exposes multiple, conflicting perspectives we are asked to respect—as I discuss in the "Bhutan" (PU S11E8) chapter, bell hooks' "mutual recognition."[10] Rather than dichotomous, Bourdain understands both imaginations are similar in that they are attempts to "make a place" for oneself within a "wretched and oppressive present," to achieve autonomy by embracing a "life of paradox and contradiction." The differences in how we understand death are what unites us.

Bourdain's worldview, which shapes his filmmaking in ways I have explored throughout this book, echoes the modernist belief in the need for constant evolution, constant change. As Bourdain explains near the beginning of "Jerusalem" (PU S2E1), "I was raised without religion. I don't believe in a higher power. I am instinctively hostile to any kind of devotion. Certainty is my enemy. You know, I'm all about doubt, questioning oneself and the nature of reality. Constantly." Similarly, the tattoo on his arm, which reads, "I am certain of nothing. I'm not even sure I'm certain of that." Or, as in this chapter's first epigraph, his belief "enlightenment" is not an attainable goal, but rather a worthy image to seek through an endless journey, "wisdom" an awareness of how much further one must travel; as with the hobo-hero, physical movement across space serving as a metaphor for ontological evolution.

At every stage, Bourdain's words and films embrace nuance, complexity, and a search for answers; they refuse genre, style, and intellectual normative structures and often embrace chaos; they result in a self-reflexivity and a need to constantly perfect one's thought and one's craft, never arriving at any destination. Further, much like hobo-hero protagonists, Bourdain's belief in a perpetual ontological journey is often expressed on spatial terms. For instance, cookbook author Nigella Lawson says Bourdain told her he feared arriving at a "dark space . . . if he kept still too long,"[11] and his longtime director and co-producer Nick Brigden claims, "he was a guy who liked, embraced, and invited change. I think he needed that. He wasn't in the same place for two weeks. He was a shark, always on the move. He had to move to survive."[12]

Such a view also explains the evolution of his shows at their most basic levels. Think, for instance, of their titles, progressing from *A Cook's Tour*, which emphasizes consumption, to *No Reservations*, which is more about individual autonomy and a search, but still primarily about the host, to *Parts Unknown*, a title which emphasizes the places he visits, and even more specifically, their unknowability, their unshareability. Similarly, think of their opening title sequences. *A Cook's Tour* has no theme song, only a first-person narration explaining Bourdain's biography and that the point of his trip is to expand his own knowledge, cataloguing discoveries. *No Reservations* and *The Layover* both trim the narrative down to be more minimalist, and add catchy background theme songs, but the *basic* point is similar to *A Cook's Tour*. *Parts Unknown*, however, opens with an original song written by Queens of the Stone Age that deconstructs narrative structure, declares the world beautiful but associates it with dark, modernist images (e.g., "I felt the rain getting colder"), and denies Bourdain's voice altogether; we simply *see* Bourdain, and, even then, mostly in still, black-and-white images, panned across and edited together to create a sense of motion, bright colors pasted over them, all of which emphasizes their constructed nature. In other words, Bourdain's themes were present from the beginning but evolved and intensified over time. More than anything, those themes evolved more and more toward embracing his modernist nature.

The fact Bourdain's worldview and artistic approach are so shaped by modernist philosophy is not shocking when one considers his influences. First, the novelists who wrote the books which most shaped Bourdain's youth, Graham Greene, Joseph Conrad, and Malcolm Lowry, are all canonical modernists. Similarly, several of the filmmakers whom Bourdain most frequently cited, Federico Fellini, Michelangelo Antonioni, and Pier Paolo Pasolini, were canonical modernists; Pasolini's belief in free indirect subjectivity, which I discuss in chapters 5 and 10, seems particularly relevant to discussions of Bourdain's modernism. Further, I believe the French and American New Wave movements I use as context for Bourdain's filmmaking approach clearly fit Berman's broader definition of modernism, and one can also trace a tendency of Bourdain seeking out opportunities to reference modernist texts even when they do not necessarily adhere to the arch of his story—such as hiring a nearly nude dancer and shooting in black and white to re-create a key scene from Fritz Lang's *Metropolis* (1927) during the end credits of *Parts Unknown* "Berlin" (S11E6).

Such perspective also offers a window into Bourdain's own journey. Upon his death, audiences and critics expressed shock that a successful travel host could have struggled with mental illness, but Bourdain had always been quite upfront about his foibles, both in his writing and on TV. Behind a brash demeanor that used machismo as a shield, he was always one of the most sensitive figures on television, and as screen surrogate, often used his struggles, insecurities, and self-doubt as a means of shaping the spectator's experience. Another of his longtime directors, Tom Vitale, found an electronic journal after Bourdain's death in which Bourdain "describe[s] himself as wandering from place to place haunted by crushing loneliness. A lost soul trapped in a perpetual state of dissatisfaction, always longing for more, he was the very embodiment of a hungry ghost."[13]

Considering the way Bourdain used his own presence in his filmmaking, and considering how that filmmaking consistently expressed a modernist perspective, is it really that shocking the real-life Bourdain might share qualities with the hobo-hero's long, dissatisfied search for a stable home, finding truth only in questions? If his legacy is, in fact, tied to his ability to force us to ask questions about the assumptions we are asked to make of Others, is it really that surprising he did not possess all those answers himself? Or, as Ben Rhodes, deputy national security advisor to US President Barack Obama, wrote for *The Atlantic*, "At his best he stripped away the filters that a superpower imposes on the world—good and evil, victor and victim—and found an essential humanity that we all share. In a time when social media elevates bombastic voices certain of their righteousness, Bourdain offered ambiguity that was somehow reassuring: It's possible, his shows suggested, to look honestly at the world's diversity, complexity, and occasional depravity, and be better for it."[14] To a modernist, truth typically can only be found by facing the darkness, searching uncertainty.

A superficial reading, however, might see Bourdain's work as postmodern rather than modern because postmodernism is largely defined by its deconstruction of truth narratives. Other self-reflexive documentarians are similarly misread. Writing about Errol Morris, to whom I compare Bourdain in chapter 6, Lucia Ricciardelli claims, "For the sake of analysis, I label Morris' documentary style as *postmodern* [because it] favors self-reflexivity, adopts a provocative tone, rejects the totalizing meta-narrative as a way to organize knowledge of the past, and mixes fact with fiction."[15] The problem with that perspective is that neither filmmaker rejects truth; in fact, their films reflect a perpetual search for it. What Bourdain and Morris reject is certainty in any *single* truth because, as Bourdain tells Christopher Doyle in "Hong Kong" (PU S11E5), "we are changing the world by looking at it through cameras as happens every time you look at real people, the real world, real places." Both Bourdain and Morris see truth as a subjective process, not a concrete destination, something closer to Werner Herzog's "poetic, ecstatic truth" discussed in chapter 3. As David Resha writes of Morris, the "films *do not* primarily function to problematize the relationship between documentaries and the world they depict. Rather, they often make resolute claims about reality and truth . . . [and] often provide a clear sense of what is real and true."[16] The same is true of Bourdain.

Labeling Bourdain (or Morris, for that matter) postmodern thereby hinges on a denial (or confusion) of Herzog's distinction between truth and fact. I once more return to Resha's analysis of Morris, in which he posits, "Morris' films do reveal a truth, but it is a truth about the documentary tradition rather than a truth about the real world beyond it,"[17] which may, at first, appear a critique of documentary filmmaking, instead, "demonstrate[s] the power and not the problems of documentary representation. Morris does not reject the documentary tradition. He experiments with many of its conventions to investigate reality and truth."[18] Again, the same can be said of Bourdain.

As I discuss in chapter 3, Bourdain's truth lies in the power of cinema, a constructed fallacy which, in its best moments, illuminates. Such belief in the power of art to express individual consciousness and enable autonomy is wholly modernist. As Berman explains, "Post-modernists maintain that the horizon of modernity is closed, its energies exhausted—in effect that modernity is passé. Post-modernist social thought pours scorn on all the collective hopes for moral and social progress, for personal freedom and public happiness. . . . These hopes, post-moderns say, have been shown to be bankrupt, at best vain and futile fantasies, at worst engines of domination and monstrous enslavement."[19] Instead, Bourdain shows his subjects as constructed to get as close to a *subjective* truth as possible. Bourdain's tone remains hopeful as he asserts the power of art to express the desire of individuals to connect and realize a shared humanity, such as his depiction of the young woman staring back at the camera in the final shot of "Bhutan."

Confusion about Bourdain's self-reflexive approach not only informs debate about his work and legacy, but largely explains the conflicting responses to Morgan Neville's documentary biopic *Roadrunner: A Film About Anthony Bourdain* (2021). Choosing a title that uses movement as a metaphor for identity, Neville forgoes a narrator, editing audio clips of interviews with Bourdain and narration from his shows to render him, posthumously, narrator of his own biopic. In addition to controversy about not interviewing Asia Argento,[20] Neville found himself the center of heated debate the week of the theatrical release when interviews by Brett Martin[21] and Helen Rosner[22] exposed his use of artificial intelligence (AI) to generate three lines "spoken" by Bourdain. A wide array of voices, including critics Sean Burns[23] and Cory Stillman,[24] criticized the ethics of using Bourdain's voice without permission and using AI to create voice, and many fans on social media argued that the use of AI was offensive to Bourdain's legacy of authenticity.[25] Within days, Rosner wrote a second article in *The New Yorker* evaluating the controversy and largely defending Neville. Her defense on grounds of authenticity is particularly well made, as she points out authenticity is a very "slippery concept, especially in the world of food and travel,"[26] a concept disavowed even by Bourdain. I have similarly argued Bourdain rejects notions of authenticity, but Rosner points to a compelling moment when Bourdain told *Time*, "The word 'authentic' has become a completely ridiculous, snobbish term."[27] Similarly, Rosner effectively explains why worrying about posthumous "consent" for the use of words and art is problematic, both because it is another slippery slope and because it is antithetical to art's very nature.[28]

Rosner's postmodern defense of the *way* Neville uses AI, however, is problematic, in ways that shed light upon my discussion of Bourdain as modernist. Rosner focuses a lot of her attention on the fact Bourdain did write the words, even if we do not know if he ever spoke them. More to the point, Rosner uses Bourdain's belief in self-reflexive documentary to diminish ethical questions about Neville's use of AI, pointing out Bourdain's own shows often challenge accepted notions of authenticity. Ironically, she uses Morris and Herzog as precedent, the two documentarians I have most used to contextualize Bourdain. For Rosner, "Creating a synthetic Bourdain voice-over seem[s] far less crass than, say, a CGI Fred Astaire put to work selling vacuum cleaners in a Dirt Devil commercial, or a holographic Tupac Shakur performing alongside Snoop Dogg at Coachella, and far more trivial than the intentional blending of fiction and nonfiction in, for instance, Errol Morris's *Thin Blue Line*."[29] Elsewhere, she explains Herzog's "ecstatic truth," adding, "Given Bourdain's formalist cinematic approach to his TV storytelling—not to mention his documented love of Werner Herzog—it's not unreasonable to imagine that he would have subscribed to Herzog's notion."[30] Rosner also reminds us Neville told her, "If you watch the film, other than that line you mentioned, you probably don't know what the other lines are that were spoken by the A.I., and you're not going to know. We can have a documentary-ethics panel about it later."[31] All in all, while Rosner chastises Neville's glibness, for which she attributes some of the criticism, she mostly agrees with him that using AI to give an audible voice to Bourdain's written words is not a big deal, precisely, she implies, because Bourdain and the directors who most influenced him took a postmodern, self-reflexive approach in which ideas of truth are passé.

And this misreading of these filmmakers explains the root of the disparate reactions. Rosner thinks Neville's use of AI is less problematic than the Astaire and Shakur examples because those are even less authentic (and aim to sell something). This perspective ignores two things. First, a primary aim of postmodern critique asserts all things, especially art, are fake, defined only by capitalist value; grading things on a sliding scale of authenticity would therefore seem superfluous. Second, a modernist argument can be made that Rosner's examples are *more* palatable precisely *because* they are obviously fake, as the spectator's joy lies in the realization the images are being manipulated to express something new, even if they are marketing ploys. Neville's AI is "not clearly faked, nor is it clearly real, and the fact that it *was* his actual words just muddles that even more."[32] In fact the AI is sufficiently disguised that Neville glibly and confidently asserts no one will identify it.

As modernist filmmakers, Morris, Herzog, and Bourdain blatantly draw their spectator's attention to the space between reality and its depiction; typically, as with Bourdain's restaging of the train scene in "Madagascar" (PU S5E4) discussed in chapter 2, making that space explicit is their entire point. Herzog's "ecstatic truth" relies on making spectators aware that truth is subjective, aware of their active participation in its construction. It is therefore reasonable to assert Bourdain's filmmaking is not an effective precedent for Neville's decision precisely *because* of Bourdain's devotion to ecstatic truth, precisely *because* he did not believe in authenticity, precisely *because* his films are about seeking (subjective) truth. As Cory Stillman claims in *Film Cred*, "Bourdain may have written those words that Neville has him artificially read aloud, and as a fan of film himself, he may have been comfortable with the director's application of a new technology, but Neville's . . . unwillingness to acknowledge his own manipulations within *Roadrunner* itself, suggests he was never all that interested in doing right by his subject."[33]

In the end, doing right by his subject, exploring difficult truths about the shared human experience—how we are all interconnected *because* of difference—is Bourdain's greatest achievement. I have examined how Bourdain's ability to break traditional Self-Other dichotomies lay in the combination of great filmmaking talents, a willingness (and autonomy) to challenge conventions, and a deep level of empathy born from experience and curiosity. Ben Rhodes's *Atlantic* article was a reaction to Charles Leerhsen's biography, *Down and Out in Paradise* (2022), another text that, like *Roadrunner*, largely ignores Bourdain's work, choosing to instead chase the demons that brought about his demise. Such a focus on Bourdain's death not only ignores the realities of mental health, it also ignores that darkness is often inextricably linked to light, that Bourdain was able to see and understand precisely because he struggled himself; as Berman claims in this chapter's epigraph, "to be modern is to live a life of paradox and contradiction." Or, perhaps more precisely, as Rhodes claims in *The Atlantic*, "The tragic irony of Bourdain's life and death is that the same interior darkness he succumbed to enabled the alchemy that he performed, again and again, on television: showing us three-dimensional human beings doing their best against often insurmountable odds."[34]

As such, Bourdain's life and work embody Berman's modernist call for art to create a "unity of disunity," emphasizing the struggle for individuals to make a place for themselves in a world that would dominate them. Elsewhere, observing that the West "experienced modernity as a whole at a moment when only a small part of the world was truly modern,"[35] Berman asserts,

> A century later, when the processes of modernization have cast a net that no one, not even in the remotest corner of

> the world, can escape, we can learn a great deal from the first modernists. . . . We have lost our grip on the contradictions that they had to grasp with all their strength, at every moment in their everyday lives, in order to live at all. . . . If we can make their visions our own and use their perspectives to look at our own environments with fresh eyes, we will see that there is more depth in our lives than we thought. We will feel our community with people all over the world who have been struggling with the same dilemmas as our own.[36]

This notion brings my mind immediately back to Rhodes, who concludes his article by stating Bourdain "was someone who wasn't offering false optimism or mindless distraction. No matter where they were, the characters Bourdain introduced to us seemed to be searching imperfectly for the same simple things: community, authenticity, and integrity. It made me feel less alone."[37] No greater accolade could be laid upon a modernist filmmaker.

Bourdain applied such an approach to locations far and near—as with Coppola's *Somewhere*, even in the most postmodern of environments. One of the best examples of this mediation of difference emphasizing connection in the face of obstacles takes place in just such an environment, when Bourdain and chef Sean Brock make an impromptu visit to a Waffle House in Charleston, South Carolina (PU S6E8). The episode opens with visual references to the avant-garde filmmaker Bruce Conner, which make it difficult for the spectator to comprehend what they are shown, and Bourdain's voice-over, which explains he had to look closer to recognize Brock's genius—that, behind a country demeanor, he discovered, "without a doubt, one of America's most important chefs." The episode returns from the opening credits to find the duo in a dive bar, Brock explaining what went "wrong" with Bourdain's previous visit to Charleston (NR S3E14). The way in which their conversation critiques *No Reservations* draws attention to Bourdain's role as mediator, as well as the fact that what he is mediating is Brock's mediation of the local culture; we are, in short, dealing with multiple, diverse perspectives as we search for a truth about Charleston somewhere between. Brock's love of the city turns the conversation to his idea of "universal awesomeness" that transcends geography and culture, leading Bourdain to ask if it applies to Waffle House. Brock explains it does because the late-night chain offers the same "experience" to a diverse group of people. Surprised, Bourdain interjects, "You are talking about it like it's a magical, spiritual place," Brock responds, "It's *beyond* a magical, spiritual place," and the scene shifts to their drunken visit.

While the first, prolonged image emphasizes the postmodern, neon glow of the parking lot, the sequence is both wholly modernist and quintessential Bourdain. Bourdain's intro eventually overlaps the eerie neon hum, as he expresses his reshaped perspective to the spectator:

> It is indeed marvelous. An irony free zone where everything is beautiful, and nothing hurts. Where everybody, regardless of race, creed, color, or degree of inebriation, is welcomed. It's warm, yellow glow, a beacon of hope and salvation, inviting the hungry, the lost, the seriously hammered, all across the South, to come inside. A place of safety and nourishment. It never closes. It is always, always faithful. Always there for you.

The scene quickly moves inside, Bourdain's demeanor and tone treating the experience like a text to be studied, no different from a meal at El Bulli, a roadside tavern in Bhutan, or a Meaderville supper club. Brock emotionally explains Waffle House was foundational for him as a child because he could watch people cook and see people from all walks of life treated with respect. Bourdain's voice-over draws attention to the layers of mediation, declaring, "I am unbelievably—in spite of my world travels—new to the wonders of the Waffle House and unfamiliar with its ways. The terminology, for instance, is new to me." Brock instructs Bourdain on the menu, explaining he orders his hash browns "scattered, covered, smothered, chunked," a nomenclature so particular to the Waffle House micro-culture that Brock claims to still not know exactly what it means. Bourdain's camera and narration, in turn, try to translate Brock's phrasing to the spectator, as best they can. Next, Brock ushers Bourdain through a self-devised tasting menu Bourdain declares "better than French Laundry." Bourdain shoots the food in a standard food-film aesthetic as if it were haute cuisine and pairs it with Antonio Vivaldi's *Four Seasons*.

Almost every trademark element of Bourdain's filmmaking is present: emphasis upon conflicting perspectives, pointed contrast between subject and depiction, use of his own presence to mediate the spectator's experience, use of juxtaposition to create his intended meaning. In this case, the effect of pairing highbrow music and food representation with lowbrow diner fare serves to emphasize Bourdain's surprise at how good that food is, thereby denying arbitrary, class-based distinctions between high and popular culture.[38] More pointedly, however, it is an example of Bourdain using film as a complex tool to break down such traditional depictions, to make his audience aware he is doing so, and to render a new, unexpected truth about his subject—in this case, the idea Waffle House is special. By sequence's end, Bourdain proclaims, "After a few bites of waffle, a burger, a hunk of generic T-bone and some hash browns, one feels drawn right to the *center* of what makes our country great. An America that drives me to clamber up on the counter and start reciting Walt Whitman. . . . And you know what? I doubt I'd be the first." Bourdain next tells Brock a dirty joke about the meaning of umami, sparking a deep, uncontrollable laugh that continues past the end of the sequence. What Bourdain has to say about food is more profound than simply that it can be a text to understand culture. Rather, he says food, like film, can connect us to the world around us, that we are not alone in our struggles. Outside the Waffle House lies a lonely, postmodern parking lot, but inside lies a space of community, hope, safety, and beauty. These things are depicted by Bourdain, a filmmaker, in a manner meant to ask the spectator to recognize and share those feelings even if they are expressed differently in every culture. They are depicted by Bourdain, a modernist filmmaker. Ultimately, they are depicted by a filmmaker.

ACKNOWLEDGMENTS

I want to thank everyone at Wayne State University Press for believing in this project, helping shape it into its final form, and getting it out to the world. Specifically, I want to thank my acquisitions editor, Marie Sweetman, who has been consistently kind, articulate, observant, and helpful, as well as Stephanie Williams, Sandra Korn, Barry Grant, Katie Martelle, Carrie Teefey, Emily Gauronskas, Traci Cothran, Kelsey Giffin, Ryan Schumacher, and Brad Norr.

When I first came up with what seemed a harebrained idea to teach a class on Bourdain, the whole thing could have met a quick end if it were not for the support offered by many people. The amount of support only grew as the scope of the project grew, generating a list to whom I am indebted far too long to fit in the pages of any book. Nevertheless, I will do my best.

If Kathleen Rellihan had not seen a tweet, reached out, and written an engaging article for CNN, none of this would have happened. I am also grateful to Travel Channel's Bill Margoll for seeing that article, visiting that class, and increasing visibility.

Institutional support at Nicholls State was swift and abundant. Specifically, I need to thank my department chair, Allen Alexander; my deans, Michele Theriot and Jean Donegan; and my president, Jay Clune. Additionally, the students who comprised the first three iterations of the Bourdain class deserve my gratitude for the abundant, varied perspectives they brought to the table, and the ways those perspectives sharpened my own. Among those students, I want to single out Courteney Dufrene, Angelle-Leigh Breaux, Collin Brazan, Zoe Cancienne, Andrew Barbier, and Delaney Ligori.

Countless people offered advice, eyes, ears, time, and other help for this project when they had no real duty to do so. Some of these were colleagues at Nicholls, such as Kathy Conner, Richmond Eustis, Tiffany Duet, and Scott Banville. Others are friends from other institutions or from outside academia altogether, such as Suzanne Ferriss, Aleksandra Hogendorf, Nicole Plyler Fisk, Marti Buckley, Carolina Caballero, Jess Armstrong, Joseba Gabilondo, and Ashlie Liss. I am indebted to each of them for their mentorship and support.

There are also those I wish to thank on a more personal level. For the better part of three decades, Keen Butterworth has been the model of the type of scholar, teacher, and, quite honestly, human being, I strive to be. My mother, Mary Ann Harden, offered countless hours babysitting and cleaning our house, without which it is hard to imagine I could have found the time necessary to work on this project. Our border collie, Pivo, loyally laid at my feet most of the time I was writing. And, above all others, my fellow enthusiasts: my wife and son, Brittany and Kepa, whose patience, support, love, and time have been omnipresent. Many of the ideas in this book sprouted in conversation with my wife, and she was the first to edit each chapter. In many ways, this project is as much hers as it is mine.

EPISODES CITED

A Cook's Tour (Food Network)

S1E8, "San Sebastián: A Food Lover's Town," directed by Matthew Barbato, aired July 5, 2002.

S1E9, "Childhood Flavors: Southwest France," directed by Matthew Barbato, aired January 29, 2002.

S2E1, "Food Tastes Better with Sand Between Your Toes" (St. Martin), directed by Lydia Tenaglia and Christopher Collins, aired February 21, 2003.

No Reservations (Travel Channel)

S1E1, "Paris: Why the French Don't Suck," directed by Hal Leigh, aired July 25, 2005.

S1E3, "New Jersey," directed by Hal Leigh, aired August 8, 2005.

S2E3, "Peru," directed by Eric Lasby, aired April 10, 2006.

S2ES, "Decoding Ferran Adrià," directed by Vincenzo Tripado, aired July 3, 2006.

S2ES, "Beirut," directed by Tom Vitale, aired August 21, 2006.

S3E10, "French Polynesia," directed by Hal Leigh, aired August 20, 2007.

S4E11, "Laos," director uncredited, aired July 7, 2008.

S4E17, "Spain," director uncredited, aired August 18, 2008.

S5E2, "Venice," director uncredited, aired January 12, 2009.

S5E6, "Food Porn," director uncredited, aired February 9, 2009.

S6E20, "Rome," director uncredited, aired August 16, 2010.

S6E21, "Back to Beirut," directed by Zach Zamboni, aired August 23, 2010.

S7E9, "Cuba," directed by Tom Vitale, aired July 11, 2011.
S7E12, "El Bulli," director uncredited, aired August 1, 2011.
S7E16, "Cajun Country," directed by Nick Brigden, aired August 29, 2011.

The Layover (Travel Channel)

S1E4, "Miami," directed by Tom Vitale, aired December 12, 2011.
S2E9, "New Orleans," directed by Tom Vitale, aired January 28, 2013.

Parts Unknown (CNN)

S1E3, "Colombia," directed by Sally Freeman, aired April 28, 2013.
S1E7, "Peru," directed by Sally Freeman, aired June 2, 2013.
S1E8, "Congo," directed by Tom Vitale, aired June 9, 2013.
S2E1, "Jerusalem," directed by Sally Freeman, aired September 15, 2013.
S2E2, "Andalucía," directed by Tom Vitale, aired September 22, 2013.
S2E3, "New Mexico," directed by Tom Vitale, aired September 29, 2013.
S2E4, "Copenhagen," directed by Tom Vitale, aired October 6, 2013.
S2E7, "Tokyo," directed by Nick Brigden, aired November 3, 2013.
S2E8, "Detroit," directed by Michael Steed, aired November 10, 2013.
S4E7, "Massachusetts," directed by Toby Oppenheimer, aired November 9, 2014.
S4E8, "Jamaica," directed by Tom Vitale, aired December 16, 2014.
S5E2, "Miami," directed by Tom Vitale, aired May 3, 2015.
S5E3, "Scotland," directed by Nick Brigden, aired May 10, 2015.
S5E4, "Madagascar," directed by Tom Vitale, aired May 17, 2015.
S5E6, "Budapest," directed by Toby Oppenheimer, aired June 7, 2015.
S5E7, "Hawaii," directed by Erik Osterholm, aired June 14, 2015.
S6E3, "Okinawa," directed by Dana Currier, aired October 11, 2015.
S6E8, "Charleston," directed by Morgan Fallon, aired November 15, 2015.

S7E4, "Montana," directed by Morgan Fallon, aired May 15, 2016.
S8E1, "Hanoi," directed by Tom Vitale, aired September 25, 2016.
S8E4, "London," directed by Richard Chandler, aired October 23, 2016.
S8E9, "Rome," directed by Tom Vitale, aired December 4, 2016.
S9E2, "San Sebastián," directed by Michael Steed, aired May 7, 2017.
S9 E5, "Antarctica," directed by Erik Osterholm, June 4, 2017.
S11E1, "West Virginia," directed by Morgan Fallon, aired April 29, 2018.
S11E5, "Hong Kong," directed by Asia Argento, aired June 3, 2018.
S11E8, "Bhutan," directed by Tom Vitale, aired June 24, 2018.
S12E1, "Kenya," directed by Morgan Fallon, aired September 23, 2018.
S12E2, "Asturias," directed by Morgan Fallon, aired September 30, 2018.
S12E3, "Indonesia," directed by Tom Vitale, aired October 7, 2018.

NOTES

Preface

1 Kathleen Rellihan, "You Can Now Take a College Class on All Things Bourdain," *CNN Online*, September 28, 2018, accessed September 17, 2021, https://www.cnn.com/travel/article/anthony-bourdain-college-course/index.html.

2 Nick Ortego, host, *Class Dismissed* podcast, episode 73, "Meet the Educator That's Teaching a Class About Anthony Bourdain," October 29, 2018, https://classdismissedpodcast.com/education/educator-thats-teaching-class-anthony-bourdain/.

3 Laurie Woolever, *Bourdain: The Definitive Oral Biography* (Ecco, 2021).

4 Charles Leerhsen, *Down and Out in Paradise: The Life of Anthony Bourdain* (Simon & Schuster, 2022).

5 Tom Vitale, *In the Weeds: Around the World and Behind the Scenes with Anthony Bourdain* (Hachette Books, 2021).

6 Robert Sklar, *Movie-Made America: A Cultural History of American Movies*, revised ed. (Vintage, 1994).

Introduction

1 Maija Zummo, "Anthony Bourdain's Irresistible Impulses," *CityBeat*, June 21, 2010, accessed September 17, 2021, https://www.citybeat.com/food-drink/eats-feature/article/13014172/anthony-bourdains-irresistible-impulses.

2 All quotations from Bourdain's shows have been transcribed by the author as faithfully as possible, including possible grammatical errors.

3 Anthony Bourdain, "My 'Cinematic Dream' Filming with Asia Argento and Christopher Doyle in Hong Kong," *Hollywood Reporter*, June 2, 2018, accessed September 17, 2021, https://www.hollywoodreporter.com/tv/tv-news/anthony-bourdain-why-shooting-parts-unknown-hong-kong-was-a-cinematic-dream-1114970/.

4 Eric Kohn, "Anthony Bourdain on Asia Argento, His Favorite Movies, and Why Donald Trump Would Be a Terrible Dinner Companion," *IndieWire*, June 3, 2018, accessed September 17, 2021, https://www.indiewire.com/2018/06/anthony-bourdain-interview-no-reservations-hong-kong-asia-argento-christopher-doyle-1201970639/.
5 Zummo, "Anthony Bourdain's Irresistible Impulses."
6 Zummo, "Anthony Bourdain's Irresistible Impulses."
7 Matthew Honovic, "Anthony Bourdain's Favorite Movies of All Time," *Long Island Film Society*, June 8, 2018, accessed September 17, 2021, https://www.lifilmsociety.org/2018/06/anthony-bourdain-favorite-films/.
8 Chelsea Conaboy, "Interview with Zach Zamboni," *Maine Voices Live*, September 8, 2017, accessed September 17, 2021, https://www.youtube.com/watch?v=-e8dk6R7c_8.
9 Alexis Pichard, *Le nouvel âge d'or des séries américaines* (Editions Le Manuscrit, 2011).
10 Kevin Perry, "Francis Ford Coppola's *Apocalypse Now* Is Not an Anti-War Film," *The Guardian*, August 9, 2019, accessed September 4, 2025, https://www.theguardian.com/film/2019/aug/09/francis-ford-coppola-apocalypse-now-is-not-an-anti-war-film.
11 Andrew Barker, "Anthony Bourdain Breaks Down Cinema History for *Parts*," *Variety*, August 5, 2014, accessed September 17, 2021, https://variety.com/2014/tv/awards/anthony-bourdain-breaks-down-cinema-history-for-parts-1201275584/.
12 Barker, "Anthony Bourdain Breaks Down Cinema History for *Parts*."
13 Laura Mulvey, "Visual Pleasure in Narrative Cinema," in *Feminist Film Theory*, ed. Sue Thornham (New York University Press, 1999), 122–30. Originally published in *Screen* 16, no. 4 (1975): 6–18.
14 Eric Kohn, "Anthony Bourdain Was a Brilliant Filmmaker in Disguise," *IndieWire*, June 10, 2018, accessed September 17, 2021, https://www.indiewire.com/2018/06/anthony-bourdain-last-interview-food-movies-legacy-1201973230/.
15 Anthony Bourdain, *A Cook's Tour: In Search of the Perfect Meal* (Bloomsbury, 2001), 5.

Chapter 1

1 Joe Berkawitz, "Final Interview with Anthony Bourdain," *Fast Company*, June 14, 2018 (recorded August 2017), accessed October 5, 2021, https://

www.fastcompany.com/40585277/watch-the-full-video-of-anthony-bourdains-final-fast-company-interview?cid=search.

2 Anthony Bourdain, *A Cook's Tour: In Search of the Perfect Meal* (Bloomsbury, 2001).

3 "Zach Zamboni—Craft Truck—Through the Lens," *Through the Lens* (S1 E17), May 30, 2013, accessed October 5, 2021, https://www.youtube.com/watch?v=Mu75llJvVqY.

4 Richard Wright, *Pagan Spain* (Harper Perennial, 1957), 228.

5 Wright, *Pagan Spain*, 232.

6 Cecilia Sayad, *Performing Authorship: Self-Inscription and Corporeality in the Cinema* (I. B. Taurus, 2013), xxii.

7 Sayad, *Performing Authorship*, xiv.

8 François Truffaut, "A Certain Tendency of French Cinema," reprinted in *Auteurs and Auteurship: A Film Reader*, ed. Barry Keith Grant (Blackwell Publishing, 2008), 11. Originally published in French in *Cahiers du Cinéma* 31 (1954).

9 Truffaut, "A Certain Tendency of French Cinema," 14.

10 Truffaut, "A Certain Tendency of French Cinema," 11.

11 Truffaut, "A Certain Tendency of French Cinema," 14.

12 Bruce Kawin, "Authorship, Design and Execution," in *How Movies Work* (University of California Press 1992), 291–301.

13 André Bazin, "On the *politique des auteurs* (April 1957)," in *Cahiers du Cinéma: The 1950s, Neo-Realism, Hollywood, New Wave*, ed. Jim Hillier (Harvard University Press), 258.

14 David A. Gerstner, "The Practices of Authorship," in *Authorship and Film*, ed. David Gerstner and Janet Staiger (Taylor and Francis, 2003), 19.

15 Matthew Bernstein, "The Producer as Auteur," in Grant, *Auteurs and Auteurship*, 180–89.

16 Kawin, "Authorship, Design and Execution," 199.

17 Jenni Matz, "Emmytv interview with Anthony Bourdain," Television Academy Foundation, January 7, 2016, accessed October 5, 2021, https://www.youtube.com/watch?v=VUvM3YpnP-U.

18 Berkawitz, "Final Interview with Anthony Bourdain."

19 "Zach Zamboni—Craft Truck—Through the Lens."

20 Berkawitz, "Final Interview with Anthony Bourdain."

21 Berkawitz, "Final Interview with Anthony Bourdain."

22 *Roadrunner: A Film About Anthony Bourdain*, directed by Morgan Neville (CNN Films, 2021).

23 Lynne Rossetto Kasper, "Anthony Bourdain's Off-the-Road Adventures in Search of the Perfect Meal," *The Splendid Table*, September 30, 2013, accessed October 5, 2021, https://www.splendidtable.org/story/2013/09/30/anthony-bourdains-off-the-road-adventures-in-search-of-the-perfect-meal.

24 Joseph Conrad, *Heart of Darkness* (Penguin, 1995), 21.

25 Sayad, *Performing Authorship*, xv.

26 Martin Scorsese, Facebook post, July 8, 2013, https://m.facebook.com/scorsese/photos/a.490754917661162/499327946803859/?_se_imp=09N0PMk0GD6yZC0eM.

27 Sayad, *Performing Authorship*, xxii.

Chapter 2

1 *Parts Unknown*, season 5, episode 6, "Budapest," directed by Toby Oppenheimer, aired June 7, 2015, on CNN.

2 Laurie Woolever, *Bourdain: The Definitive Oral Biography* (Ecco, 2021), 307–8.

3 Joe Berkawitz, "Final Interview with Anthony Bourdain," *Fast Company*, June 14, 2018 (recorded August 2017), accessed October 5, 2021, https://www.fastcompany.com/40585277/watch-the-full-video-of-anthony-bourdains-final-fast-company-interview?cid=search.

4 Robert Bresson, *Notes on the Cinematographer* (Éditions Gallimard, 1975).

5 Josh Martin, "The Power and the Beauty: Behind the Table with Todd Liebler," *The Journey for More*, May 7, 2020, accessed October 28, 2021, https://joshmartin95.com/the-power-and-beauty-behind-the-table-with-todd-liebler/.

6 Martin, "The Power and the Beauty."

7 Tom Vitale, *In the Weeds: Around the World and Behind the Scenes with Anthony Bourdain* (Hatchette, 2021), 105.

8 Vitale, *In the Weeds*, 105.

9 Vitale, *In the Weeds*, 107.

10 Martin, "The Power and the Beauty."

11 Andrew Barker, "Anthony Bourdain Breaks Down Cinema History for *Parts*," *Variety*, August 5, 2014, accessed September 17, 2021, https://variety.com/2014/tv/awards/anthony-bourdain-breaks-down-cinema-history-for-parts-1201275584/.

12 Barker, "Anthony Bourdain Breaks Down Cinema History for *Parts*."
13 Martin, "The Power and the Beauty."
14 Barker, "Anthony Bourdain Breaks Down Cinema History for *Parts*."
15 Chelsea Conaboy, "*Maine Voices Live* with Zach Zamboni," *Maine Voices Live*, August 29, 2017, accessed October 28. 2021, https://www.youtube.com/watch?v=-e8dk6R7c_8.
16 "Zach Zamboni—Craft Truck—Through the Lens," *Through the Lens* (S1 E17), May 30, 2013, accessed October 5, 2021, https://www.youtube.com/watch?v=Mu75llJvVqY.
17 "Zach Zamboni—Craft Truck—Through the Lens."
18 Vitale, *In the Weeds*, 5.

Chapter 3

1 Eric Kohn, "Anthony Bourdain Was a Brilliant Filmmaker in Disguise," *IndieWire*, June 10, 2018, accessed September 17, 2021, https://www.indiewire.com/2018/06/anthony-bourdain-last-interview-food-movies-legacy-1201973230/.
2 *Grizzly Man*, directed by Werner Herzog (Lions Gate Films, 2005).
3 Cecilia Sayad, *Performing Authorship: Self-Inscription and Corporeality in the Cinema* (I. B. Taurus, 2013), 71.
4 Brian Ferguson, *Yanomami Warfare: A Political History* (School of American Research Press, 1995).
5 *The Trap: What Happened to Our Dream of Freedom*, episode 2, "The Lonely Robot," written and directed by Adam Curtis, 2007, BBC.
6 *The Trap*, episode 2, "The Lonely Robot."
7 "Zach Zamboni—Craft Truck—Through the Lens," *Through the Lens* (S1 E17), May 30, 2013, accessed November 28, 2021, https://www.youtube.com/watch?v=Mu75llJvVqY.
8 Guy Gauthier, "Jean Rouch, gourou Nouvelle Vague," *CinémAction* 104 (2002): 70–75.
9 Jamie Berthe, "Beyond the Entomological Critique: Re-Thinking Rouch and African Cinema," *Studies in French Cinema* 18, no. 3 (2008): 267–77.
10 Albert Cervoni and Muna El Fituri, trans., "A Historic Confrontation in 1965 Between Jean Rouch and Ousmane Sembène: 'You Look at Us as If We Were Insects,'" *CinémAction* 81 (1996).
11 Steven Feld, introduction to Jean Rouch, *Ciné-Ethnography* (University of Minnesota Press, 2003), 16.

12 Ronald Bergan, "Jean Rouch Obituary," *The Guardian*, February 20, 2004, accessed November 30, 2021, https://www.theguardian.com/news/2004/feb/20/guardianobituaries.film.
13 Sayad, *Performing Authorship*, 83.
14 Rouch, *Ciné-Ethnography*, 40.
15 Rouch, *Ciné-Ethnography*, 99.
16 Quoted by Bergan in "Jean Rouch Obituary."
17 *Burden of Dreams*, directed by Les Blank (Flower Films, 1982).
18 Matthew Gandy, "Visions of Darkness: The Representation of Nature in the Films of Werner Herzog," *Ecumene* 3, no. 1 (January 1996): 2.
19 Roger Ebert, "Herzog's Minnesota Declaration: Defining 'Ecstatic Truth,'" April 30, 1999, accessed November 30, 2021, https://www.rogerebert.com/roger-ebert/herzogs-minnesota-declaration-defining-ecstatic-truth.
20 Ebert, "Herzog's Minnesota Declaration."
21 *Le petit soldat*, directed by Jean-Luc Godard (Les Films Imperia), 1963.
22 Ebert, "Herzog's Minnesota Declaration."
23 Ebert, "Herzog's Minnesota Declaration."
24 Walter Murch, "Sound Design: The Dancing Shadow," in *Projections: Film-makers on Film-making*, vol. 4, ed. John Boorman, Tom Luddy, David Thomson, and Walter Donohue (Faber & Faber, 1995), 247.
25 Tom Vitale, *In the Weeds: Around the World and Behind the Scenes with Anthony Bourdain* (Hatchette, 2021), 106.
26 Ebert, "Herzog's Minnesota Declaration."
27 Matt Miller, "From Gonzo Chef to World-Renowned Traveler: Remembering Anthony Bourdain's Life Behind the Camera," *Esquire*, November 11, 2018, accessed November 30, 2021, https://www.esquire.com/entertainment/tv/a24888814/eric-ripert-sandra-zweig-remembering-anthony-bourdain-parts-unknown-interview/.

Chapter 4

1 *No Reservations*, season 4, episode 11, "Laos," produced by Christopher Collins and Lydia Tenaglia, aired July 7, 2008, on Travel Channel.
2 Anthony Bourdain, "Bourdain's Field Notes: Jamaica," CNN, November 2014, accessed January 20, 2022, https://explorepartsunknown.com/jamaica/bourdains-take-jamaica/.
3 Jeffrey Ruoff, Jeffrey, ed., *Virtual Voyages: Cinema and Travel* (Duke University Press, 2006).

4 San Sebastián trailer, *Parts Unknown*, April 28, 2017, accessed March 19, 2024, https://www.youtube.com/watch?v=DKpFJSZgqSI.
5 Bourdain, "Bourdain's Field Notes: Jamaica."
6 James F. Knapp, "Primitivize and Empire: John Synge and Paul Gauguin," *Comparative Literature* (University of Oregon) 41, no. 1 (Winter 1989): 53–68, 53.
7 Heather Waldroup, "Traveling Representations: *Noa Noa*, *Manao Tupapau*, and Gauguin's Legacy in the Pacific," *Journeys* 11, no. 2 (2010): 1–2.
8 Paul Gauguin, *D'où venons-nous? Que sommes-nous? Où allons-nous?*, 1897, oil on canvas, Museum of Fine Art, Boston, Massachusetts.
9 Paul Gauguin, *Contes barbares*, 1902, oil on canvas, Museum Folkwang, Essen, Germany.
10 Waldroup, "Traveling Representations," 21.
11 Alison Nordström, "Making a Journey: The Tupper Scrapbooks and the Travel They Describe," in *Photographs Objects Histories: On the Materiality of Images*, ed. Elizabeth Edwards and Janice Hart (Routledge, 2004), 84.
12 Lori Kido Lopez, "Eating a Meal with the Other: The Ethical Challenges of Travel Food Shows," *Popular Culture Review* 22, no. 1 (2011): 99.
13 Lopez, "Eating a Meal with the Other," 105.
14 Lopez, "Eating a Meal with the Other," 105.
15 Lopez, "Eating a Meal with the Other," 99.
16 Lopez, "Eating a Meal with the Other," 103.
17 See, for example, Téwodros W. Workneh and H. Leslie Steeves, "*Anthony Bourdain: Parts Unknown* in Africa: Cultural Brokerage, 'Going Native,' and Colonial Nostalgia," *International Journal of Communication*. 13 (2019): 5525–47; Jacob Henry, "Traveling Beyond Genre: Reviewing *Anthony Bourdain: Parts Unknown*'s Africa," *Humanity & Society* 41, no. 4 (2017): 515–18.
18 Casey Ryan Kelly, *Food Television and Otherness in the Age of Globalization* (Lexington Books, 2017), 117.
19 Kelly, *Food Television and Otherness in the Age of Globalization*, 18.
20 Ana Christoffersen, "Can Bond Movies Be Fixed? Ana de Armas and Cuba in *No Time to Die*," *LatinXFilm*, January 14, 2022, accessed January 20, 2022, https://www.latinxspaces.com/latinx-film/can-bond-movies-be-fixed-ana-de-armas-and-cuba-in-no-time-to-die (URL no longer available).
21 Christoffersen, "Can Bond Movies Be Fixed?"
22 bell hooks, *Black Looks: Race and Representation* (South End Press, 1992).

23 Claire Johnston, "Women's Cinema as Counter-Cinema," in *Feminist Film Theory*, ed. Sue Thornham (New York University Press, 1999), 37.
24 Johnston, "Women's Cinema as Counter-Cinema," 38.

Chapter 5

1 Catherine Russell, *Experimental Ethnography: The Work of Film in the Age of Video* (Duke University Press, 1999), 276.
2 Francis Vanoye, *Scénarios modèles de scenarios* (1991; repr., Armand Colin Cinéma, 2008), 207. Passage translated by Brittany Powell Kennedy.
3 Colin MacCabe, *Godard: A Portrait of the Artist at Seventy* (Farrar, Straus and Giroux, 2003), 241.
4 *Les plages d'Agnès*, directed by Agnès Varda (Les Films du Losange, 2008).
5 Emma Wilson, *French Cinema Since 1950: Personal Histories* (Rowman & Littlefield, 1999), 11.
6 Wilson, *French Cinema Since 1950*, 11.
7 Walter Murch, "Sound Design: The Dancing Shadow," in *Projections: Film-makers on Film-making*, vol. 4, ed. John Boorman, Tom Luddy, David Thomson, and Walter Donohue (Faber & Faber, 1995), 247.
8 Wilson, *French Cinema Since 1950*, 20.
9 Charles Leehrsen, *Down and Out in Paradise: The Life of Anthony Bourdain* (Simon & Schuster, 2022), 87–88.
10 Tom Vitale, *In the Weeds: Around the World and Behind the Scenes with Anthony Bourdain* (Hachette, 2021), 36.
11 Chelsea Conaboy, "Interview with Zach Zamboni," *Maine Voices Live*, September 8, 2017, accessed September 17, 2021, https://www.youtube.com/watch?v=-e8dk6R7c_.
12 Laura Rascaroli, *The Personal Camera: Subjective Cinema and the Essay Film* (Wallflower, 2009), 3.
13 A. O. Scott, "Agnès Varda: Living for Cinema, and Through It," *New York Times*, June 25, 2009, accessed October 25, 2022, https://www.nytimes.com/2009/06/28/movies/28scot.html; Cecilia Sayad, *Performing Authorship: Self-Inscription and Corporeality in the Cinema* (I. B. Taurus, 2013), 48.
14 Laurie Woolever, *Bourdain: The Definitive Oral Biography* (Ecco, 2021).
15 Anthony Bourdain, *Kitchen Confidential: Adventures in the Culinary Underbelly* (Bloomsbury, 2000), 14–17.
16 Pier Paolo Pasolini, *Heretical Empiricism*, ed. Louise K. Barnett, trans. Ben Lawton and Louise K. Barnett (Indiana University Press, 1988).

17 Rascaroli, *Personal Camera*, 112.
18 Rascaroli, *Personal Camera*, 113.

Chapter 6

1 Andrew Barker, "Anthony Bourdain Breaks Down Cinema History for *Parts*," *Variety*, August 5, 2014, accessed September 17, 2021, https://variety.com/2014/tv/awards/anthony-bourdain-breaks-down-cinema-history-for-parts-1201275584/.
2 Laurie Woolever, *Bourdain: The Definitive Oral Biography* (Ecco, 2021), 193.
3 Kanishk Tharoor, "Anthony Bourdain's Extreme Empathy," *The Atlantic*, June 10, 2018, accessed January 17, 2023, https://www.theatlantic.com/entertainment/archive/2018/06/anthony-bourdains-extreme-empathy/562454/.
4 John W. Little, "Anthony Bourdain Talks Travel, Food, and War," *BlogsofWardotcom*. July 20, 2014, accessed January 17, 2023, https://blogsofwar.com/anthony-bourdain-talks-travel-food-and-war/.
5 Kim Ghattas, "How Lebanon Transformed Anthony Bourdain," *The Atlantic*, June 9, 2018, accessed January 16, 2023, https://www.theatlantic.com/international/archive/2018/06/how-lebanon-transformed-anthony-bourdain/562484/.
6 Little, "Anthony Bourdain Talks Travel, Food, and War."
7 Little, "Anthony Bourdain Talks Travel, Food, and War."
8 Little, "Anthony Bourdain Talks Travel, Food, and War."
9 Ben Rhodes, *The World as It Is: A Memoir of the Obama White House* (Random House, 2018), 337.
10 Rhodes, *The World as It Is*, 373.
11 Tom Vitale, *In the Weeds: Around the World and Behind the Scenes with Anthony Bourdain* (Hachette, 2021), 16.
12 Amanda Erickson, "Anthony Bourdain Just Got Banned from Azerbaijan," *Washington Post*, October 27, 2017, accessed February 2, 2023, https://www.washingtonpost.com/news/worldviews/wp/2017/10/26/anthony-bourdain-just-got-banned-from-azerbaijan/.
13 Little, "Anthony Bourdain Talks Travel, Food, and War."
14 Little, "Anthony Bourdain Talks Travel, Food, and War."
15 Barker, "Anthony Bourdain Breaks Down Cinema History for *Parts*."
16 Lucia Ricciardelli, "Documentary Filmmaking in the Postmodern Age: Errol Morris and *The Fog of Truth*," *Studies in Documentary Film* 4, no. 1 (2010): 43.

17 Gilberto Perez, "Errol Morris's Irony," in *Three Documentary Filmmakers: Errol Morris, Ross McElwee, Jean Rouch* (SUNY Press, 2004), 3–14.
18 David Resha, *The Cinema of Errol Morris* (Wesleyan University Press, 2015), 2.
19 Ricciardelli, "Documentary Filmmaking in the Postmodern Age," 37.
20 Resha, *Cinema of Errol Morris*, 1–2.
21 Anthony Bourdain, "Bourdain's Field Notes: London," CNN, October 2016, accessed February 7, 2023, https://explorepartsunknown.com/london/bourdains-field-notes-london/.
22 Woolever, *Anthony Bourdain*, 433.

Chapter 7

1 Jamie Soja, "An Interview with Anthony Bourdain and Éric Ripert," *HuffPost*, April 23, 2013, accessed November 4, 2024, https://www.huffpost.com/entry/an-interview-with-anthony_b_3119080.
2 Cynthia Baron, Diane Carson, and Mark Bernard, *Appetites and Anxieties: Food, Film, and the Politics of Representation* (Wayne State University Press, 2014), 17.
3 Eric Kohn, "Anthony Bourdain on Asia Argento, His Favorite Movies, and Why Donald Trump Would Be a Terrible Dinner Companion," *IndieWire*, June 3, 2018, accessed March 9, 2023, https://www.indiewire.com/2018/06/anthony-bourdain-interview-no-reservations-hong-kong-asia-argento-christopher-doyle-1201970639/.
4 Baron, Carson, and Bernard, *Appetites and Anxieties*, 8.
5 James Keller, *Food, Film and Culture: A Genre Study* (McFarland, 2006), 1.
6 Laura Lindenfeld and Fabio Parasecoli, *Feasting Our Eyes: Food Films and Cultural Identity in the United States* (Columbia University Press, 2017), 1.
7 Keller, *Food, Film and Culture*, 1.
8 Lindenfeld and Parasecoli, *Feasting Our Eyes*, 3.
9 Lindenfeld and Parasecoli, *Feasting Our Eyes*, 5.
10 Lindenfeld and Parasecoli, *Feasting Our Eyes*, 184.
11 Lindenfeld and Parasecoli, *Feasting Our Eyes*, 16.
12 Baron, Carson, and Bernard, *Appetites and Anxieties*, 8.
13 Baron, Carson, and Bernard, *Appetites and Anxieties*, 22.
14 Lindenfeld and Parasecoli, *Feasting Our Eyes*, 214–15.
15 Lindenfeld and Parasecoli, *Feasting Our Eyes*, 183.

16 Rachel Laudan, "Slow Food: The French Terroir Strategy, and Culinary Modernism. An Essay Review of Carlos Petrini, Trans. William McCuaig," *Food, Culture & Society* 7, no. 2 (2004): 133–44.

17 Anthony Bourdain, "Bourdain's Field Notes: Copenhagen," CNN, October 2013, accessed April 3, 2023, https://explorepartsunknown.com/copenhagen/bourdains-field-notes-copenhagen/.

18 Lindenfeld and Parasecoli, *Feasting Our Eyes*, 183.

Chapter 8

1 Anthony Bourdain, "Bourdain's Field Notes: Hong Kong," CNN, May 30, 2018, accessed December 31, 2021, https://explorepartsunknown.com/hong-kong/bourdains-field-notes-hong-kong/.

2 Anthony Bourdain, "Anthony Bourdain: My 'Cinematic Dream' Filming with Asia Argento and Christopher Doyle in Hong Kong," *Hollywood Reporter*, June 2, 2018, accessed December 31, 2021, https://www.hollywoodreporter.com/tv/tv-news/anthony-bourdain-why-shooting-parts-unknown-hong-kong-was-a-cinematic-dream-1114970/.

3 Matt Wilstein, "The Dark Reality of Anthony Bourdain's Final Days," *Daily Beast*, July 12, 2021, accessed December 17, 2021, https://www.thedailybeast.com/anthony-bourdains-dark-final-days-revealed-in-new-documentary-roadrunner.

4 Cory Stillman, "*Roadrunner* Threatens to Leave Anthony Bourdain's Legacy in Ruins," *Film Cred*, August 2, 2021, accessed December 17, 2021, https://film-cred.com/roadrunner-anthony-bourdain-morgan-neville/.

5 Chelsea Conaboy, "Interview with Zach Zamboni," *Maine Voices Live*, September 8, 2017, accessed January 1, 2022, https://www.youtube.com/watch?v=-e8dk6R7c_8.

6 Bourdain, "My 'Cinematic Dream' Filming with Asia Argento and Christopher Doyle in Hong Kong."

7 Stillman, "*Roadrunner* Threatens to Leave Anthony Bourdain's Legacy in Ruins."

8 Eric Kohn, "Anthony Bourdain on Asia Argento, His Favorite Movies, and Why Donald Trump Would Be a Terrible Dinner Companion," *IndieWire*, June 3, 2018, accessed December 31, 2021, https://www.indiewire.com/2018/06/anthony-bourdain-interview-no-reservations-hong-kong-asia-argento-christopher-doyle-1201970639/.

9 Bourdain, "My 'Cinematic Dream' Filming with Asia Argento and Christopher Doyle in Hong Kong."
10 Heather Cho, "Behind the Camera: *Parts Unknown* Guest Director Asia Argento," CNN, May 30, 2018, accessed December 31, 2021, https://explorepartsunknown.com/hong-kong/hong-kong-behind-the-scenes/.
11 Cho, "Behind the Camera."
12 Kohn, "Anthony Bourdain on Asia Argento, His Favorite Movies, and Why Donald Trump Would Be a Terrible Dinner Companion."
13 Ackbar Abbas, "The New Hong Kong Cinema and the 'Déjà Disparu,'" *Discourse* 16, no. 3 (Spring 1994): 65.
14 Abbas, "The New Hong Kong Cinema and the 'Déjà Disparu,'" 66.
15 Abbas, "The New Hong Kong Cinema and the 'Déjà Disparu,'" 67.
16 Jenny Leung, "One of Hong Kong's Last Remaining Traditional Cafes Closes Down After 55 Years," *Time Out*, December 17, 2019, accessed December 30, 2021, https://www.timeout.com/hong-kong/news/one-of-hong-kongs-last-remaining-traditional-cafes-closes-down-after-55-years-121719.
17 Abbas, "The New Hong Kong Cinema and the 'Déjà Disparu,'" 69.
18 Abbas, "The New Hong Kong Cinema and the 'Déjà Disparu,'" 69.
19 Allan Cameron, "Trajectories of Identification: Travel and Global Culture in the Films of Wong Kar-Wai," *Jump Cut: A Review of Contemporary Media* 49 (Spring 2007), https://www.ejumpcut.org/archive/jc49.2007/wongKarWai/index.html.
20 Cameron, "Trajectories of Identification."
21 Emily VanDerWerff, "Anthony Bourdain Was a Modern Mr. Rogers," *Vox*, June 10, 2018, accessed December 31, 2021, https://www.vox.com/culture/2018/6/10/17443144/anthony-bourdain-parts-unknown-hong-kong-recap-mister-rogers.
22 Abbas, "The New Hong Kong Cinema and the 'Déjà Disparu,'" 67.
23 VanDerWerff, "Anthony Bourdain Was a Modern Mr. Rogers."

Chapter 9

1 Frederick Jackson Turner, "The Significance of the Frontier in American History," *Annual Report of the American Historical Association* (1893): 197.
2 Turner, "The Significance of the Frontier in American History," 197.
3 Turner, "The Significance of the Frontier in American History," 197.

4 Steven Spielberg in *Directed by John Ford*, directed by Peter Bogdanovich (American Film Institute, 2006).
5 Edward Buscombe, "Painting the Legend: Frederic Remington and the Western," in *John Ford Made Westerns: Filming the Legend in the Sound Era*, ed. Gaylyn Studlar and Matthew Bernstein (Indiana University Press, 2001), 154.
6 Buscombe, "Painting the Legend," 166.
7 Gaylyn Studlar and Matthew Bernstein, introduction to Studlar and Bernstein, *John Ford Made Westerns*, 3.
8 Jim Harrison, "Seven in the Woods" (2019), as quoted in *Parts Unknown*, "Montana" (S7E4).
9 Harrison, "Seven in the Woods."
10 Jim Harrison, "Time" (2016), as quoted in *Parts Unknown*, "Montana" (S7E4).
11 Jim Harrison, "Wolves of Heaven" (2016), as quoted in *Parts Unknown*, "Montana" (S7E4).
12 Harrison, "Wolves of Heaven."
13 Studlar and Bernstein, introduction to Studlar and Bernstein, *John Ford Made Westerns*, 5.
14 Peter Lehman, "How the West Wasn't Won: The Repression of Capitalism in John Ford's Westerns," in Studlar and Bernstein, *John Ford Made Westerns*, 133.
15 John Baxter, *The Cinema of John Ford* (AS Barnes, 1971), 79–80.
16 Baxter, *The Cinema of John Ford*, 81.
17 Bruce Glasrud and Michael Searles, *Black Cowboys in the American West: On the Range, on the Stage, Behind the Badge* (University of Oklahoma Press, 2016).
18 Gail M. Nomura, "Significant Lives: Asia and Asian Americans in the History of the U.S. West," *Western Historical Quarterly* 25, no. 1 (Spring 1994): 69–88.

Chapter 10

1 Jacqui Kong, "Feasting with 'The Other': Transforming the Self in Food Adventuring Programs," *Asian American Literature: Discourses & Pedagogies* 2 (2011): 46.
2 Kong, "Feasting with 'The Other,'" 46.
3 Lori Kido Lopez, "Eating a Meal with the Other: The Ethical Challenges of Travel Food Shows," *Popular Culture Review* 22, no. 1 (2011): 99.

4 Anthony Bourdain, "Anthony Bourdain in Rome: Our Most Beautiful Show," CNN, December 6, 2016, accessed March 11, 2022, https://www.cnn.com/travel/article/anthony-bourdain-parts-unknown-rome-essay/index.html.
5 Bourdain, "Anthony Bourdain in Rome."
6 Manuela Mariana and Patrick Barron, "Cinematic Space in Rome's Disabitato: Between Metropolis and Terrain Vague in the Films of Fellini, Antonioni, and Pasolini," *Modernism/Modernity* 18, no. 2 (2011): 309.
7 Bourdain, "Anthony Bourdain in Rome."
8 John Davis Rhodes, *Stupendous Miserable City: Pasolini's Rome* (University of Minnesota Press, 2007), xiii.
9 Mariana and Barron, "Cinematic Space in Rome's Disabitato," 329.
10 Mariana and Barron, "Cinematic Space in Rome's Disabitato," 329.
11 Mariana and Barron, "Cinematic Space in Rome's Disabitato," 329.
12 Rhodes, *Stupendous Miserable City*, 111.
13 Rhodes, *Stupendous Miserable City*, 5.
14 Rhodes, *Stupendous Miserable City*, xv–xvi.
15 Bourdain, "Anthony Bourdain in Rome."
16 Anthony Bourdain, "Stornelli: An Italian Rap Battle," CNN, April 4, 2017, accessed March 11, 2022, https://explorepartsunknown.com/rome/stornello/.
17 Ackbar Abbas, "Hong Kong: Other Histories, Other Politics," *Public Culture* 9, no. 3 (1997): 304.
18 Abbas, "Hong Kong," 304–5.
19 Rhodes, *Stupendous Miserable City*, 135.
20 Rhodes, *Stupendous Miserable City*, 128.
21 Rhodes, *Stupendous Miserable City*, 111.
22 Rhodes, *Stupendous Miserable City*, 127.
23 Lino Micciché, *Pasolini nella città del cinema* (Marsilio, 1999), 116.
24 Rhodes, *Stupendous Miserable City*, 127.
25 Jordi Maiso, *Precariedad, exclusión, marginalidad. Una historia conceptual de la pobreza* (Zaragoza University Press, 2022), 257.

Chapter 11

1 Marlowe Stern, "Anthony Bourdain's Deep into the Heart of Trump Country: 'I Was Utterly Disarmed,'" *Daily Beast*, April 23, 2018, accessed March 31, 2022, https://www.thedailybeast.com/anthony-bourdains-journey-deep-into-the-heart-of-trump-country-i-was-utterly-disarmed.

2 Anthony Bourdain, "Bourdain's Field Notes: West Virginia," CNN, April 26, 2018, accessed March 31, 2022, https://explorepartsunknown.com/west-virginia/bourdains-field-notes-west-virginia/.
3 Neal Conan, "Poverty Porn: Education or Exploitation?," *Talk of the Nation*, March 5, 2009, accessed March 31, 2022, http://www.npr.org/templates/story/story.php?storyId=101487893.
4 Eric Kohn, "Anthony Bourdain Was a Brilliant Filmmaker in Disguise," *IndieWire*, June 10, 2018, accessed March 31, 2022, https://www.indiewire.com/2018/06/anthony-bourdain-last-interview-food-movies-legacy-1201973230/.
5 Kohn, "Anthony Bourdain Was a Brilliant Filmmaker in Disguise."
6 Meredith McCarroll, "Anthony Bourdain Listened to the Voices *Hillbilly Elegy* Ignored," CNN, May 31, 2019, accessed March 31, 2022, https://www.cnn.com/2019/05/31/opinions/bourdain-west-virginia-mccarroll/index.html.
7 Anthony Harkins and Meredith McCarroll, "Introduction: Why This Book?," in *Appalachian Reckoning: A Region Responds to "Hillbilly Elegy,"* ed. Anthony Harkins and Meredith McCarroll (West Virginia University Press, 2019), 1–20.
8 Meredith McCarroll, "Hillbillies Need No Elegy," *Bitter Southerner*, accessed March 31, 2022, https://bittersoutherner.com/hillbillies-need-no-elegy-appalachian-reckoning.
9 F. Jack Hurley, *Marion Post-Wolcott: A Photographic Journey* (University of New Mexico Press, 1989).
10 McCarroll, "Hillbillies Need No Elegy."
11 John Tyson, "Anthony Bourdain Shares His Experience in McDowell County," *Bluefield Daily Telegraph*, September 20, 2017, accessed March 31, 2022, https://www.bdtonline.com/news/anthony-bourdain-shares-his-experience-in-mcdowell-county/article_b1f10120-9e0e-11e7-95c8-87243b1cb19a.html.
12 Elizabeth March Catte, "Stereotypes on the Syllabus: Exploring *Hillbilly Elegy*'s Use as an Instructional Text at Colleges and Universities," in Harkins and McCarroll, *Appalachian Reckoning*, 60–79.
13 Eleanor Krause and Richard V. Reeves, *Rural Dreams: Upward Mobility in America's Countryside* (Center on Children and Families at Brookings, 2017), 12–13, accessed February 5, 2026, https://www.brookings.edu/wp-content/uploads/2017/08/es_20170905_ruralmobility.pdf.

14 Catte, "Stereotypes on the Syllabus," 67.
15 Ivy Brashear, "Keep Your 'Elegy': The Appalachia I Know Is Very Much Alive," in Harkins and McCarroll, *Appalachian Reckoning*, 159–60.
16 Brashear, "Keep Your 'Elegy,'" 160.
17 John Yau, "Poetry in Motion," *The American Poetry Review* 34, no. 1 (January–February 2005): 35.
18 Brashear, "Keep Your 'Elegy,'" 162.

Chapter 12

1 Anthony Bourdain, "Bourdain's Field Notes: San Sebastián," CNN, September 25, 2017, accessed April 29, 2022, https://explorepartsunknown.com/san-sebastian/bourdains-field-notes-san-sebastian/.
2 Bourdain, "Bourdain's Field Notes: San Sebastián."
3 Bourdain, "Bourdain's Field Notes: San Sebastián."
4 Bourdain, "Bourdain's Field Notes: San Sebastián."
5 Bourdain, "Bourdain's Field Notes: San Sebastián."
6 Homi Bhabha, *The Location of Culture* (Routledge, 1994).
7 Benedict Anderson, *Imagined Communities: Reflections on the Origin and Spread of Nationalism* (Verso, 1983).
8 Anderson, *Imagined Communities*, 6.
9 Joseba Gabilondo, epilogue to Jaume Martí-Olivella, *Basque Cinema: History of an In/Visibility* (Barbaroak, 2020), 599.
10 Gabilondo, *Basque Cinema*, 597.
11 Nathan Richardson, "Animals, Machines, and Postnational Identity in Julio Medem's *Vacas*," *Journal of Iberian and Latin American Studies* 10, no. 2 (2004): 202.
12 Brittany Kennedy and Todd Kennedy, "Basqueing on the Bayou: Conflicting Visions of Authenticity in Julio Medem's *Vacas* and Benh Zeitlin's *Beasts of the Southern Wild*," *Transnational Cinemas* 8, no. 2 (May 2017): 12.
13 Martí-Olivella, *Basque Cinema*, 561.
14 Gabilondo, *Basque Cinema*, 599.
15 Gabilondo, *Basque Cinema*, 602.
16 Ackbar Abbas, "The New Hong Kong Cinema and the 'Déjà Disparu,'" *Discourse* 16, no. 3 (Spring 1994): 69.
17 Gabilondo, *Basque Cinema*, 611–15.
18 Gabilondo, *Basque Cinema*, 611–15.
19 Gabilondo, *Basque Cinema*, 600.

20 Gabilondo, *Basque Cinema*, 613.

21 "'80 egunean' filmak nazioartean arrakastatsu darrai: Guadalajara eta Washington-en izango da aurki," Euskalkultura.eus, March 22, 2011, accessed December 27, 2020, www.euskalkultura.eus.

22 Gabilondo, *Basque Cinema*, 614.

23 Gabilondo, *Basque Cinema*, 626.

24 Abbas, "The New Hong Kong Cinema and the 'Déjà Disparu,'" 69.

25 Gabilondo, *Basque Cinema*, 652.

26 Kennedy and Kennedy, "Basqueing on the Bayou," 10.

Chapter 13

1 Darren Aronofsky, "A Road Trip Through Bhutan with Anthony Bourdain," CNN, June 22, 2018, accessed May 12, 2022, https://edition.cnn.com/travel/article/darren-aronofsky-anthony-bourdain-traveling/index.html.

2 Eric Kohn, "Anthony Bourdain's Season-Finale Episode of *Parts Unknown* Is Heartbreaking," *IndieWire*, June 24, 2018, accessed May 12, 2022, https://www.indiewire.com/2018/06/anthony-bourdain-parts-unknown-bhutan-darren-aronofsky-1201977936/.

3 Anthony Bourdain, "Bourdain's Field Notes: Madagascar," CNN, May 17, 2015 (updated September 26, 2017), accessed May 12, 2022, https://explorepartsunknown.com/madagascar/bourdains-field-notes-madagascar/.

4 Shelby E. Ward, "Anthony Bourdain's Cosmopolitan Table: Mapping the Ethni(c)ity Through Street Food and Television," *Otherness: Essays and Studies* 7, no. 1 (March 2019): 62.

5 Jacques Derrida, *On Cosmopolitanism and Forgiveness: Thinking in Action* (Routledge, 2001).

6 John Urry, *Consuming Places* (Routledge, 1995). Quoted by Ward in "Anthony Bourdain's Cosmopolitan Table."

7 Ward, "Anthony Bourdain's Cosmopolitan Table," 46.

8 Ward, "Anthony Bourdain's Cosmopolitan Table," 49.

9 Ward, "Anthony Bourdain's Cosmopolitan Table," 60–61.

10 Ward, "Anthony Bourdain's Cosmopolitan Table," 57–58.

11 Oliver Strand, "Anthony Bourdain on Authenticity, Expectations, and Opening the Country's Most Ambitious Food Hall," *Variety*, October 21, 2016, accessed August 10, 2022, https://www.vogue.com/article/anthony-bourdain-food-hall-manhattan-waterfront-new-york.

12 Alice Vignoles-Russel, "Creating Interiority in Darren Aronofsky's *Black Swan*: An Issue of Composition, Space, and Visual Distortion," *Film Matters* (Fall 2015): 34.
13 Vignoles-Russel, "Creating Interiority in Darren Aronofsky's *Black Swan*," 35.
14 Kohn, "Anthony Bourdain's Season-Finale Episode of *Parts Unknown* Is Heartbreaking."
15 Todd Kennedy, "Bob Dylan's 'Highway Shoes': The Hobo-Hero's Road Through Modernity," *Intertexts* 13, nos. 1–2 (Spring/Fall 2009): 37–58.
16 Kohn, "Anthony Bourdain's Season-Finale Episode of *Parts Unknown* Is Heartbreaking."
17 Aaron N. Oforlea, "[Un]veiling the White Gaze: Revealing Self and Other in the Land Where the Blues Began," *The Western Journal of Black Studies* (Winter 2012): 289–90.
18 bell hooks, *Black Looks: Race and Representation* (South End Press, 1992).
19 Jacqui Kong, "Feasting with 'The Other': Transforming the Self in Food Adventuring Programs," *Asian American Literature: Discourses & Pedagogies* 2 (2011): 52–53.
20 Kong, 53.
21 Anthony Bourdain, Twitter, August 31, 2017, https://twitter.com/Bourdain/status/903080058541285377.

Conclusion

1 *No Reservations*, season 2, episode 3, "Peru," directed by Eric Lasby, aired April 10, 2006, on Travel Channel.
2 Marshall Berman, *All That Is Solid Melts into Air: The Experience of Modernism* (Penguin Books, 1988), 11.
3 Berman, *All That Is Solid Melts into Air*, 5.
4 Berman, *All That Is Solid Melts into Air*, 15.
5 Berman, *All That Is Solid Melts into Air*, 5.
6 Todd Kennedy, "Bob Dylan's 'Highway Shoes': The Hobo-Hero's Road Through Modernity," *Intertexts* 13, nos. 1–2 (Spring/Fall 2009): 40.
7 Tom Vitale, *In the Weeds: Around the World and Behind the Scenes with Anthony Bourdain* (Hachette Books, 2021), 158.
8 Todd Kennedy, "On the Road to 'Some' Place: Sofia Coppola's Dissident Modernism Against a Postmodern Landscape," *Miscelánea* 52 (December 2015): 53.

9 Anthony Bourdain, "Bourdain's Field Notes: Jamaica," CNN, November 2014, accessed April 27, 2023, https://explorepartsunknown.com/jamaica/bourdains-take-jamaica/.

10 bell hooks, *Black Looks: Race and Representation* (South End Press, 1992).

11 Laurie Woolever, *Bourdain: The Definitive Oral Biography* (Ecco, 2021), 250.

12 Woolever, *Anthony Bourdain*, 250.

13 Vitale, *In the Weeds*, 284.

14 Ben Rhodes, "What Kind of Man Was Anthony Bourdain?," *The Atlantic*, November 29, 2022, accessed May 6, 2023, https://www.theatlantic.com/books/archive/2022/11/anthony-bourdain-down-and-out-in-paradise-book/672284/.

15 Lucia Ricciardelli, "Documentary Filmmaking in the Postmodern Age: Errol Morris and *The Fog of Truth*," *Studies in Documentary Film* 4, no. 1 (2010): 36.

16 David Resha, *The Cinema of Errol Morris* (Wesleyan University Press, 2015), 7.

17 Resha, *Cinema of Errol Morris*, 231.

18 Resha, *Cinema of Errol Morris*, 11.

19 Berman, *All That Is Solid Melts into Air*, 9–10.

20 Jen Maravegias, "Controversies over Anthony Bourdain Documentary Hurt the Women He Loved," *Pajiba*, July 16, 2021, accessed May 9, 2023, https://www.pajiba.com/film_reviews/controversies-over-anthony-bourdain-documentary-hurt-the-women-he-loved.php.

21 Brett Martin, "What Was Anthony Bourdain Searching For?," *GQ*, July 13, 2021, accessed May 2, 2023, https://www.gq.com/story/anthony-bourdain-morgan-neville-roadrunner-documentary.

22 Helen Rosner, "A Haunting New Documentary About Anthony Bourdain," *New Yorker*, July 15, 2021, accessed May 2, 2023, https://www.newyorker.com/culture/annals-of-gastronomy/the-haunting-afterlife-of-anthony-bourdain.

23 Sean Burns, Twitter, July 15, 2021 (cited by Rosner and others).

24 Cory Stillman, "*Roadrunner* Threatens to Leave Anthony Bourdain's Legacy in Ruins," *Film Cred*, August 2, 2021, accessed May 2, 2023, https://film-cred.com/roadrunner-anthony-bourdain-morgan-neville/.

25 Helen Rosner, "The Ethics of a Deepfake Anthony Bourdain Voice," *New Yorker*, July 17, 2021, accessed May 2, 2023, https://www.newyorker.com/culture/annals-of-gastronomy/the-ethics-of-a-deepfake-anthony-bourdain-voice.

26 Rosner, "Ethics of a Deepfake Anthony Bourdain Voice."
27 Jack Dickey, "Ten Questions with Anthony Bourdain," *Time*, August 6, 2015, accessed May 2, 2023, https://time.com/3987009/10-questions-with-anthony-bourdain/.
28 Rosner, "Ethics of a Deepfake Anthony Bourdain Voice."
29 Rosner, "Ethics of a Deepfake Anthony Bourdain Voice."
30 Rosner, "Ethics of a Deepfake Anthony Bourdain Voice."
31 Rosner, "Haunting New Documentary About Anthony Bourdain."
32 Rosner, "Ethics of a Deepfake Anthony Bourdain Voice."
33 Stillman, "*Roadrunner* Threatens to Leave Anthony Bourdain's Legacy in Ruins."
34 Rhodes, "What Kind of Man Was Anthony Bourdain?"
35 Berman, *All That Is Solid Melts into Air*, 36.
36 Berman, *All That Is Solid Melts into Air*, 36.
37 Rhodes, "What Kind of Man Was Anthony Bourdain?"
38 Perry Meisel, *The Myth of Popular Culture: From Dante to Dylan* (Wiley-Blackwell, 2009).

INDEX

Note: Page numbers appearing in italics refer to figures.